THE FALKLANDS AFTERMATH

By the same author:

Grains of Sand

There Are No Frontiers

MBFR – The Preliminaries And The First Half Year

The European Defence Community – A History

THE FALKLANDS AFTERMATH

PICKING UP THE PIECES

Major-General Edward Fursdon
CB MBE DLitt

LEO COOPER
LONDON

First published 1988 by Leo Cooper Ltd

Leo Cooper is an independent imprint of
the Heinemann Group of Publishers,
10 Upper Grosvenor Street, London W1X 9PA

LONDON   MELBOURNE   JOHANNESBURG   AUCKLAND

ISBN: 0-85052-205-6

Printed by Butler & Tanner Ltd,
Frome and London

CONTENTS

ILLUSTRATIONS

Acknowledgements

The author is indebted to the MOD for permission to reproduce photographs, Nos 37, 39 and 41; to Sir Rex Hunt, Vice-Admiral Sir Derek Reffell, Air Commodore Bill Wratten and Captain Richard Gill for the photographs of themselves and to the 1st Battalion The Queen's Own Highlanders for the photograph of Piper Gillies. All the other photographs were taken by the author.

Maps

Drawn by John Mitchell

Sketch

FOREWORD

by SIR REX HUNT C.M.G.
Former Governor of the Falkland Islands and High Commissioner of the British Antarctic Territory

General Fursdon was one of the first of many correspondents and media men to come down to the Falkland Islands after the war in 1982. Unlike most of the others, however, he stayed for almost six weeks and was thus able to absorb the flavour of what he calls the 'unique Falklands factor', which eluded his more transient colleagues. As a military man, he writes with understanding and knowledge about the bewildering assortment of units that comprised 'Biffy' (British Forces Falkland Islands) and the variety of problems that confronted their energetic Commander in the aftermath of victory. Finally, as a keen observer and sensitive writer, he is able to convey to the reader what it meant to be a part of 'the inescapable and oft-neglected postscript' to a military campaign. How I wish the *Daily Telegraph* had been receiving his despatches from the battlefield *during* the campaign.

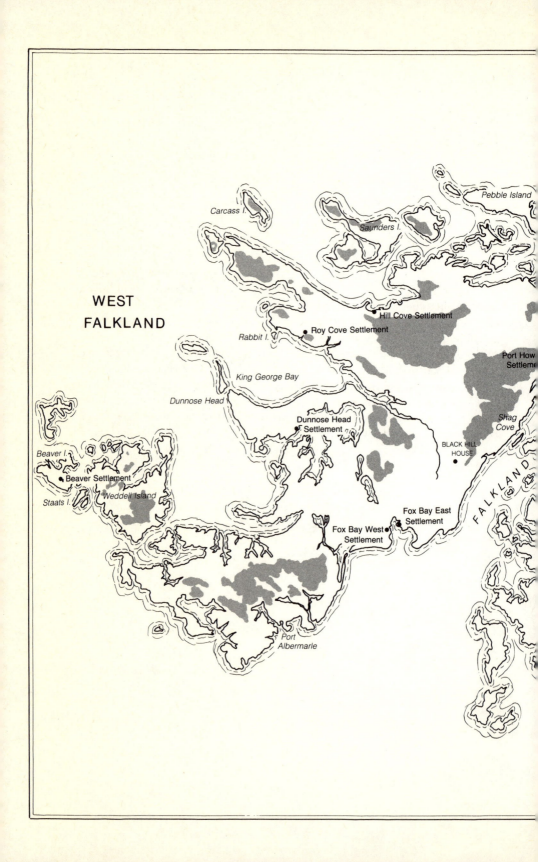

WEST
FALKLAND

Carcass I.

Saunders I.

Pebble Island

Hill Cove Settlement

Roy Cove Settlement

Rabbit I.

Port How
Settleme

King George Bay

Dunnose Head

Shag
Cove

Dunnose Head
Settlement

BLACK HILL
HOUSE

Beaver I.

Beaver Settlement

Weddell Island

Staats I.

FALKLAND

Fox Bay East
Settlement

Fox Bay West
Settlement

Port
Albermarle

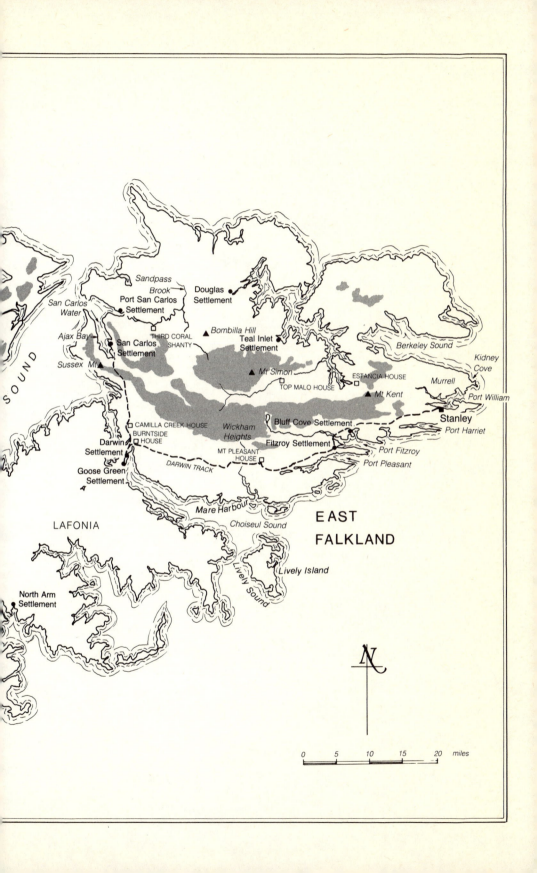

Sandpass
Brook
Douglas
Settlement
Port San Carlos
Settlement
San Carlos
Water
Ajax Bay
THIRD CORAL
SHANTY
▲ Bombilla Hill
Teal Inlet
Settlement
Berkeley Sound
Kidney
Cove
San Carlos
Settlement
▲ Mt Simon
ESTANCIA HOUSE
Murrell
Sussex Mt ▲
TOP MALO HOUSE
Port William
S O U N D
▲ Mt Kent
CAMILLA CREEK HOUSE
Wickham
Heights
Bluff Cove Settlement
Stanley
Port Harriet
BURNTSIDE
HOUSE
Darwin
Settlement
Fitzroy Settlement
Port Fitzroy
MT PLEASANT
HOUSE
Goose Green
Settlement
DARWIN TRACK
Port Pleasant

Mare Harbour
LAFONIA
Choiseul Sound
EAST
FALKLAND
Lively Island
North Arm
Settlement

N

0   5   10   15   20   miles

Author's Note

The content of this book stems from July and August of 1982. The delay in its publication until now is accounted for firstly by the simple difficulty, within the confines of a hectic daily job, of finding the time 'to get it all together', and secondly by the subsequent time actually required to realize publication.

The result of this passage of time is that there have been a number of significant developments in the Falkland Islands in the intervening years – notably the opening of the new airfield at Mount Pleasant. Although this book is about the early Aftermath of the Falklands campaign, nevertheless I have felt it incumbent upon me to add an Epilogue in which, non-politically, I have briefly recorded some of the developments since 1982, especially the military ones.

Inevitably there has to be a 'cut-off' date when writing a book about any continuing saga. This is particularly so when it features the Falklands where the situation could change so rapidly and unexpectedly as the result of any combination of political, military or economic developments – domestic or international – including any significant reduction in Garrison Force levels consequent upon one of the British Government's periodic threat reassessments. This book's Epilogue necessarily ends in late 1986.

I take this opportunity publicly to give my thanks to the many who have helped me so much in making my self-imposed task possible. Firstly, to all ranks of the Royal Navy, the Army, the Royal Air Force and the Merchant Navy during my time spent in the Falkland Islands, at sea in the South Atlantic, and in South Georgia, for their consistently unfailing courtesy, good humour and tolerance, and for the warm welcome extended to me whenever and wherever I intruded into their various lives and activities.

To those individuals whose exploits have not been included in this book, and to any Service unit or vessel which has been inaccurately recorded or even omitted altogether, I offer my very sincere apologies in advance. I realize only too well that such things, regrettably, can happen. Whereas I dated my own notes at the time, I found when checking the updating additions that some public records differed in their version of the dates of certain events. This was an added problem and I realize that the solution I adopted may well upset some expert participants; my apologies go to them too.

Secondly, I must especially thank Sir Rex Hunt, Civil Commissioner at the time, and the Falkland Islanders I met, for their valuable views, insights and continued patience in answering my many questions. In particular, I am very grateful to the Davidson family for making me so welcome and for looking after me so well.

Thirdly, my thanks are due to Peter Eastwood, now retired, and Andrew Hutchinson, both of the *Daily Telegraph*, for permission to use material originally written for them; to Graham Bound and Lieutenant-Colonel George Elliott for permission to quote from *Penguin News* and the Royal Green Jackets' *Regimental Chronicle* respectively: to Mark Mathewson for permitting me to quote his 'Ode to Tumbledown', to Ted Shipsey for use of his material on the mysterious South Georgia cat and to Major Ian Winfield for the diagram on p 127. Fourthly, to several Departments of the Ministry of Defence, especially the various Service Historical Branches, the Royal Marine Records and the Fleet Air Arm Museum for their help in producing the detail of Annexes E, F. and G.

I must also especially thank Major-General Sir David Thorne, Major-General P. E de la C de la Billière, Brigadier G. W. Field, Brigadier D. Brownson, Colonel N. J. Ridley, Colonel B. Tasker QARANC, Lieutenant-Colonel J. Mills, Captain J. Mullin and Major R. Macdonald of the Royal Engineers, Wynn Kenrick, and many other friends for their constructive comments and suggestions, the Ministry of Defence for permission to use certain Crown Copyright photographs and the Falklands Airfield Joint Venture and other individuals who kindly allowed me to use some of their own.

Finally, I must commend my wife Joan for all her invaluable help with the book, and for having so patiently 'lived the Falklands' with me for over five years; my daughter Sabina Palley, Gillian Wettern and Kathy Turner for deciphering parts of the manuscript and helping me type it; and last, but certainly not least, my publisher Leo Cooper for his constant encouragement.

To one and all, I am deeply grateful.

PROLOGUE

The final defeat and surrender of the enemy normally marks the end of a successful military campaign; the Captains and Kings and the victorious troops return home to a well-deserved and triumphal reception to celebrate the hard-won peace. What is left behind is the Aftermath – a kind of vacuum – a politically, economically and militarily difficult environment in which the winning military power is immediately faced with immense problems. In this the Falkland Islands campaign was no exception.

The military machine which wins a war, and which by its nature has hitherto been ultimately responsible for everything that has happened within its geographical sphere of influence, has been necessarily geared to fighting the enemy on land, on and under the sea and in the air.

Peace having been declared and the inescapable dictum of total responsibility having assumed much wider dimensions, the military commander eagerly seeks the earliest restoration of a civilian governmental authority to which he can hand over the appropriate civilian mandates.

The victorious forces have not been designed, geared or structured suddenly to deal with the broad spectrum of the politically sensitive and complicated humanitarian tasks of feeding, housing, caring for and administering the population and terrain over which the war has just been waged. Public utilities, communications and the supporting infrastructure of economic life may have been destroyed. Both participants will have strewn great areas of territory with the potentially lethal litter of war.

The installation of a Civil Commissioner in the immediate Aftermath of the Falklands campaign, however, did not of itself solve the practical problems of 'putting the Islands together again'. Because resources were so scarce, and with much of what little there was having been destroyed, the onus of providing resources of all kinds for the initial attempts at returning to normal fell to the Military Commissioner, as the Commander British Forces Falkland Islands was called.

This book sets out to sketch in something of what the Aftermath was all about, and of how this unique subject – the inescapable and oft-neglected postscript to any military operation – was tackled after the Falklands campaign.

Wihout doubt 'Mines' and 'The Airfield' were the immediate priorities, and therefore these subjects inevitably tend to dominate this book, some may feel overwhelmingly so, but that was the reality.

In order to help set out the contents in context, and to refresh memories, I have deliberately brought to the front of the book, and thus chronologically out of written sequence, my penultimate despatch of 30 August, 1982, which briefly summarizes the Falkland Islands land campaign.

It seemed a strange anomaly to me that, whereas as a Defence Correspondent I had been expected to risk my life in the front line of other people's wars, such as the Iraq-Iran conflict, I was not allowed to participate in our nation's own one in so-called peacetime. I was no exception, however, for not one regular or even 'instant' Fleet Street Defence Correspondent sailed with the Task Force – an editorial decision which in my own case, as a retired soldier, still rancours. Fleet Street rumour has it that some of those who did go just happened to be reporters on shift duty hanging around the News Room when the Editor looked up, saw them and said, 'You'll do. You're expendable. Get on the next train to Portsmouth'.

A few of the journalists who became instant war correspondents wrote or broadcast exceptionally well; one went allegedly hoping to make a fortune out of his claims for expenses!

One regional newspaperman is said to have ridden to the quayside on his motor-bike, parked it and gone on board one of the troopships for a quick visit. He was busy interviewing 'the lads' when he suddenly realized the ship had sailed. A fellow journalist, with him on board, said to me later, 'To hell with the campaign. All he was worried about was that someone would nick his parked bike before he got back.'

The role of the Fleet Street Defence Correspondents during the Falklands Campaign was to try and draw together the many different threads of the unfolding saga, while commuting between the Ministry of Defence (MOD) and Fleet Street at all hours of the day or night. Doing this without a break for the seventy-four days it took from the Argentine invasion on 2 April to the surrender on 14 June had many similarities to fighting a campaign in itself. Certainly one felt one had fought it every pavement step of the way.

The leaks from Parliament were notorious, frequent and not always accurate. Information would come back via different means from the South Atlantic before the Ministry of Defence knew about it. Confidentiality was not always respected; the operational implications of some published and broadcast information were not appreciated by some media men who, understandably, had no operational background, and, for some time, iniquitously, established and recognized British Defence Correspondents were given no more information by the MOD than their Argentinian and other foreign colleagues in London, a situation which could not have happened in any other country in the world. Suffice it to say that, contrary to the views of some on both sides and leaving aside an expected touch of arrogance from some of the media involved, short-comings were evident both in the MOD and the media.

Anchored, as I had been for so long, with one foot in the MOD and the other in Fleet Street, the longer the campaign went on the more unanswered questions it raised in my militarily-trained mind. There were strange gaps in information, incomplete pictures and frustratingly fragmented briefings which disturbed my privileged professional experience.

I received a few anonymous cryptic letters direct from the front. Gradually there seemed to emerge a unique Falklands factor about the whole operation which was totally elusive in form or content. So strong did this feeling become that, quite regardless of my job as a Defence Correspondent, I resolved at an early date that by hook or by crook I would just have to get 'down South' and find out for myself what was this strange Falkland dimension.

Still very much the amateur Correspondent, I was intrigued that many of my colleagues had a totally different approach to the campaign, and certainly did not share my military craving to go down to the South Atlantic and conduct my own post-mortem on what, to me, were some of the strange happenings which had gone on down there. One or two thought I was quite mad. To them the Falklands had been just another story which had now ended: 'Where, what and when was the next one?' was what was important to them as the career professionals.

The media men with the Task Force were now returning to Britain, but for a Defence Correspondent to go down to the Falklands in the immediate Aftermath proved virtually impossible.

In the meanwhile the Ministry of Defence had quite rightly invited a number of foreign journalists down to the Falklands to see the scene of the campaign for themselves, experience the conditions and talk to some of those who had taken part in it. One of these was Claudio Sanchez Venegas from Chile's Channel 13 TV network. He was a Spanish-speaking correspondent, the first one to visit the Falklands, and he was duly flown down to Stanley where Lieutenant-Colonel John Mills took him over.

Although from Chile, Claudio was regarded both by the MOD and by the world's media as being the unofficial representitive of all the Spanish-speaking peoples, and as such everyone was somewhat anxiously awaiting his reactions to the Falklands, and to reading what he subsequently wrote.

In conversation at supper on the day of Claudio's arrival, it became very clear to Lieutenant-Colonel Mills that his guest was convinced that HMS *Invincible* had been damaged during the campaign. Indeed he had referred to the pictures of damage to the vessel that he had seen which had been put out by the Argentine Government during the actual campaign. The record obviously needed putting right instantly. Excusing himself for a moment, John Mills dashed to the nearest telephone and rang up the General. 'We've just got to get Claudio out to the *Invincible* at once', he explained.

Early next morning a Royal Navy Sea King helicopter took Mills and Claudio 200 miles out to the *Invincible*, where they flew very slowly along the vessel's port side on which the sun shone brightly. Claudio's camera was clicking away, but at the end of the pass John Mills realized, through a shouted conversation, that Claudio was still not completely convinced;

he thought that the damage was obviously on the vessel's hidden starboard side. So down the starboard side they duly flew, with Claudio's camera recording the undamaged scene, and then landed on the flight deck where Captain Jeremy Black met them himself and took them up to his day cabin for a briefing. Perhaps not without coincidence, a head later popped around the door – that of HRH Prince Andrew.

The gratifying result of this exercise was that Claudio was finally converted to the reality of *Invincible*'s invincibility, and later reported accordingly to his Spanish-speaking audiences.

Of course there were high-priority Servicemen to be flown down there on the limited Hercules aircraft seats available, and, as always, the MOD gave favoured treatment to television as opposed to the printed word.

Although the three Service Directors of Public Relations were keen for particular aspects of the Aftermath to be urgently covered, and pressed my case hard, the MOD was unco-operative. Frustratingly, and regrettably, I therefore missed the vital immediacy of the first month of getting the bulk of fighting Servicemen back to Britain and the Argentinian prisoners-of-war back to Argentina.

Eventually on official stand-by from 13 July, it was not until late in that month that at last I managed to work my passage via Ascension to the Falkland Islands, and later to South Georgia. I had a tricky moment when, waiting to fly out from RAF Brize Norton, someone very senior from my newspaper rang up intending to veto my departure. Not getting very far with him on the telephone, I just hung up the receiver – and went.

It is the lot of any specialist newspaper correspondent that much of what he writes will never be published. For understandable editorial or news reasons, no matter how carefully he has written his piece or researched its accuracy, or how important he personally feels it to be, his masterpiece may well end up on the News Editor's or the Copy Taster's 'spike' (thrown out), may be severely cut down, altered or re-written by the sub-editors, or even have insets cut into it from other sources which he considers highly questionable or even downright inaccurate – all without any reference to him as the 'by-line' author. Very seldom will his original piece appear in print as it was written.

The great majority of the despatches I sent home from the South Atlantic, only a proportion of which were printed and then often in well-pruned form, appear correctly dated and in full in this book. These despatches appear in smaller print. One about submarines, necessarily written later for security reasons, is also included. Deliberately, for the sake of preserving their immediacy and the reflected mood 'down South' at the time, the despatches are as written. The other pieces and notes that appear were never transmitted to my newspaper; they supplement and inevitably at times partially repeat or overlap with the despatches. The passage of time allows me to include, enclosed in square brackets, items relevant to subsequent events and additional details which, for operational reasons, were security classified at the time and therefore could not be given.

The discerning may well notice points in my narrative which the subsequent revelations of Falklands history may have shown to be inaccurate; for these I apologise, but hope for understanding. Full, accurate knowledge at the time is always difficult for a gipsy to maintain when wandering widely over the oceans, especially when it is so often tightly wrapped up in separate compartments of national security.

I spent nearly six weeks experiencing the Aftermath. With the help of friends, with a number of whom I had previously served, I was able to travel all over West and East Falkland, visit the Royal Air Force's flying and air defence squadrons, and not only visit the Royal Navy Task Force at sea but spend six days on a frigate. I saw the breathtaking splendour of dawn over South Georgia.

That July I was indeed fortunate that there was still a large number of men of all ranks around who had served right through the campaign. Some, like Lieutenant-Colonel Geoff Field, the Task Force's Sapper, had been in command. They were all marvellously patient in answering my endless questions and, on the ground, 'walking me through' the San Carlos landings, the yomping route to Teal Inlet and Estancia House, the Battles of Goose Green, Longdon and Tumbledown, and much else besides. The Ship's Company of HMS *Andromeda* were kindness itself.

There has been strain in varying degrees in every military campaign throughout history, when men have been required to risk their lives for the cause of the moment. The build-up resulting from primitive-style living in the shadow of imminent death for a prolonged period brings its own psychological challenges and difficulties which all must face in their own way, aided by inner strength, morale, faith, previous experience, discipline and training.

In the immediate Aftermath, once the strain of the ever-present threat is suddenly removed, perhaps by victory, a very natural relief sets in with most people which is related to the intensity of the preceding experience, and takes them in different ways. Suffice it to say that, as military commanders down the ages have found, such states can bring their own Aftermath problems and need shrewd and firm handling.

One Falklands Commanding Officer told me that, although he had not personally experienced this phenomenon before, his father, who had served in Italy during the Second World War, had warned him about it before he sailed. In the event, therefore, the signs came as no surprise and he was ready to deal with it, although it proved a particular challenge on a desolate island 8,000 miles from home, lacking virtually any immediate facility to help those who had fought so bravely to unwind before sailing for home.

Because of the circumstances that applied, this book is essentially the very personal story of one man's involvement in a unique situation. Inevitably, the number of different aspects of the Aftermath I wanted to record were legion. Because I was working alone, however, I could only be at one place at a time, and thus could only report consequentially what were in fact concurrent activities. At times this caused chronological difficulties, as when reporting from South Georgia and from HMS *Andromeda*.

In trying to cover the wide variety of tasks being undertaken by the Services, of necessity I had to dovetail in my visits as and when Service resources and security allowed; and of course I could only fit in where it did not cause detriment to the operational-type activity still being intensively pursued by everyone around me.

Regrettably my time 'down South' had to be limited, and so, even though I managed to stay down there four weeks longer than others had originally intended I should, and was thus lucky enough to be the first post-campaign Falklands Correspondent to report out of South Georgia and from a Royal Navy frigate at sea, there remained parts of the Aftermath, especially as it affected the civilian community, which I could not myself experience and for this the book is the poorer.

As I explored and talked, gradually that elusive Falklands factor began to take on an identity. The Argentinians' mood being what it was, and because very deliberately they had not agreed to end hostilities, the threat of further planned or rogue military action by them against the British was considerable; so, for reasons of operational security, I had to be circumspect in what I wrote.

Whereas there is no way of bridging the threshold that for ever divides those who participated in the campaign and those who did not, nevertheless, within that limitation, by the end of my six weeks in the South Atlantic I felt I had begun to understand just a little of that Falklands factor which had for so long troubled and eluded me. Certainly the Falkland Islands are unique, as is the outlook and way of life of the people who inhabit them.

Whatever the Aftermath may ultimately turn out to be, life can never go back to what it was before the Argentine invasion and the subsequent British campaign. By their very remoteness and their newly assumed high political profile, the Islands are destined to be living in the Aftermath for a long time to come. Thanks to an irreparable nocturnal knee injury caused one black pre-dawn by a length of three-inch pipe, I too am reminded of the Aftermath every day of my life.

1 | THE LAND CAMPAIGN

30 August, 1982

No one who has not actually been to the Falklands, be he a Government Minister, Serviceman, Whitehall official, MP or journalist, can ever speak or write convincingly about them with any acceptable sense of conviction or degree of credibility. Having been there for some while, and having travelled all over East and most of West Falkland, I believe this to be a fundamental truth.

Of course they can comment on facts and hold forth on the principles of why Britain went to war, but they certainly have no licence to pronounce upon the stark reality of the actual event. No amount of rhetoric or fine words can substitute illusion for personal experience of the Islanders' outlook, the uniquely desolate 'yomping' terrain, 'hacking' the bitter weather, seeing the overpowering under-development of facilities, and sensing the prevailing ambiance of somewhere 8,000 miles away.

Similarly, no imagination can do justice to the bare grass hillocks of Darwin and Goose Green, or the frighteningly open voids, bereft of any cover, separating the mountain features such as Two Sisters from Tumbledown. It cannot portray the searing razor climate, hung with perpetual damp, or the vicious intensity of battle through which the British troops stormed to overwhelm the well-prepared, dominating Argentine defensive positions.

Their actions were determined and earthy, sharp and bitter, grim and mounted with tremendous guts – persistently brave; it was thus that they won. Throughout history enemies have misjudged the British character, which even combines humour with danger, and the Argentines were no exception.

No wonder that now there is a distinct and graded Falklands fraternity to which only those who have plumbed its peculiar dimension, many to the limits of physical and battle exhaustion, can ever truly belong.

It is this highly individual, almost emotive, element which separates the Falklands campaign from any other in which British Forces have been engaged since the Second World War. As ever, there are those who now want to forget and those who want to remember; some publicly, but others, for good reason, privately within themselves.

The Argentinians invaded on Friday 2 April this year, yet only seven weeks to the day – Friday 21 May – 3 Commando Brigade of some 4,000 men landed from San Carlos Water at three separate beaches. 45 Commando landed at Red Beach – Ajax Bay; 3rd Battalion The Parachute Regiment at Green

Beach – Port San Carlos; and 2nd Battalion The Parachute Regiment, followed by 40 Commando, at Blue Beach – San Carlos Settlement. 42 Commando, initially held embarked as a reserve, landed later in the day at Green Beach.

Necessary consolidation of the Bridgehead occupied the first five days ashore. Air defences were deployed, patrols went forward and observation posts were established. Vital stores and equipment were unloaded under frequent Argentine air attacks on the Royal Navy, the merchantmen and the ground forces ashore.

On 27 May came the outbreak from San Carlos. In the north 45 Commando made for Douglas Settlement and 3 PARA for Teal Inlet and on to Estancia. In the south, with a company of 42 Commando held back in reserve and with only three 105 millimetre guns of 29 Commando Regiment in support, 2 PARA headed out to attack Darwin and Goose Green, reaching Camilla Creek House by last light. On 28 May they advanced through Burntside House to Darwin and the hills overlooking Goose Green, having bitterly outfought successive lines of excellently prepared Argentine positions, and having survived intensive shell mortar, heavy machine gun, ground-firing anti-aircraft guns and Pucara aircraft fire.

Goose Green surrendered on 29 May. It was a key turning point in the campaign and deeply affected the morale of the remainder of the Argentine Garrison.

In the north 3 PARA advanced on to Mount Estancia and Vernet, where they were joined by 79 Battery, Royal Artillery. On 30 May 42 Commando seized the dominant Mount Kent, an area in which Special Forces had been operating, and later reinforced it. On the same day the advance element of 5 Infantry Brigade arrived at San Carlos to establish contact with 3 Commando Brigade.

Having trans-shipped from the QE2 to the Canberra and other vessels at South Georgia, 5 Infantry Brigade landed at San Carlos – Blue Beach – on 2 June. 1st/7th Gurkha Rifles (1/7 GR) initially moved south to Sussex Mountain, from whence they moved on to Goose Green to relieve 2 PARA. 2nd Battalion The Scots Guards (2 SG) and 1st Battalion The Welsh Guards (1 WG) moved out to the Verde Mountains and Bonners Bay respectively.

In the meanwhile 2 PARA had moved forward by helicopter to Fitzroy and Bluff Cove, where they were joined by 29 Battery Royal Artillery, and by the two troops of B Squadron of the Blues and Royals who had crossed over to the south to support them. On 5/6 June, with 45 Commando relieving them on Mount Kent, 42 Commando moved forward to occupy Mount Challenger. 2 SG disembarked at Bluff Cove, having moved round there by sea.

On 7 June, having embarked at San Carlos the previous evening, 1 WG disembarked its HQ, one Company and some of the Support Company at Fitzroy and the rest returned to San Carlos. The following day the LSL Sir Galahad returned to disembark these remaining companies of 1 WG, plus a Royal Artillery battery and 16 Field Ambulance, at Port Pleasant where it and the LSL *Sir Tristram* were disastrously attacked by Argentinian aircraft.

On 9 June 1/7 GR, less one company, also arrived in the Bluff Cove area and two companies of 40 Commando were put under command of 1 WG to make up its strength. Helicopters had been flying stores, equipment and gun ammunition to the forward areas, and the 'Build up' phase, with some regrouping, was complete.

The final attacks almost ran one into the other and lasted from 11 to 14 June. First, on the night of 11/12 June 3 Commando Brigade made three initial night attacks, all involving heavy hand-to-hand fighting, and all of which were successful by first light. 3 PARA, with 2 PARA in reserve, gained Mount Longdon. 45 Commando, from Mount Kent, captured Two Sisters. With 1 WG protecting the start line on Mount Challenger, 42 Commando secured Mount Harriet and Goat Ridge.

Second, on the night of 13/14 June, and under cover of a diversionary attack by elements of 2 SG and the Blues and Royals from Mount Harriet towards Mount William, the main body of 2 SG stormed and, delayed somewhat by heavy hand-to-hand fighting, captured the dominant feature of Mount Tumbledown. In the north 2 PARA took Wireless Ridge. 1/7 GR then moved to assault Mount William, and this seemed to be the ultimate 'trigger' collapsing the Argentine resistance. 1 WG headed for Sapper Hill and, according to reports, white flags came out in Stanley. [*This was later denied by many. One explanation given to me by a Falkland Islander, when I questioned him on the point, was that the so-called 'white flags' were put out by some civilians who wanted to identify their houses as not being Argentine-occupied, and therefore hopefully safe from possible attack in what they saw as being 'the final assault'.*] Sappers accompanied the leading elements of the Battalions throughout.

Inevitably, the above is only the very barest bones of the framework of the land campaign, many parts of which deserve whole chapters to themselves. But, even at this early stage, what lessons already stand out? Of course they are legion, but none are revolutionary or surprising, and many really reaffirm the importance of old ones which perhaps had been undervalued or forgotten. One must be very careful, however, because the Falklands created a unique set of military circumstances not necessarily applicable elsewhere. For example, there were no battle tanks.

First, without doubt, was the old lesson that high morale and bravery, guts and determination, even when outnumbered and faced by a wall of enemy fire from seemingly unassailable positions, against all the accepted teaching, carried the British troops through to victory. Second was the value of responsible leadership, initiative and drive shown not only by junior officers, but also by young junior NCOs and at times private soldiers – a comparatively new world-beating dimension encouraged by adventurous training and developed by service in Northern Ireland.

Third was the dividend from superb fitness and hard training which enabled the men to fight and travel, man-packed, in appalling conditions. Survival on Mount Kent, for instance, taxed even the fittest almost to the limits; it certainly defeated the few Argentinians there. Fourth the campaign re-emphasized the importance of basic infantry skills, night fighting techniques, independence from vehicles, and the closest All Arms working. Also, as was well proved on a number of occasions, deception, bluff and flexibility, skilfully applied at the right moment, can still turn a difficult situation into a winner.

Fifth was the inestimable value of helicopters – be they the deep-throated, chud-chudding heavy-lift RAF Chinooks, the roaring piratical Royal Navy's Wessexes or heavily-jowled Sea Kings, or the bee-whining reconnaissance 'teeny weenies' of the Army Air Corps. Sixth, operational experience in the campaign fully confirmed the effectiveness of the three rather than the two sub-unit organizational structure some are now advocating as an economy. It also clearly demonstrated the value of all formations having their own organic logistic units in peacetime, and that never again must the MOD economize by pruning out the small but vital 'fringe' logistic skills contained in the Port Operating, Air Despatch, Bakery, Laundry and Bath, and other specialist units. They are indispensable. The loading and discharge of merchantmen, about which much can be learned from 'Operation Corporate' (codename for the Falklands Operation), is also worth special mention.

Seventh, the contribution to overall victory of boldly-handled, fearless Special Forces, whose daring exploits can produce effects out of all proportion to their numbers, and not necessarily only on the immediate battlefield. The use of satellite communications was revolutionary.

The operation also produced many equipment lessons, both good and not so good: areas of special interest are air defence, radar, night fighting aids, clearance of plastic mines, and the need for high-mobility low-pressure vehicles for infantry and logistic use. The CVT light armoured vehicles of The Blues and Royals did well. Artillery and naval gunfire support proved invaluable, and of course there are never really enough Sappers to go round! Finally, in the immediate Aftermath of the war, some valuable intelligence was lost by not being quick enough in securing it intact, an art well perfected in the Second World War.

Now, today, there is a fine balance to be struck between how much and when to stop Headquarters in Britain 'backseat driving' and leaving it to the responsible and experienced men on the spot who have to live with their decisions. The military are well organized, highly talented, and are commendably forging ahead with their rightful job of defending the Falkland Islands. At the same time, they are giving a tremendous lead and helpful partnership to the Falkland Islanders themselves in the short term. One just hopes that the Government, in particular the Foreign Office, are as alert, and right behind them for the longer term. After all, it is nearly three months since Victory Day in Stanley which celebrated the end of a sharp campaign of a little over two months which had galvanized the whole of Britain. But out here we still await publication of the revised Shackleton Report – one can now appreciate the brilliance of the original one – and the visit of any Minister or Senior official from Whitehall.

2 | 'GOING SOUTH'

It was a brilliant sunny day as RAF VC 10 flight 2394 lifted off from the Brize Norton runway at 10 am, climbed steeply to 35,000 feet and headed south for Dakar. On board were a variety of reinforcements from all three Services for the newly-established Falklands garrison — mainly RAF — including a sprinkling of specialists whose expertise was urgently required for the Aftermath.

The cloud base quickly faded away to reveal the endless clear blue of the Atlantic far below. Smooth, efficient and comfortable, the sleek VC 10 landed at Dakar in Senegal five hours later and taxied to the remote part of the airfield set aside for refuelling British aircraft in transit for Ascension. Passenger facilities were nil and the studied French-style outward 'non-person' approach was very evident. It was a long, hot one-and-a-half-hours stay on the ground during which I came to know the concrete apron and stretch of grass-fringed monsoon drain, which comprised the main features of our view, very well.

Grateful to be back on board, we flew the last leg to Ascension and arrived at 7.30 pm local time, Monday 26 July. It was a good flight, and I was glad to have the opportunity, naturally on an unclassified basis, to talk at length to fellow-passenger Lieutenant-Colonel Johnny Ricketts, Commanding Officer of 1st Battalion The Welsh Guards. It was his battalion which suffered so appallingly from the Argentine air attacks on the Logistic Landing Ships, *Sir Galahad* and *Sir Tristram*, the previous month at Fitzroy Sound (so often wrongly referred to as Bluff Cove).

Colonel Ricketts had flown back to England from the Falklands earlier, but was now returning to Ascension to rejoin his battalion due to arrive there by sea from Stanley the next day, en route home by RAF VC 10s. His authentic, wide-ranging and penetrating scene-setting for my visit, touching both on the campaign and its immediate Aftermath, was invaluable.

Ascension Island, about the size of the Isle of Wight, is a stretch of volcanic rock surrounded by a hostile constantly heaving sea and topped by the strange Green Mountain. The American astronauts' moon buggy is said to have undergone its trials on Ascension's moon-like surface. But high on Green Mountain, near the remains of the Royal Marines' 19th century farm, you could be forgiven for imagining yourself in a Devon lane with its banks of ferns and flowers. The contrast with the rest of the Island is almost unimaginable.

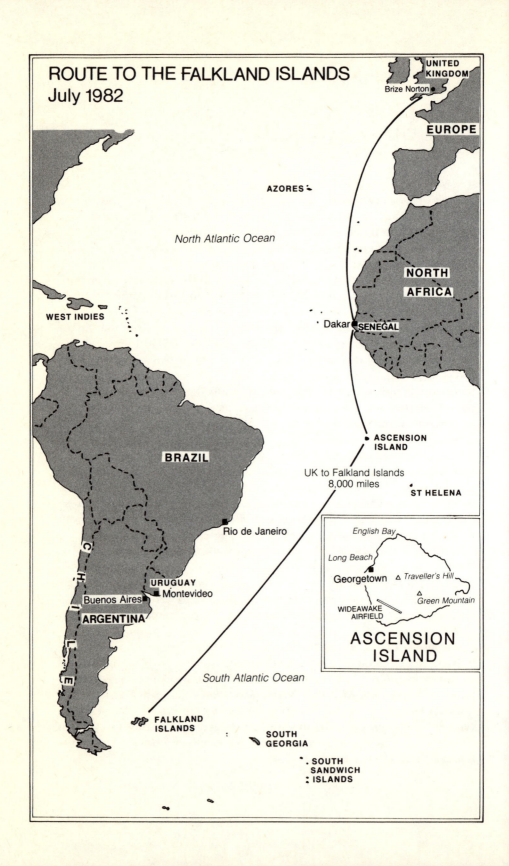

The Island has no indigenous population. It is administered by a Foreign Office official who owes his allegiance to the Governor of St Helena 700 miles away. In normal times it has an imported population of about 1,000, including fifty-five families, all on contract, who serve specific tours of duty on the Island and then have to leave. Similarly, children reaching the age of sixteen, if they have no job, must also leave the Island. The expatriates belong almost exclusively to Cable and Wireless, the BBC and the United States Air Force Base (including its National Aeronautics and Space Administration (NASA) element) and include a number of people from St Helena. Many find the tour very attractive, and some Cable and Wireless families are on their fourth or fifth tour. The USAF base is run on contract by Pan-Am. No American families can stay on the Island unless the wife has an official job.

The Falklands campaign shattered these people's peaceful existence. So long as the Falklands need a British garrison, so Ascension will require one too. The current problem is to decide how big this needs to be, and then to build a permanent camp for it. Whatever its future size turns out to be, the pressure of a garrison will ensure that life in Ascension will never be the same again, and it will be important to avoid future friction between the two 'populations'.

Nestling far below Green Mountain, and en route to it from Georgetown the capital, lies the bungalowed and green-lawned 'ex-pat' village, mainly for BBC and Cable and Wireless employees, vividly coloured by bougainvilleas and typical of the many others around the world.

In Georgetown is the Club (the old Royal Marine Garrison House), its open balcony and ambiance a reminder of colonial days, but now tempered by an 'invasion' of Servicemen of all kinds who are received by the residents with mixed feelings. Georgetown also has a small jetty where the sea can quickly change from calm to thirty-foot waves, thus putting a premium on ship-to-shore movement being done by helicopter.

In the American area between Wideawake Airfield and Georgetown, RAF aircrews are living in American air-conditioned expanded, folding huts looking like elongated versions of the old railway carriage connecting corridors. Other troops are spread around in a variety of local accommodation, including a tented camp at English Bay which, protected by nets and because of the very treacherous currents everywhere else, is the only safe place on the Island to bathe.

Space is at a premium in Ascension, be it for living or working, and no one is retained whose presence cannot be well justified. The airfield apron and parking area is very limited, and the crowding VC10s, C130 Hercules transports, Victor tankers and the various air defence fighters have to be jigsawed into a dense, workable pattern.

The transit passengers' arrangements at Wideawake Airfield on Ascension are primitive – a large open-ended canvas hanger. Our VC10 load of men, once fed, soon became spaced-out rows of blanket-wrapped bundles on the low canvas camp beds, snatching what hours of sleep they could before our early start the next day. Some time before midnight I was aroused from fitful snatches of sleep to be told, in cheering style, that as our Flight 'DEE' would be delayed for over an hour I could have a longer sleep!

Of course there was no guarantee that we would actually land after our fourteen-hour flight to Stanley. If we missed any one of our mid-air refuellings, we would have to turn round and fly back to Ascension and try again another day. The same thing would apply if the weather had closed in when we arrived overhead Stanley airfield; there is no diversionary airfield handy. The day before, an RAF Warrant Officer told me, a Hercules had only made its landing on the Falklands at the third attempt. Twice it had had to turn round in mid-air and fly all the way back to Ascension – some twenty-six hours continuously in the air on each occasion.

Noisily re-awakened a couple of hours later, we waited around in long-established Service pattern to emplane. It was just after 4 am when we finally lined up and snaked our way out under the eerie floodlighting to the huge-bellied ground-beetle shape on the tarmac which was our Hercules. The forward half of its stripped-down, gymnasium-like interior was filled by two enormous fuel tanks, barely leaving room for two side rows of narrow nylon 'para' seats, let alone the feet of their occupants. The centre part of the rear of the aircraft was filled with a pile of miscellaneous stores for the Falklands garrison, plus our kit, all securely netted to the aircraft floor. By the rear door was the crudely screened-off Elsan lavatory. A Royal Navy Lieutenant near me wished loudly that he was on a ship.

Like some overalled Batman, the Air Loadmaster descended from the flight deck hatch to brief us on the journey – two mid-air refuellings using the 'ski down' dropping altitude technique; over water all the way so nothing much to look at; a thirteen- to fourteen-hour trip depending on the weather, but twenty-six to twenty-eight hours if we had to turn back after arrival at Stanley; and safety drills. We rumbled down the runway in the dark, and when the shaking stopped we were airborne. Those who had not quickly taken into use Batman's parting present of cotton wool for our ears soon rolled theirs up into earplugs to keep out the forthcoming half a day's incessant penetrating roar of four powerful old-fashioned engines grinding their way through 3,000 miles of upper South Atlantic air.

Batman appeared again with Tarzan and, by swinging along the high ribs of the fuselage structure above our heads, they reached the rear of the plane. With swift cuts of their escape knives the securing tapes of a pile of pristine white boxes were severed and, with much 'passing the parcel', we ended up with two each. These were our rations for the journey. 'Eat 'em both now – or starve for 10 hours and have a feast – the choice is yours', said Tarzan.

This welcome invasion by the crew did, however, open up new horizons for the alert, crafty or previously well-briefed. Having perforce looked well upwards towards the aircraft's 'ceiling' during the acrobatic display, the dim lighting had revealed eight horizontally lashed stretchers spaced out high above the constraining narrow 'para' seating. These were for bringing back casualties from the Falklands on the return trip. It did not take long before eight of the braver, taller and quicker 'old soldiers' had scaled the fuselage walls and were comfortably ensconced on the stretchers, with their two white boxes tucked in beside them, ready to ride out the long journey in as cosy 'pull-the-ladder-up' style as they could. 'Bet they won't last out to Stanley', growled a jealous prostrate Glaswegian bundle of combat clothing, roughed at its top end with carrot-coloured hair.

After a few hours the last of the humourists, story-tellers and wise-crackers had run dry. The aircraft's high portholes did not let in much light and this, combined with the low-intensity interior lighting, made reading virtually impossible.

The earlier rows of separate individuals now melded into a loose jelly of adhering bodies slumped inertly against each other in resigned slumber, regardless of rank or Service. This still life of exhausted humanity occasionally flickered when a leg was re-stretched or an arm re-positioned. It hardly stirred even when Batman and Tarzan made their periodic acrobatic tours to check on the functioning of the aircraft's vital systems.

The white food boxes soon lay half-opened among the netted stores, while the various discarded portions of sandwich, cheddar cheese, orange and the occasional hard-boiled egg, variously unappetizing to their aerial picnic owners either at the first or second time of eating, dried and curled and gathered dirt between the tightly packed and angled feet.

Batman suddenly appeared above my wearying head. 'The Captain's compliments, Sir, but would you like to come up on the flight deck for the in-flight refuelling due shortly?' I swung my way forward over the prostrate bodies and heaved myself up on to the spacious flight deck. An extra Captain and Navigator were being carried in case the trip to Stanley had to be aborted in flight. They would take over flying the aircraft back to Ascension when the original crew ran out of flying hours. Our Captain, from his left-hand seat, half-turned and waved me welcome as everyone eagerly searched the sky rendezvous for our tanker aircraft. 'What a huge, great lonely place the South Atlantic is,' I wrote in my notebook. 'It just goes on for ever.'

Flight Lieutenant Ernie Bishop, home-based with No. 24 Squadron at Lyneham and Captain of my Hercules transport aircraft flying the 3,000-mile 'Air Bridge' from Ascension Island to the Falkland Islands, notched up two firsts on Tuesday. It was his first operational in-flight refuelling and his first landing at Stanley Airfield. Both were successful.

Two refuellings are required during the fourteen-hour flight. This ensures that if, on arrival, the weather over Stanley is too bad for a landing or, for instance, as with the Hercules ahead of us, an engine fails, the aircraft has enough fuel to return to Ascension safely. The technique demands intense concentration on behalf of the Hercules pilot, plus a high degree of professional skill and strong nerves. It also requires a high standard of teamwork and mutual confidence between him and the pilot of the Victor tanker aircraft.

At the pre-arranged mid-air rendezvous in the middle of nowhere, high above the featureless expanse of the South Atlantic, our Victor tanker descended from 35,000 feet behind us to appear by the starboard wing. It then moved just ahead and stationed itself only fifteen to twenty feet above us, with its flexible fuel delivery hose trailing aft. The hose's maximum length is ninety feet and a large cone-shaped basket is fitted to its trailing end. When the receiver aircraft is in contact with the tanker and the hose pushed in, however, the effective free length of hose is reduced to some sixty feet.

The Hercules pilot's task is then to fly his aircraft gently forward so as to insert his rigid fuel receiving probe, projecting from just above his cockpit, into the Victor's hose end, the connection being aided by the cone-shaped basket. But there are problems as the basket looms bigger and comes to within only a few feet of the Hercules' cockpit window. With the two very large aircraft so close together, the pilot must concentrate on flying it very accurately and safely. Since he cannot do this and watch both probe and basket at the same time, he first lines himself up on a special form of cross on the Victor's rear boom.

His co-pilot's job is then to 'talk him in blind' over the intercom with the last fine adjustments. 'Left a bit – more left – that's it – nice and relaxed – steady now – steady now – a bit more throttle – up a bit.' At last the probe enters the basket's cone, pushes into the fuel hose and the tension eases. At the last moment, however, air turbulence, as in our case, can make the basket bounce around. The probe can hit the basket's outside rim and the whole hose then lashes around the sky. The Hercules pilot must instantly drop back until all is steady again and have another try. It is not easy to get a bull's eye first time; we only got the probe in at the fourth attempt.

Another difficulty is that the Victor's minimum speed of 235 knots at height coincides with the upper range of the Hercules' speed. Because it becomes increasingly heavier as it takes on the fuel, however, the Hercules cannot maintain this top speed at constant height as it does so. The two hose-coupled aircraft therefore have to execute a joint continuous gradual descent in order to enable the Hercules to maintain its connection to the Victor tanker, a difficult manoeuvre known as the 'tobogganing' or 'skiing down' technique. The result of our thirty minutes of umbilical cord-connected display of difficult extremely close formation flying was a drop in altitude from 24,500 feet to 9,000 feet and the transfer of just over eleven tons of fuel.

The telling white grip of our pilot's knuckles eased. Relieved, I returned to my seat. The Victor applied full power, turned back towards Ascension and was gone in an instant. Down below the breaking patches of the flecked South Atlantic showed clearly its winter anger as we flew on to Stanley.

Ernie Bishop invited me back to the Flight Deck for his and my first landing on Stanley airfield. Although there was a lot of low cloud about, I could easily pick out the geography of the terrain about which I had written so much for so long – the airfield, the beaches, the causeway joining the airfield to Stanley, the Cathedral, and the peaks of Tumbledown, Harriet, Wireless Ridge and distant Mount Kent.

We touched down at six forty pm, and I was soon bumping my way in Lieutenant-Colonel John Mills's ex-Argentinian Mercedes 'Jeep' through the minefield gap, past the abandoned litter of war and up to the Upland Goose Hotel. There I found myself sharing a table with the initial reconnaissance team for the proposed new Falklands international airfield which consisted of Colonel Robin Jukes-Hughes, Royal Engineers, and Mr Maurice Chammings of the Property Services Agency. I quickly checked in at the British Forces Headquarters with Colonel Roger Wheeler, the Chief of Staff, Colonel Gerald Blakey, the Colonel AQ, and Colonel Derek Brownson, the Commander Royal Engineers. I also met Major Tony Reed-Screen, whose excellent introductory briefing and subsequent extensive plans ensured I experienced as much Aftermath as possible, Captain Jimmy James, the Senior Naval Officer Falkland Islands (SNOFI), and Group Captain Bill Wratten, the Air Force Commander. As Roger Wheeler put it to me, the Headquarters had been started up from six big mail bags 'stuffed with signals'.

Within the hour I was at Government House, talking to Rex Hunt, previously the Governor but now the Civil Commissioner, who had arrived back on the Islands on 25 June, and to Major-General David Thorne, the Military Commissioner/Commander British Forces who had arrived on 17 July to take over from Major-General Jeremy Moore. I had last seen General Thorne when he was a student at the Army Staff College and I was an instructor. He had played a star role even then – in the end-of-course pantomime.

At last, but a month too late, I had arrived in the Falklands – for the Aftermath.

3 | SCENE SETTING

Stanley Airfield is the top Aftermath priority. During the campaign it had suffered five craters and some 1,000 'scabs' which are small scoops cut out of the runway as a result of the impact on it of different types of ordnance, especially cannon shells and rocket fire. There was no operative system for aircraft fuel.

First the airfield had to be rehabilitated into a safe, operationally efficient condition which could be defended and into which the Hercules from Ascension could bring reinforcements, specialists and the urgently required stores. These were all crucial for the Garrison's own administrative survival, the Falkland Islanders' initial rehabilitation, and the continued deterrent defence of the Islands against what is still assessed as a threat – even if only from rogue elements – from Argentina.

It was therefore very correct that on my first cold, wet, blustery Falklands day I was taken out by Colonel Derek Brownson, the Commander Royal Engineers, from Wrangle in Lincolnshire, to visit the airfield and 'get the message'. The scene resembled my father's descriptions of the Somme – there was deep mud everywhere, through and in which dark green parka-clad, muffled, mittened, gum-booted men slithered and strove to work. The challenging conditions made everything more than twice as difficult to do, yet there were cheery grins behind the grey breath clouds, a running commentary of wise-cracking earthy humour and obvious steely determination to get the work done.

The Harrier force was still operating from a Forward Operating Base, flying from an airstrip of aluminium matting running parallel to the patched-up main runway. The extent of this was such that a culvert had had to be built by Sappers – made of empty Exocet missile containers! Nothing else available had been suitable – thus making it probably the most expensive culvert in the world. When we arrived, the exceptional Falklands gales – gusting up to 100 mph – had just collapsed two of the large Rubb aircraft shelters. [Two of the all-too-few Harriers had been struck by the falling arched roofs and had been badly damaged; another looked pretty sick, and it was some time before they were fit to fly again – a story which for operational reasons could not be written at the time.] Airmen were busy lashing down the remaining aircraft, whilst the Sappers were busy trying to work out how to strengthen the design of the shelters' footings.

Colonel Brownson next took me to see the Emergency Fuel Handling Equipment System which had recently been installed. This used a pipeline

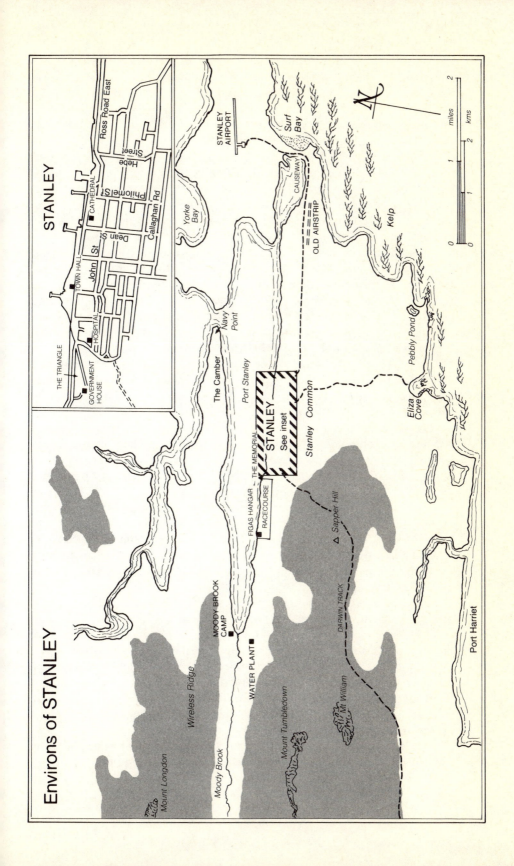

Environs of STANLEY

STANLEY (inset)

THE TRIANGLE
Ross Road East
Hebe Street
Philomel St.
Dean St.
Callaghan Rd
John St.
TOWN HALL
CATHEDRAL
HOSPITAL
GOVERNMENT HOUSE

Mount Longdon
Wireless Ridge
Moody Brook
MOODY BROOK CAMP
WATER PLANT
Mount Tumbledown
Mt William
Sapper Hill
DARWIN TRACK
Port Harriet
Port Stanley
The Camber
Navy Point
Yorke Bay
STANLEY AIRPORT
Surf Bay
CAUSEWAY
OLD AIRSTRIP
Kelp
Pebbly Pond
Eliza Cove
STANLEY See inset
Stanley Common
THE MEMORIAL
FIGAS HANGAR
RACECOURSE

N

0   1   2   miles
0   1   2   kms

to pump aircraft fuel ashore direct to the airfield from a beached fuel dracone. When empty, the dracone had to be towed by a Royal Corps of Transport work-boat out to a tanker, anchored in Port William, for refilling. Although somewhat laborious, it was a far better system than ferrying fuel out to the airfield in drums by truck – a very tedious task tying up valuable men and other resources.

The line of the pipe ran from the airfield, through an Argentine minefield and down into the attractive, small Yorke Point beach, on which sat a sad-looking wrecked D6 bulldozer. Another expensive casualty also stranded there was a Combat Engineer Tractor which had driven over an anti-tank mine. Although the Colonel assured me the immediate run of pipe had been cleared of mines, one kept open-eyed and rather near it. The little beach had also been cleared, but the sea and sand movement drifted and brought in a nearby anti-tank mine which had caught the dozer by surprise. The dunes and beaches were, and will remain, a nastily treacherous area of 'now you see it, now you don't'.

We moved on through a new kind of deep mud, this time creamy grey-white. We were by the granite quarry, once used by civilian contractors for the construction of the original Stanley airfield, now reopened by the Sappers. There had been trouble with the rock-crusher, but new ones were due to be landed shortly. The rock-drills had also been jamming in the exceptionally hard rock, and a civilian expert was flying out from Britain to advise on a solution to the problem.

Nevertheless, the quarry's output was sufficient to keep several hundred Sappers of 3 and 50 Field Squadrons busy extending the previous totally inadequate aircraft parking aprons and providing the elements of an operational lay-out which would subsequently form part of the planned extended and re-surfaced main runway system.

After a tour of some of the RAF's tented and battened-down accommodation, and the troglodyte quarters of some of the RAF Regiment's detachments, we had a quick look at the Argentine defences arrayed along the airport's southern beach approaches. These had been given priority initially; the defenders had had plenty of time, and hence had 'gone to town' in developing them.

The defences were based upon line behind echeloned line of well-prepared, deeply-dug trenches with overhead cover and bristling with interlocking fire. The whole was meshed with barbed wire and laced with booby traps. Mortars and machine-guns were plentiful and in close support with, presumably, a very detailed pre-registered fire plan. To the rear, on Stanley Common, were 105 mm and 155 mm guns for further support. We agreed that any British force that had landed there would have had the greatest difficulty in surviving. San Carlos, despite all its peculiar problems, was well chosen.

We land-rovered back to Stanley over the pot-holed and disintegrating only metalled road the Falklands possessed, past a huge rusting pile of rifles removed from Argentinian prisoners.

Yes, this was the Aftermath indeed – the stark sculptured still-life of abandoned artillery angled to the sky, the twisted chassis of vehicles blasted to scrap, the miserable droop of a knocked-out Argentine helicopter, the frayed roofs and sagging wires of shell-torn buildings and the endless filth, mud and glinting carpet of haphazardly strewn cartridge cases by the thousand.

Thankful even for the vehicle's windows that tempered the chill of bitter darkening cold, at least I had a warm glow inside me that said 'This is what I came so far to see'.

The next day, out on a wide-ranging tour with Lieutenant-Colonel Geoff Field, we landed at Ajax Bay – the Red Beach of the initial landings – a dark, depressing place full of the rusting débris of war and of lately abandoned mountains of assorted stores. I explored the gaunt windowless caverns of the one-time meat refrigeration plant which, during the campaign, had been turned into the miraculous 'Red and Green Life Machine' Falklands Field Hospital, commanded by Surgeon-Commander Rick Jolly.

Right Flank Company of 2nd Battalion, The Scots Guards, had been stationed there after the surrender until returning home with the Battalion on the *Norland* in late July.

Inscribed in old English writing by Lance-Sergeant Jim Leslie on one of the factory's huge gaunt interior walls, and flanked by his drawings of the cap star of The Scots Guards and the badge of 9 Parachute Squadron Royal Engineers, was the '*Ode to Tumbledown*' written by Lieutenant Mark Mathewson. Made the more poignant by its immediacy, this instant tribute to the Battalion's epic battle, and especially to those killed in it, ran thus:

ODE TO TUMBLEDOWN

It was the Guardsmen of the Crown
Who scaled the heights of Tumbledown
And fought that night a bloody fight
To see victory by dawn's first light.
From crag to crag amongst the rock
They skirmished on, numbed by shock;
Through shell and mortar fire they moved
Till at last the ground they'd proved,
Port Stanley lay there – just ahead
As they began to count their dead.
But where the glory, where the pride
For those eight brave men who died?
They who made that lonely sacrifice
And through each death paid the total price,

In their final and heroic act
Did surely speed the warring armies' pact,
Each one who there his life laid down
Saved countless others from their own unknown.
So those of you who live to talk
Let your pride hover as does the hawk
And never let men these acts forget
Nor the memory of our dead neglect,
But once returned across this vast sea
Remember then just what it was to be . . .
A Scots Guardsman.

20 June, 1982.

Colonel Geoff Field and I walked the hundred yards or so up the hillside
to the wind-stretched Union Jack, bright-coloured against the surrounding
drab of the peaty braeside, which, together with the little plot of white
crosses, marked the temporary resting place of those who died in the
Argentinian bombings on the landings and 2 PARA's historic attack on
Goose Green.

It was a poignant place, made all the more so by its simplicity, and the
visible equality in death of those who had died doing their respective jobs
in war: Colonel 'H' Jones buried alongside his men – helicopter pilot
beside Sapper corporal.

4 | THE MINES

The biggest hazard to life and limb of both Falkland Islanders and the British Servicemen after the Argentine surrender is the vast quantity of live mines and unexploded ammunition of all kinds that lie everywhere. Children wanting to go out and play are at especially high risk.

The sheer scale of this nightmare problem had become apparent to the men of 59 Independent Commando Squadron Royal Engineers when they entered Stanley with 2nd Battalion, The Parachute Regiment from Wireless Ridge. Major Roddy Macdonald, the Officer Commanding, who tackled it first, said, 'For the first time in the campaign, I was faced with a huge problem without the means of being able to solve it – a very isolated position to be in, and I felt very lonely.'

Lieutenant John Mullin of 9 Parachute Squadron, Royal Engineers, which during the campaign had mainly supported the units of 5 Infantry Brigade, told me that the mines were thick around Sapper Hill, by the Darwin track coming into Stanley from the south-west, and north of Wireless Ridge. There were mines scattered around the main mountain battle areas to the west of Stanley and reaching down to the sea near Port Harriet. Mines had been laid in West Falkland, too, and at Grytviken and Leith in South Georgia.

Another threat comes from the many unexploded bombs, shells and missiles of all kinds, fired by both the British and the Argentinians, lying buried and unburied in the same areas. There are also booby-traps of both crude and highly sophisticated design, often attached to attractive items like abandoned binoculars or just to a series of hidden grenades.

Coating the streets, strewn across gardens and pavements and tucked into odd corners of garages and stores, sometimes hidden in the filth, is a vast quantity of half-opened, discarded and exposed ammunition of all kinds. 'It is an Aladdin's Cave defying description,' said Captain Dick Gill RAOC, the Task Force's Ammunition Technical Officer.

On 14 June Major Macdonald tracked down the Argentinian Chief Engineer, Lieutenant-Colonel Dorago, and asked him to produce not only all the data and records he had on the minelaying but also the men who had done it. It quickly became clear that the Argentinian Marines and Army engineers had both been laying mines and in some areas had overlapped.

On 15 June 59 Commando Squadron's Recce Troop, led by Lieutenant Clive Livingstone, RE, and now joined by Warrant Officer Class 2 Pete

Ellis, teamed up with fourteen selected key Argentinian engineer prisoners-of-war. Splitting up into small groups, they went out to see what they could actually find 'on the ground'.

A 'mines warning' was broadcast on the local radio to the civilians and the Squadron established a Mines Operation Centre in the Government Secretariat building to collate information and direct the work.

By the end of the day a gruesome picture emerged. The Argentinians did not know how many mines they had really laid, or where, and could not even vouch for those for which records did exist. The map traces were often inaccurate, and maps to which they referred were missing.

Some key pickets driven into the ground as marking reference points had been removed. Many mines laid on the beaches had been shifted by the sea or were now deep-buried under wind-lashed sand. In the latter stages of the final battles, Argentinian marine, gunner and infantry units had all used mines which were largely unrecorded.

By now 59 Commando Squadron had an exceptionally co-operative group of volunteer Argentinian Marine and Army engineer prisoners-of-war working with them on the mine clearance task. On 18 June, however, Corporal 'Bas' Morgan lost a foot on a mine, and three days later Lance-Corporal 'Molly' Millinson, who was following immediately behind one of the Argentinians, also lost a foot. But it was peacetime now, and Major-General Jeremy Moore, Commander Land Forces, made the decision that, apart from vital priority tasks which made mine clearing unavoidable, only the identification and fencing off of Argentine minefields would henceforth be undertaken.

29 July, 1982

Horrific is the only word to describe the problem of the Argentine mines in the Falkland Islands. Over 12,000 are currently estimated to have been laid around Stanley alone, but the total figure could well be much higher. It is too soon yet to be sure, if ever one can be.

In the early days of their Garrison's occupation, the Argentinians densely mined the areas which they thought most likely for the British seaborne invasion. In the main, these were the beaches and inland areas around Stanley airport and near Stanley town, especially to the south.

Once they realized that the British had landed at San Carlos, however, the Argentinians hurriedly laid new belts of minefields in places like Mount Longdon, to the west of Stanley, and also to cover the northern and southern routes to it. They also reinforced others in their previous defences. In the last stages of the battle, they hastily issued even more mines to units for quick desperate laying, and many more were reported to have been laid indiscriminately direct from helicopters. Some areas were not proper minefields at all, but simply areas of dangerous booby-traps to catch the unwary. Certainly some of these were set out extremely late on in the battle.

Lieutenant John Mullin, whose Field Troop from 9 Parachute Squadron, Royal Engineers, has recently been responsible for the mines problem, showed me the range of mines found to date. Basically these are four types of anti-personnel mine, varying from three to six inches in diameter, three of which are difficult for current British mine detectors to pick up because their metallic content is too low. They are of Spanish, Italian, Argentine and other origin – sophisticated, modern and deadly.

The anti-tank mine range includes five types, of similar national origins, plus an American model. One of these, very cunningly, acts both as an anti-personnel and an anti-tank mine simultaneously. Three types float. Only two of them are readily detectable by standard British equipment. [*Details of the mines used by the Argentinians in the Campaign are given in Annex A.*]

Lieutenant Mullin told me there were 105 separate known mined areas around Stanley to date. Those laid early on had usually been fenced in, the mines buried and reasonably recorded. Those laid following the British landing were poorly marked, if at all, and unrecorded. Those sown from helicopters could have landed on the surface, ready armed, anywhere. Most minefields contained both anti-personnel and anti-tank mines.

The task of initially clearing Stanley was undertaken by 59 Independent Commando Squadron, Royal Engineers, but in five days they had suffered three casualties. The order was then given to suspend all actual mine lifting, except for vital areas, until new techniques and equipment were available. The emphasis was switched to locating and fencing in the mined areas, and the task passed to 9 Parachute Squadron.

Thirty-five Argentinian prisoners-of-war volunteered to help and gave valuable assistance. They are now back in Argentina. They showed the Sappers the location of many of the minefields laid, and also taught them the Argentinian methods of laying and recording. Having visited a number of the minefields, I was surprised at the lack of depth of some of them, often with only four rows of mines at quite wide spacings. In some areas the Argentinians had not even bothered to remove their tell-tale empty mine boxes from the sites. When laying properly, their method was to use long lines, with D-rings fitted at the ends to fit over marking pegs. These lines were also fitted with circular rings at designated intervals to indicate the correct point at which each mine was to be laid and buried. [*Details of the Standard Argentine Minelaying Procedure are given in Annex B.*] The main mine-affected areas around Stanley were split into four, each the responsibility of a team led by an NCO. Sergeant Sweeney, who had been in the battle for Mount Longdon, was responsible for the area of Stanley Airfield. Sergeant Strettle, who had been with 2nd Battalion The Scots Guards, was given the maze-like area of Stanley Common. Sergeant Corck, who had been with 2 PARA on Wireless Ridge, took the Darwin Road approach and the south-western end of Stanley. Corporal Foran [*later awarded a Military Medal for his work in the Battle of Tumbledown*] became responsible for the north-western area of Stanley.

Lieutenant Mullin estimates his teams have now fenced in some seventy per cent of the known mined areas, marked down a further twenty per cent and know where another five per cent should be. But even this is a dangerous job because there may be others, and you have first to find the minefield 'edge'. One of the Argentinian Corporal POWs lost a limb on a mine near Pebbly Pond.

Many problems affect progress. The rough seas pounding on the beach shift the mines in the sand. Snow on the ground covers up everything, and so all mine activity has to come to a halt. Mines have appeared in places previously checked. In one instance, on the Darwin Road, it may have been only the fact that the ground was frozen solid that failed to set off a deadly mixture of a bomb topped by an anti-tank mine when a British Land-Rover went over it. This interesting combination was only unearthed after an Argentinian Lieutenant POW actually travelling in the Land-Rover with Lieutenant Mullin remembered laying it!

The policy today is still that no mines should be lifted unless absolutely necessary, but obviously there are certain areas of ground which are operationally vital to clear. Quite apart from the Stanley area, there are more minefields yet to be dealt with at Fox Bay and at Port Howard in West Falkland; many have now been lifted at Goose Green; there were none at San Carlos.

Mines are also expected to have been laid on Mount Murrell, to the north of Stanley. Helicopter reconnaissance has confirmed a number of injured and three-legged animals there, mainly sheep. No records exist for it, and obviously the real total size of the mine problem has yet to be fully circumscribed. The possibility of some future casualties cannot be excluded despite the detailed safety precautions which are taken.

In the vital areas mine clearance still has to be done by prodding by hand, using something resembling a long meat skewer. Each one found has then to be dealt with. But some other techniques are soon to be tried out here. New American and German detectors, which operate by detecting anomalies and density variations in the ground, will soon be tried out. Trials are to be made of infra-red linescan equipment from a Gazelle helicopter in the hope of revealing hitherto unknown minefields.

Whereas the peat's peculiar smells have defeated traditional forms of 'sniffer', mine dogs will soon arrive to see if they can do any better. Much hope is set on a 1982 adaption of the Second World War 'Flail Tank' technique, it uses a bulldozer with an armoured cab, with a rotating bar mounted forward to which are attached short pieces of heavy chain. As the bulldozer moves forward, the chains flail the ground and should either detonate or disintegrate the anti-personnel mines, but it is no good in very wet or rocky ground. Driving the dozer on its trials is Lance-Corporal McCartney, a Royal Engineer plant operator. [*This technique proved unsuccessful on live trials – it could not guarantee 100 per cent clearance – and was therefore abandoned.*] The use of vehicle-mounted very high pressure water jets of up to 3,000 pounds per square inch is another idea being canvassed for the beaches and for the peat.

This peculiar Falklands terrain, however, varies from peat to rock outcrop very quickly, so no one technique can be universally applied; each method brings its own difficulties and has its own limitations. One captured Senior Argentinian officer, asked how he would have cleared the mines if they had won, answered simply 'with sheep'.

The Falklands mine problem is now, and will remain, a tremendous challenge for the Royal Engineers. They have done, and will continue to do, much dangerous and valuable work; their enthusiasm is unabated and very encouraging. They are determined to 'crack the problem' one way or another. It may well be, however, that in due course the Government may decide mined areas must so remain into the future, perhaps marked 'no entry – grazing only'.

Now deep into the cold and biting South Atlantic winter, the civilian population does not venture out much. But, come the Falklands spring, they and their children will want to be out and about again. Their favourite beaches and much of the surrounding countryside will necessarily, however, still be denied to them for their own safety. More particularly, in September each year they start cutting the peat banks for their vital annual fuel supply and many of these will still be behind mine fences. It may therefore become necessary to import alternative fuel – coal or anthracite – for the Falkland Islanders. The cost of it would be just another extra to put down to the unique Falkland experience. [*Fresh peat banks were later opened up.*]

The Argentine Marine Officer and the other thirty-four POWs (twenty Army, fourteen Marines) were what Lieutenant Mullin described 'as the key to the puzzle' in the early days of trying to get to grips with the Argentine mine problem.

They worked cheerfully, proved eager to please and were proud of their specialist skills as professionals. Retention of their continuing co-operation in what was proving to be a good joint working relationship was obviously important.

Warrant Officer Class 1 Canessa, a Spanish linguist from the Engineer-in-Chief's Branch in the MOD, joined the 9 PARA team. A wit, the possessor of a lively quick mind and a tireless worker, his job was to look after the volunteer mine POWs who were being kept together as a separate group.

Although always under strong armed guard, and only allowed out of their accommodation for specific purposes, nevertheless the POWs did gain some return for their volunteered services. They were paid, had showers and were given captured Argentine clothing and food. Devout men, Roman Catholic services were arranged for them. A bugler and joint Guards of Honour were provided at the burials of Argentinian casualties discovered by the continuing mine-clearance work. The Red Cross had right of access to the POWs at any time, and exercised this on a number of occasions.

On 2 July, as mentioned earlier, an Argentinian mine-clearing POW working on Stanley Common stepped on an anti-personnel mine. He was immediately given first aid, and as a result of Lieutenant John Mullin gallantly running through the minefield to radio for help, within fifteen minutes the POW was on his way to the operating table in a Royal Navy Wessex helicopter. He lost his leg from above the knee, but survived.

On 4 July the Argentinian POW mine team invited the OC 9 PARA, Major Chris Davies, and the British mine team to a barbecue. It was paid for and cooked by the Argentinians themselves who said they wished to thank the British for saving the life of their Corporal.

On 8 July a load of Argentinian POWs including the 'Mine Team' were embarked with their comrades onto the ferry *St Edmund* in preparation for their repatriation. The next day, however, when invited to do so, all thirty-five members of the 'Mine Team' re-volunteered to stay on and continue their dangerous work, subject to three conditions they required to be met to protect their personal position on their eventual repatriation. These were, firstly, that they would go back into the same accommodation that they had occupied previously. Secondly, that they would not have to do any mine fencing work although they would advise where the fences should run. Thirdly, they wanted specific assurances that they would go back to Argentina not before or after the rest of the POWs, but with the main body so that in no way could they be branded by any of their compatriots as specially collaborationist. General Mario Menendez, the Argentinian Falklands Garrison Commander and himself a POW, accepted the first two conditions, but baulked at the third, saying neither 'yes' nor 'no', only that he would trust the British to carry out whatever they wanted to do.

The whole incident arose because the thirty-five 'Mine Team' POWs had all been put on board the *St Edmund* early, and had thus been re-united with their friends. In the end, the 'Mine Team' stayed on board and sailed for Argentina with their compatriots.

9 PARA sailed for Britain on 17 July leaving behind Lieutenant Mullin and Sergeant Wrega [later awarded a Military Medal for his part in the campaign] to hand over responsibility for the Falklands mine problem to 69 Gurkha Independent Field Squadron RE.

5 | EOD

The Argentine mines are one thing, but there is also a vast array of other dangerous explosive objects lying about much of the Falklands today. A tremendous amount of clearing-up work has been done already, especially in the streets and public areas of Stanley. But the whole place is still something of an Explosives Ordnance Disposal (EOD) man's paradise. There is enough work here to keep him busily employed for at least another two years; on average one meets some items of ammunition on the ground every five paces.

'A fantastic EOD experience' was how Major Guy Lucas, the Royal Engineer who leads the Joint Service EOD Cell and who is also Officer Commanding 49 EOD Squadron, described it. He co-ordinates the work of the Royal Engineers Mine Clearance Teams, his own EOD specialists and, when necessary, that of the RAF experts, the Royal Navy Fleet Clearance Divers and the Royal Army Ordnance Corps ammunition specialists. The RN divers specialize in underwater clearance, and the RAF experts deal with items like the napalm 'bombs' found at Goose Green. Major Lucas's main responsibility is the area clearance of all these dangerous bits and pieces, whereas the problem of the minefields, known and unknown, is currently delegated to a designated Royal Engineer Field Squadron.

At the end of the war Goose Green and all the Falkland Islands from roughly east of Mount Kent contained a very large complex of overrun Argentine defensive positions which still held vast quantities of live ammunition, grenades, rockets, flares and other explosive objects of every kind. Some were in good unused condition; some had been damaged and were therefore now unstable. Much of this Aftermath is clearly visible, as I have witnessed myself in the Argentine trenches on Mount Tumbledown and Mount Longdon. Many other items, however, are now hidden amongst the general debris of war and in half-collapsed defensive positions. At the rear of Mount Kent we checked a still-unexploded 1,000 lb bomb – one of those dropped by the Argentine Skyhawks which attacked 3 Commando Brigade's Headquarters on the afternoon of 13 June.

The abandoned Argentine 155 mm dug-in gun positions near Stanley, which I visited with Major Lucas, are now heavily flooded with peat water, and much deadly material is lying just below its chocolate-coloured surface.

To make matters worse, there are also items which the Argentinian Infantry and Gunners fired at the British, and which the British fired at the Argentinians, which for one reason or another failed to explode. These items can either be still lying on the surface or, following their point of impact, firmly lodged underground. Sometimes their tail fins are protruding, and sometimes there is just a hole in the ground like a little rabbit burrow. Peat makes tracing the latter more difficult, since it tends to shatter and make a projectile's entry tunnel more ragged. Some unexploded items have sunk right down into the very soft areas of bog where they landed and thus may remain an unknown irrecoverable hazard for ever.

Both the British and the Argentine Air Forces fired cannon at, and dropped bombs on, each other's positions, and the Royal Navy fired many shells on to the mainland. Not all of this ordnance exploded, and in the case of cluster bombs not all the distributed bomblets exploded. This is another whole area of work for the EOD men. The earlier problem of dealing with unexploded bombs in the Royal Navy ships by experts in both Services is already well known. The very gallant Staff Sergeant who died doing this work, and the Warrant Officer who was severely wounded, were both Royal Engineer EOD men. [*Staff Sergeant James Prescott RE was later posthumously awarded the rare Conspicuous Gallantry Medal. WO2 John Phillips RE was awarded the Distinguished Service Cross.*]

The Argentinians were very keen on creating major areas of booby-trapped devices. These consisted mainly of a variety of push and pull switches and igniters, often tripwire operated, connected to large packets, even boxes, of explosives. They were also attached to grenades – a favourite trick – mines and large conventional bombs.

More deadly, they placed booby-traps in some of their abandoned trenches; for instance a number of grenade 'traps', invitingly laid, were set for those in a hurry. These were often simple devices, as Major Lucas showed me up on Mount Longdon, like grenades without a safety pin leant against another object, ready to explode when dislodged, or two grenades linked together for maximum effect. Lance-Corporal Budhaparsad Limbu of 1st/7th Gurkhas was killed by such an object in the early Aftermath, while clearing the Argentinian trenches at Goose Green.

After the surrender, horrifyingly, a large number of booby-traps were found set amongst the civilian houses in Stanley itself; and at Government House the defending Argentinians had set up a number of command-detonated explosive charges designed to be fired from within the House in the face of any British assault. The day after the surrender Lieutenant-Colonel Geoff Field personally neutralized one of these devices consisting of three anti-tank mines coupled up to two large propane gas cylinders.

The Argentinians, contrary to some reports earlier in the war, were not short of ammunition of any kind. It is still here heaped pile upon pile, much of it in unopened new boxes and much else spilling out like rows of evil teeth. There are containers of every nature from rifle bullets, through grenades – including some previously quite unknown varieties – mines, cannon shells and rockets of every possible size and shape, to heavy shells, missiles and bombs.

One area of collection alone covers several acres full of assorted Cobra and SAM missiles; mines; 60, 81 and 120 mm mortar rounds; 155 and 105 mm shells; 35 and 30 mm cannon shells; nasty 'two-time' EA-M5 and other grenades; and even some dum-dum rifle cartridges. A number of types have yet to be traced to the country of manufacture.

The EOD area clearance problem, like that of the mines, is enormous in itself. It calls for painstaking research, knowledge, skill, confidence – and nerve. All the available records of firings in the campaign are now being analysed in order to try and establish what areas have actually been under fire, by what type of projectile, and with what known effect. For example, known numbers of a particular type of bomb dropped on a particular area can be checked against the known characteristic crater burst for that type. This gives some idea of what may be around in that area and still unaccounted for. Sensitive EOD instruments can then start an appropriate detailed search for the remainder. With the best will in the world, however, no one can ever guarantee a war area 100 per cent safe.

In the uniquely intense Falklands EOD situation, everywhere is having to be subjected to keen-eyed initial visual search to spot and then neutralize the surface-spread ammunition and other explosive items. Much of this can be safely collected. This initial search can then be followed up by more specialist techniques. Stanley Town, of which about thirty per cent has been checked out by Search Teams, is an obvious top priority. A number of house gardens still await this treatment. The current advice to everyone is 'do not walk on grass areas unless you know it has been cleared'. The area beside the road leading out of the town towards Darwin is currently particularly dangerous. Whereas the Stanley civilians and the troops are well aware of the situation, the safety of stray visitors landing from ships, who may not be, are one of Major Lucas's perpetual worries. Searching the huge areas around Stanley, let alone the mountain battle areas, has yet to start. Much remains to be done, also in the outlying ground of Goose Green, San Carlos, Pebble Island and Fox Bay.

At Goose Green, for instance, I saw an enormous collection of assorted ordnance which has already been gathered together at the end of the grass airstrip – and there is plenty more to be added to it yet. Not far away is a damaged and upended Argentine Pucara aircraft.

The British cluster bombs' unexploded scattered bomblets are among the more dangerous items to tackle. Even now one of Major Lucas's senior NCOs is dealing with some lying in shallow water near Port Howard. The whole of the affected areas of danger throughout the Falklands will take ages to work over.

Much of the 'Aladdin's Cave' haul of dangerous EOD and mines material already collected is now being disposed of safely. Most of this is done by controlled explosions. Among the items destroyed since 18 June are forty-three 1,000-pound and cluster bombs, a sea mine and forty-eight large missiles. Also 'cleared' are twenty-six crashed aircraft. The Team had additionally dealt with some napalm, countless shells, mortars, bombs, rockets, mines and a good weight of bulk explosive.

Yesterday, out with Captain Brian Lloyd of 49 EOD Squadron, I fired the circuit blowing up two damaged Tigercat missiles, and visited a 1,000-pound bomb whose explosive was in the process of being steamed out.

Travelling around with Major Lucas, and since, I find I have developed a strong inclination – particularly when having to walk on grass tufted peat out in the 'Camp' (countryside) – to keep at least one eye trained on the ground just ahead of my large size eleven feet. It is very different for the solitary smug-looking penguin I saw walking along a beach minefield, he was obviously happy in the knowledge that he was well below the minimum weight for activating any fuses.

Tremendous gallantry was shown by many of all ranks of the three Services involved in the Falklands campaign, a number of whom were deservedly awarded decorations and medals. There was bravery shown in the Aftermath, too, by those who risked the hazards of discovering, marking and clearing the mines; rendering safe the booby traps cunningly laid in the abandoned Argentine trenches and other fire positions; and disposing of the unexploded bombs, cluster bomlets and other lethal ordnance, together with large quantities of unstable damaged Argentine ammunition and missiles.

After the Second World War those actively engaged on post-hostilities bomb and mine disposal in Britain up until as late as 31 December, 1949, were awarded the General Service Medal with an appropriate clasp for this hazardous work. Following this precedent, Parliamentary moves were made post-Falklands to mark the service of those so engaged in the South Atlantic after the Argentine surrender. But all these efforts, to the dismay of a number of MPs and even though they reached the personal attention of the Prime Minister, regrettably proved unsuccessful.

6 | ACCOMMODATION

In July the bulk of the Falklands Garrison is neccesarily based on Stanley. It is the seat of Government and contains the Headquarters and most of the British Forces. It has the only airfield link with the outside world and possesses the only comparatively sheltered suitable anchorage for the shipping which has brought down all the logistic, engineering and other stores the British Force requires both to administer itself and to create the basis of some sort of more permanent garrison.

The main problem, never fully appreciated by some back in Britain, is the absence of any of the proper port or other infrastructure support such as would be normal elsewhere in the world in the early Eighties. What very little there was has been damaged and is virtually unusable. Stanley, really a fair-sized coastal village, has no unloading facilities, no spare accommodation and no storage ashore to take the huge quantities that need to be handled.

The shipping therefore has to stay at anchor as floating store-houses, whilst either their contents are used up, or it is their turn to be unloaded by ship's derrick into lighters and the stores brought ashore through Army tracking-matted, specially bulldozed slipways. Such is the queue that some vessels have to go back to top up with more stores at Ascension whilst some of their other holds still contain stores awaiting unloading at Stanley.

The sheer numbers of the British Garrison mean that some ships have to be kept just as sources of readily available but crowded accommodation from which the men 'commute' ashore daily by powered raft.

If I had not personally witnessed it, I would not have believed that the Falklands winter weather could be so changeable that on some days, even though the accommodation ships are anchored in the comparative safety of Stanley less than 200 yards out, the water state can become too rough for men to be brought across to work and the scheduled timetable for several projects suffers thereby.

The Settlements out in the country – 'the camp' as it is called – vary greatly in size but all are comparatively small. There are not that many – only forty in all – and they range from one or two farming families up to about 180 souls in Goose Green, the largest Settlement. The only spare accommodation out 'in the camp' are the bunk-houses in the large Settlements which are normally kept for the transit stay of the sheep-shearing gangs at fleecing time, farm sheds that happen just to be empty, or the rare house unoccupied between tenancies.

Fitzroy Sound, scene of the disastrous Argentine air attack which descended so suddenly on the *Sir Galahad* and the *Sir Tristram* on 8 June, was tranquil yesterday. Overlooking it, contrasting with the pale green hillside into which they are set, shine the brilliant white boulders which form a huge leek, the Regimental badge of the Welsh Guards. It is a fitting and poignant memorial to the men who died there. Nearby the dug-outs and trenches in the peat still bear witness to the fact that, not long since, war had passed that way.

But in the green-roofed Fitzroy Settlement things have moved on. Major John Tulloch with his men from 137 Battery of 40 Field Regiment Royal Artillery have come out from Colchester to replace those of 4 Field Regiment who, their battle over, are now bound for home. Fresh and enthusiastic, they were hard at work catching up on their gun drills when I arrived. The Battery is normally equipped with heavy FH 70 155 mm guns and supports 19 Infantry Brigade. Its men were having to re-learn their drills on the 105 mm Light Gun. Delighted with the soft hills and quiet beaches of the Sound, these cheerful gunners are already talking in terms of what they will do 'in the summer'.

The men are at present accommodated in the sheep-shearers' bunkhouse, spare houses, and sheds in the Settlement. The local community offer them baths. Within three days of their arrival, however, seventy-five per cent of their number had been through the distressing and almost universal initiation test faced by most troops arriving in the Falklands. They had suffered from the dreaded 'Galtieri's Revenge', as it is locally known, which is a particularly virulent form of tummy bug. It lasts for about forty-eight hours but, once endured, it is unlikely to strike again.

Major Tulloch praised Mr Binney, the Settlement Manager, and the rest of the community for their marvellous help. It is quite a large Settlement by Falklands standards, being twenty-five families and about 16,000 sheep. The unit is keen to help the community in return, and Bombardier Jimmy Jenkins has become the local schoolmaster for the five children aged six to fourteen attending school. He is a surveyor by training 'and is good at maths'. He checks in weekly with the civilian Educational Authorities in Stanley for his next 'pack' of material and is 'chuffed' when the children call him 'Sir'.

The influx of soldiers obviously makes demands on the Settlement's water supply. To ease this situation, Lance-Corporal Alastair Simpson, from Kirriemure, and Sapper Ken Menzies, from High Wycombe, run a 'water point'. This pair, from 3 Field Squadron Royal Engineers, pump water up from the Sound into 2,500 gallon tanks for storage and treatment. The Gunners then call daily with a farm tractor and trailer, borrowed from the Settlement, to fill up their water jerricans from the purified supply.

The extraordinary cheerfulness and ready acceptance by all ranks of the difficult problems of accommodation in the Falkland Islands is most striking. It is matched only by the genuine concern strongly felt by those responsible, from General David Thorne downwards, to improve things just as soon as they can.

Everyone here now lives in a house of some sort, on an accommodation ship or in a heated tent. 'Field conditions', yes, but no one sleeps out, or rough. No one expects star hotel treatment, but for housing what is now really an alert peacetime garrison, of course much has yet to be done and will be done. At least the weather should be improving from now on. There are, however, several basic factors relevant to the Falklands accommodation situation about which a number of people in England seem to be unaware and do not appreciate.

The continuing assured defence of the Falkland Islands against any enemy threat must remain the overriding British priority. The most important element of this is the introduction of RAF Nimrod Airborne Early Warning aircraft and Phantom air defence fighters, land-based at Stanley airfield. But they cannot arrive until the airstrip itself is lengthened by the special American AM2 surfacing Britain has bought for the purpose. In the meantime the Naval Task Force's air cover, supplemented from the land, is still essential.

The Royal Engineers will undertake this major airfield task, once the design is completed and the necessary stores are on site. But there are port operating limitations and priorities. Port Stanley has no deep-water jetty or other ship-to-shore cargo handling facilities which can cope with the task. All the required items have to be offloaded by derricks and cranes on to Mexeflote powered pontoons from the two merchant ships lying out in Port William.

The military then have to sail the Mexeflotes into Stanley Harbour and bring them into a specially built military slipway. Offloaded by soldiers using fork lifts, and then loaded on to trucks, the airfield parts are then driven several miles up through the minefields beside the road to the airfield. This laborious and time-consuming process is now well under way, but the tonnage of stores required is huge; helicopters have been tried out, but are of no real help. When, as frequently happens, the 'Easterlies' blow in from the South Atlantic, the Mexeflotes cannot operate in the resultant sea state; the 'Westerlies' or 'Southerlies' make things even worse! In the meanwhile there is much import-ant associated preparatory work for the Royal Engineers to do which has to be completed on time, so as not to delay construction of the extension once the stores for it are ready. The minefield work must also continue.

Permanent 'hard' accommodation, Portakabins and the like, can only be constructed by the Royal Engineers and many associated services are required. This work can only be done once the priority task of the airfield has been completed. Everyone wants all this to be done as quickly as possible, but the problem is not one which could be speeded up just by providing more Royal Engineers, even if this were possible. First, the final Falklands force level for the Services has to be agreed, and the related deployment plan made for where the troops are to be stationed.

Engineer reconnaissance is then required in each selected deployment area to see where best, in conjunction with the local community, the permanent camps can be sited. Next, the resultant detailed plans have to be drawn up. Negotiations must then take place with the owners of the necessary land which, given Falkland soil conditions, may contain good sheep grazing.

All the stores required to build the permanent camps, including the large Portakabins, have first to be unloaded from the deep-water ships in Port William in which they are now held, using military resources. They must then be transported to the various sites. Because there are no roads in the Falklands countryside, all this distribution must be done the long way round by suitable shipping, supplemented by helicopter, farm tractors and trailers, and port facilities in the Settlements are very limited indeed.

Electric power, water, drainage, sewerage and recreational facilities – none of which will exist at the chosen sites – must also be provided for the troops for whom the camp will be home for the months of their overseas tour. If not, then the Portakabins will be no more than just so many hard tents. There is simply no instant solution to the longer term 'hard' accommodation problem. It will progress just as quickly as the peculiar Falklands factors allow it to, and hopefully by the end of the year much will have been done.

At present more than 4,000 Army and RAF live in a wide variety of accommodation. Some Royal Navy are also ashore. In talking informally to many men in each Service – and contrary to some reports recently circulating in Britain – I heard no complaints whatsoever. All the men with whom I spoke fully appreciated that, even with the war over, they had necessarily to live in field conditions for the present. Indeed, a detachment of RAF Regiment manning Rapiers – affectionately known as 'The Rock Apes' to their friends, and who probably live in the toughest conditions anywhere in the Falklands – told me they were angry at what they considered a false representation in the British Press of their situation and of their cheerful acceptance of it.

Accompanied by Captain David Harding, the HQ Staff Officer responsible, I visited every type of accommodation occupied by troops – private houses, tents, accommodation ships and even the Royal Corps of Transport Port Regiment's small craft on which the crews live. The TEV *Rangatira* currently houses 1,200 men on board in adequate bunk bed comfort; the soldiers say 'it is the only ship in the world that farts'. They are warm, dry and well fed but, because the vessel has to lie out, there is a daily commuting problem ship-to-shore for the troops. She could take more men, but feeding and water might then be difficult.

The Landing Ship Logistic *Sir Bedivere* (5,674 tons)* currently alongside, takes 298 men with full ship's facilities and reportedly excellent food. Again,

*Full Load Tonnages have been used throughout for Royal Navy and Royal Fleet Auxiliary vessels.

she could take more at a pinch, but is soon required for another important operational task.

The ferry *St Edmund*, now on her way back from Ascension, is seriously being considered for use as an extra accommodation ship for some 800/900 men. Like the *Rangatira*, she cannot come alongside, and her troops too would have to commute by boat to work ashore. Lastly there is the LSL *Sir Tristram* (5,674 tons) her superstructure a sad distorted mass of twisted burnt metal as a result of her bombing off Fitzroy. Moored over at Navy Point, she is not in current use, but exploring below deck I was astonished to find bunk bed, cabin and dormitory accommodation for 270 men, complete with light, heat, water and washing facilities. Her tank deck was still intact. Development plans are now in train to replace her lost catering facilities and to provide some recreational area. When these are implemented, she will provide invaluable additional accommodation.

Thanks to the help offered by the civil population, nearly 1,700 troops live in Stanley. Some are billeted with families, normally in ones or twos, but feed in Army cookhouses. Others live in houses offered completely to the Army; there were sixty-five men in one I visited. Many live in Government buildings, like the Town Hall or the Gymnasium, or in the Church Hall.

Conditions obviously vary widely from excellent to adequate, but in each case the men are dry and warm at night. Only a fool stays uncomfortable for long in such circumstances, and I can assure readers that the characteristic capability of the British soldier for self-help, improvisation and traditional 'curvaceous' wall adornment (usually '*Star*' birds) is as strong as ever!

Captain Harding stressed that acceptance of billeting by the householder is entirely voluntary, and of course the Army immediately relinquishes the house of any returning civilian who wants it back. Buildings essential to community life, like schools and churches, are not occupied. Nevertheless it is a fact that the number of billets with civilians, despite a system of payment, is significantly decreasing with time.

Outside Stanley, the troops live in the Settlements either in houses, sheep-shearers' bunkhouses or sheep sheds. Some of the latter can be a bit draughty. As one soldier put it, 'I'm not a sheep with a fleece'. Come shearing time in October, however, there may well be a temporary problem which can only be solved by tents. At present only the RAF's No. 18 Squadron of Chinook helicopters and some small deployed Rapier detachments out in the 'camp' have to live in tents, but the men are rotated periodically.

At Stanley Airfield 440 RAF men are currently living in tents, most of them Arctic type, but all have heaters. As several airmen told me, they, unlike soldiers, were not used to tents or field conditions, and found it 'tough going to begin with'.

Of course mud and the sponge-like peat are uncomfortable neighbours to live with, and 'wellies' have become part of daily life. The men had had to learn the art of tent living, with the cutting of surrounding drains, bunds and suchlike.

The airfield has to be ready-manned for operations twenty-four hours a day, and so the required number of RAF simply have to live out there. As an RAF Corporal said cheerfully, 'It would make no sense us swopping over with the Army's billets in town'. He and his mates told me they were warm and dry in their tent, and that was what mattered. He certainly had no complaint. The Rapier Air Defence crews, necessarily deployed in tactically suitable but exposed positions, undoubtedly have the toughest time. But there is currently a scheme which gives them two nights of 'rest and recreation' on the *Rangatira* every fourteen days. 'Wonderful it was to have a hot shower, get my laundry done and have someone else cook the food', a grinning airman told me in the fug of his shelter dug well down below the peat.

Britain's Servicemen fought excellently in the war out here. To me, however, there is something still tremendously commendable about all those now here in the very difficult phase of transition to proper peace. Morale is very high and they are all working extremely hard, twenty-four hours a day, determined 'to get it all sorted out'. They are still earning the nation's pride and deserve its admiration, and 8,000 miles from home, must not ever become forgotten.

Guardsman Phillip Williams, aged eighteen, of 2nd Battalion The Scots Guards, has just (2 August) found his way back into civilization at Bluff Cove Settlement. Previously posted as 'Missing believed killed', he was last seen with the Battalion on 14 June near Mount Tumbledown. Somehow he has miraculously survived forty-eight days on his own in an extremely hostile and well-mined environment – it is not yet fully clear how. [*It was later reported that he had found shelter for a while in an isolated building towards Port Harriet, earlier occupied by the Argentinians, containing some abandoned rations. Guardsman Williams was flown back to Britain where he was welcomed home by a rejoicing family, and rejoined his Battalion.*]

7 | THE DAVIDSONS

On 30 July I moved out of the famous Upland Goose Hotel overlooking Stanley's waterfront and into a small guest house called 'Malvinas', run by the kind and generous Davidson family, which better suited the circumstances of my stay in the South Atlantic.

Don Davidson originally worked in Antarctica with the British Antarctic Survey, but decided to come out and settle on a small island off the west coast of West Falkland. The temperature there is a few degrees warmer than in East Falkland, and he made a living out of horticulture, particularly selling salad produce and other vegetables to vessels like the *Lindbad Explorer* which regularly called in during its specialist tourist expeditions.

The Falklands have hardly any trees. There are some around Government House in Stanley, some at Roy and Hill Coves, at Carcass and at Teal Inlet, but that is virtually all. Deciding that trees could be useful as windbreaks or as shelter for stock, Don spent much time and effort experimenting with the problems of growing trees for what he saw as a potential Falklands market. After a number of failures due to the harsh, bleak climate, he eventually devised a successful way of raising them in a nursery but, to his regret, could not interest either the Falkland Islands Company or any other big landowners in his project. Presumably it would have been an investment for them on which there would have been no visible extra return. He had to give up his project.

In fact, a Government Forestry Officer ran a scheme from 1920 to 1926 trying to produce trees to grow in sheltered areas, and as shelter belts. But the scheme was eventually abandoned because it was very expensive and uneconomical. It was too cold and too windy for the young trees and, surprisingly, there was not enough rain for them!

Initially there were two families on their island, but the other one moved away and for the last few years the Davidsons lived entirely on their own. Occasionally they visited their neighbours on an adjacent island by boat. They educated their children themselves; but eventually, when their daughter was nearing seven, they decided that for the sake of her education, combined with the uncertainty of their horticultural outlet to passing ships, they had to give up their island home and move into Stanley.

The Davidsons had stayed in the Falklands throughout the Argentinian occupation. The Argentinians were very superstitious, they said, and were on the look-out for omens. In the first week a huge Argentine flag was hoisted on a flagpole outside the Government Secretariat building; but it was too heavy, and the flagpole blew down, a setback which many Argentinians regarded as a bad omen. It stayed down for a week. It was then replaced by a tiny flag on a tiny flagpole.

Then Post Office signs were erected in Spanish carrying rosettes in Argentina's national colours, but these were blown away by a sixty-knot wind and were never replaced.

Argentina's real failure over 'Las Malvinas' across the years, Don told me, was that they had totally failed to understand the fundamental British character, psychology and outlook of the Falkland Islanders. Argentinians used to fly over and spend holiday week-ends in Stanley. Incidentally, the Argentine National Airline's representative was an Air Force Officer. A number of Falkland Islanders used to visit Argentina, and the Argentine Government offered scholarships there for secondary education.

But none of this really affected the basic issue or reached out to the heart of the problem, he said. The Argentinians' psychological approach had, for them, been totally wrong. If they had really sat down and studied in depth the problem of regaining possession of 'Las Malvinas' some years ago, they would have come up with a very different solution based upon peacefully trying to woo the Islanders over a period of years.

For example, Don said, one obvious move would have been to give a commitment to take over the Falkland Islands Company, whose near monopoly on some important aspects of life was, apparently for some, one of the most irksome aspects of living in the Falklands. Investment and absentee landlords would have been other sensitive subjects for diplomatic manipulation. Of course such an approach could well have got the Argentinians nowhere anyway, but at least it would have been a more intelligent angle and might possibly have helped towards achieving some acceptable peaceful 'arrangement' or compromise in the long run. But for the Argentinians to opt for a military invasion of the Islands was an act of madness which could never have succeeded permanently. After all, it is an elementary fact that an alien government cannot ever win over a population by force.

The Argentine Garrison, Don said, was 'shattered' by the fact that they were not made welcome by the local population – something they simply could not understand. After a while it became obvious that many of the soldiers 'had no heart in it and didn't want to be here. For them the real killer was the deterioration in the weather at a crucial moment, which lost for many what little will to continue they had'. The officers were certainly very politically minded, 'with the régime', and fully accepted the claim for 'Las Malvinas' sovereignty.

The Argentinian soldiers hated their officers – 'which was why the Globe Store was burnt down just after the surrender. In fact the soldiers had made a mistake – they had meant to burn down the main officers' accommodation and mess building (which was opposite the Globe) but got the wrong house.' The ironic twist was that the Globe Store was one of the very few Argentine-owned buildings in town. Not only was the gulf between officers and men wide, Don said, but also that between the NCOs and the men. It was reported that on one occasion an Argentinian officer leading a patrol went inside a house and sat down for coffee and a talk for half-an-hour, whilst the rest of his patrol had to stand outside in the bitter cold. On another, a patrol leader, carrying no equipment, literally threw his binoculars back at his orderly which the poor man, already carrying both his own and his officer's equipment, was expected to catch. In the absence of an officer, the Argentine NCO was very much 'God' and quickly ensured the men knew it.

Many of the soldiers were illiterate. One patrol, completely lost, eventually stumbled in to Estancia. The soldier leading it was offered the use of the telephone to call up his HQ in Stanley, but it very soon transpired that not only could he not use one but had never even seen one before.

The Davidsons' home was warm and friendly. They were kindness itself to me, and nothing was too much trouble. After the surrender they had played host to the men of the Royal Marines Mountain and Arctic Warfare Cadre – 'a marvellous group' they said – who, on their departure, gave the Davidsons a signed Group souvenir drawing which hung proudly on the sitting-room wall. [*The Cadre's excellent forward patrolling and surveillance work during the campaign has been well recorded in Major-General Julian Thompson's book* No Picnic. *They were also involved in a sharp action at Top Malo House (in central East Falkland, east of Mount Simon) against a group of Argentinian Special Forces, on which a film was later based. I was privileged to watch it some months later in the Cadre's Mess in Norway, punctuated by the pertinent comments of those who had taken part in the original action.*]

Margaret Davidson's reputation for good cooking, despite the very limited range of foods then available in Stanley, soon spread throughout the Garrison until catering for farewell dinners became her forte, and faced the family with the dilemma of either remaining a guest house or becoming a restaurant; either would obviously be a success. [*The Davidsons are now back in Britain.*]

8 | RATIONS

The homely hot smell of freshly baked bread, wafting up Dean Street, next to the Cathedral, guided me unerringly to the Army's Bakery. The warmest and driest place in Stanley, it produces a twelve-ounce loaf per day for every man in the Garrison.

The Bakery Section, run by Master Baker Warrant Officer Class 1 Rob Ross from Nairn, is part of 9 Ordnance Battalion, Royal Army Ordnance Corps, stationed at Devizes. The Section has an operational role with NATO's Allied Mobile Force (Land) and normally spends about five months a year on exercises ranging from Northern Norway to Greece and Turkey. It left Britain on 19 May in the *St Edmund* and baked its first Falkland loaf on 30 June.

In charge of the shift duty was Sergeant Mick Jarwood, from Plymouth. He reckons to make 100 loaves from each fifty-five pound bag of strong wheat flour. Mixed, chopped into fourteen-ounce blocks, and then hand-rolled into balls, the dough mixture spends thirty minutes in the 'prover', followed by a further thirty-five minutes in the oven.

I was there when the oven door opened, and the six trays each of eighteen newly baked hot loaves came out. The Section's record – it works in two shifts – is 6,000 loaves in a day; it now bakes something like 4,000. In wet and cold Stanley fresh bread added to basic field rations makes all the difference and is excellent for morale.

6 August, 1982

The deep distinctions which so obviously existed in the Argentine Army between officers and men extended even to their twenty-four-hour ration packs. The officers' one was exactly twice the size of, and very different from, that of the men. In the British Army, needless to say, all ranks have exactly the same ration packs.

The Argentine soldiers' pack ration for a day contained four packets of water biscuits, jam, a small bar of chocolate, a tin of meatballs, drinking chocolate powder and half-a-dozen boiled sweets. It also had a small carton of fuel tablets, matches, and a metal frame upon which to heat up any item. In the officers' pack, by contrast, was a quarter bottle of whisky and a packet of cigarettes. There were also two large packets of biscuits, jam and honey, one tin of corned beef and one of beef with macaroni in tomato sauce, orange juice, tea bags and drinking chocolate powder. Finally the officers' pack contained toilet paper, a can opener, matches, a plastic mug and spoon, heating tablets and a better cooking stand. Officers' and soldiers' ration packs both contained political slogans and religious tracts.

The difference between the two packs – particularly the whisky and cigarettes touch – is almost unbelievable to anyone brought up in the British military tradition, but, as many people here have told me, 'It's perhaps indicative of why the Argentinians lost the war'. No wonder it is very difficult these days to find an Argentine officer-type ration pack around – they're much too popular!

9 | CRE WORKS

On the last day of the war Stanley's water plant at Moody Brook had been put out of action by a heavy shell. The sewerage system, being waterborne, was not working properly, and the way the Argentinians had simply used the floors in houses or sheds bore stark witness to this fact. Only one of the electricity station's three generators was functioning, and many of the overhead power distribution lines, cut by shellfire, were draped around town like so much loose knitting.

This was the situation faced by Lieutenant-Colonel Leslie Kennedy and his team who flew in from San Carlos on the morning after the surrender. His task, as Commander Royal Engineers (CRE) Works, Falkland Islands, was to use his Royal Engineers Civil, Electrical and Mechanical engineering experts, and other resources, working together with those available from the Falkland Islands Public Works Department (PWD), to rehabilitate the town. Colonel Kennedy's domain was formally declared a 'Military Works Area', the first to be so designated since Aden. [*This declaration stayed in effect until 1 April, 1984, when the 'Area' was handed over to the Property Services Agency (PSA): the CRE Works Unit was formally disbanded on 15 May, 1984.*]

Colonel Kennedy's priorities were water and electricity. He told me he had found fire hydrants turned on and Argentine-occupied houses with all the taps running. Since the town's daily leakage loss from its elderly pipe system was around fifty per cent, it was not surprising that the storage tanks emptied in a day with the result that the civilians were then down to their house reserves of water.

The presence of a large number of British ground forces and Argentinian prisoners-of-war, plus the fact that the town's 500,000 gallon reservoirs were down to only two days' supply, complicated the problem and gave it added urgency. The burning-down of the PWD's plumbers' workshop on surrender night, destroying all tools and spares, compounded it even further. Military water points were quickly established, however, and water dracones filled from the 'water ship' anchored off Stanley were brought into use in order to get by.

Intensive repair work at the Moody Brook water plant restored the supply source, but then further major damage to the pipe mains system was discovered which was difficult to repair. But after four days of feverish work by 9 Parachute and 61 Field Support Squadrons RE, water was back on again to parts of the town. The latter unit's welders, under Major Richard Nicholas's direction, did especially good work in repairing not only the cast iron pipes in the Moody Brook plant, but also the main pipeline leading from there into Stanley, which had been cut by shellfire. After a further six days of intensive effort the water was back on everywhere and the sewerage was in business again. Later 3 Field Squadron constructed and operated the major military water supply point at Moody Brook which supplemented the normal town system.

The Royal Engineers are still giving strong support to the PWD, and Warrant Officer Class 1 Gordon Hinds, from Newcastle, was in charge of Stanley's water supply out of Moody Brook yesterday. Explaining to me the problems and the repairs that had had to be carried out, he said that normally the town used 100,000 gallons a day. By supplementing it with military resources and storage tanks, this had now been upped to 120,000 gallons daily. But the RAF still have to come in daily to town from Stanley airfield to collect their supplies by truck. He showed me how the huge filtration tank had been moved sideways off its base by the force of the shell which hit it, and spoke of the difficulties experienced in getting it back onto its seating again.

Initially the RE assistance to the PWD on the electrical side was limited, as Colonel Kennedy put it, 'to tying knots in the overhead distribution cables in order to link them up again'. Before long, however, the increased calls for more power by all concerned began to overload the sub-stations whose fuses repeatedly blew. The decision was therefore made to set up a military power station, using two 255 kilowatt Army generators, to ease the PWD's load.

Staff Sergeant Keith Walker, a Clerk of Works from Aberdeen, is in charge of it, and he now supplies a quarter of the town's total power requirements. He told me he had only recently completed his training course and was very lucky to be having to put his new knowledge to good use so soon.

Of Stanley's total of 368 houses, twenty-seven were uninhabitable, of which at least four had been completely destroyed. More than half had suffered some minor damage. There was no system working for the supply of petrol for civilians.

Captain Bob Jenkinson originally supervised the technical aspects of the very successful Emergency Fuel Handling Equipment (EFHE) in the San Carlos area which, between 25 May and 14 June, dispensed 550,000 gallons of fuel ashore over Blue (San Carlos) and Green (Port San Carlos) Beaches. The installation at Green Beach is still very much in action. Terminating at the temporary aluminium-panelled airstrip initially laid during the campaign for use by the Harriers, it now supplies the RAF Chinook helicopter squadron based at Port San Carlos Settlement, which I visited, and also refuels any other passing RN or Army helicopters en route to or from West Falkland. Now Captain Jenkinson is establishing other key civilian and military fuel points on the Islands. He is planning bigger and better ones for the future, including the use of Argentine Company YPF's tank farm's facilities in Stanley, completed in 1975, but which thereafter remained unused because there was no jetty and also, rumour has it, because of disagreement over which flag the re-supplying tankers would fly!

Plans inevitably change, and the other urgent task that instantly came to the CRE Works was to get the cratered and 'scabbed' airfield open for RAF Hercules aircraft. With hectic work by 59 Independent Commando Squadron RE, using unorthodox but very effective techniques, and by initially repairing only half of the runway width, the first aircraft was able to land on 24 June. Now he and his Specialist Team are fully committed on the design and development work required for the Stanley Airfield runway extension. His draughtsmen are working in an improvised drawing office in an upstairs room in town. This is a technically interesting, unique and difficult task. The site work is being undertaken by 50 Field Squadron (Construction) RE. Apart from continuing to help the PWD out with materials and RE tradesmen to repair Stanley's house and building damage, and its 'heavily bashed' roads, Colonel Kennedy has the responsibility for designing the new 'hard' accommodation camps for the future Army and RAF garrison to be deployed in the Falklands. Because the parameters of every chosen and acquired military detachment site will be different – and the required strengths of men in them will vary – careful detailed engineer reconnaissance of each one is vital.

Each camp will need to be individually designed and then RE-built. The accommodation units will need bases and the camps will all require full mains services ab initio. Designing, delivering and installing self-contained water, electric power, drainage and sewerage systems at remote places, with no access roads, will be just another big challenge to the Royal Engineers, and of course they must 'get it right' first time. Thereafter there will also be a sizeable continuing requirement for the appropriate skilled RE maintenance tradesmen to live on site in addition to the camp's regular occupants.

There is no doubt whatever that the Falkland Islands will remain one huge Sapper 'paradise' for a very long time to come.

10 | THE PWD

An absolute minimum of £35 million, totally excluding anything at Stanley Airport, is the cost of war damage to the Falkland Islands, according to Mr John Brodrick, Director of the Falkland Islands Public Works Department (PWD). This costing is based on Falkland rates for labour which are something like a quarter to a third lower than in Britain. 'And that total is a low estimate of the cost,' he told me.

The PWD staff never stopped working during the Argentine occupation and then, with very limited resources of manpower and equipment, they were hard put, in the immediate Aftermath, to start restoring Stanley to normality.

Amid the plethora of problems, however, there were a few cheering moments such as when Les Harris, the senior local PWD electrician, managed to save the power station at the time of the disastrously destructive fire in the plumbers' store next door to it.

Mr Brodrick returned to the Islands on 25 June with the Civil Commissioner, Mr Rex Hunt. He has been stranded in Britain, at the time of the invasion, whilst on an official trip home. The Falklands PWD with its force of only 120 men has responsibilities approaching those of a municipal authority in Britain. These include the provision of water and electricty, construction and main-tenance of all Government buildings, roads and transport, and even grave-digging and the supply of fuel. Now, with the assistance from the Army's CRE Works, the Director is trying to put the town back on its feet.

But Mr Brodrick faces many difficult problems. With water, for instance, he needs to replace all the many old leaking galvanized service pipes leading into houses, largely installed in the late 1950s and 1960s, which the acidity in the peat soil has begun to eat away, thus losing half of all the total treated water his Moody Brook plant supplies. In one place he investigated, he found that twenty feet of galvanized pipe had just disappeared without trace. Modern heavy-duty plastic pipes are the answer, but there have been problems in the past with the Falkland Islands Council over payment for new pipes, and the same problem remains today. An up-to-date water treatment plant is also necessary to cater for the expanded permanent population of Stanley.

'There is an on-going social problem with the war-damaged houses,' he told me, 'but, with the Army's help and that of the few small contractors in Stanley, we are slowly winning the battle of repairs.' 'Twenty-seven pre-fabricated three-bedroom houses have now been ordered from Britain,' he said, 'as replacements for accommodation lost.'

Unique to the Falklands, Mr Brodrick has a Peat Officer whose job it is to allocate a peat bank to each house in Stanley. All the banks are on Crown Land. The Peat Officer tells the householder which bank faces to cut, to what limits, and what drainage is required. There are special Peat By-Laws governing the whole process. Contracts are let for the supply of peat to all Government buildings, including Government House. There is a long cycle to be followed before peat is ready for use. It is cut in September, thrown up on to the top of the banks and then 'rickled' into beehive-shaped stacks to dry. It is brought back into house storage the following March/April by which time it can be burnt. The peat is best for burning, however, if kept another year for use the following March/April. [*The Argentinian occupation forces' own heavy and random use of peat exacerbated the Aftermath problem of restoring control over, and reverting to, the accepted Falklands system of cutting peat.*]

Peat is the traditional fuel for the Falklands, whether in Stanley or out 'in the camp'. Free peat, if you go out and cut it, is a normal part of a wage out in the Settlement farms. The fact that today many of the best and nearest peat banks for Stanley now lie within areas of uncleared Argentine mines is very serious and could have a long-term effect on the local population. Mr Brodrick told me that phurnacite had now been ordered from Britain as an emergency replacement for peat. He foresaw it becoming a permanent form of fuel for the future, together with perhaps an increased use of propane gas and kerosene for heating and cooking. [*These alternatives were later to prove too expensive.*] For the immediate present, many people will be using kerosene. 'The fuel problem is now something of an Island emergency,' he said, 'but everyone is pulling together – both civilian and military – to make the existing peat stocks last until the supplies of phurnacite and propane gas arrive on 15 September. Those inhabitants of Stanley who have good stocks of peat in hand are being very forthcoming in helping out those who are without.'

The aim now is to get 'back on course again,' Mr Brodrick told me. Inevitably there will be a wage adjustment because it will all now be related to UK levels. 'We'll end up like the Isle of Wight', he said. 'There never was a "down and out" Falkland Islander,' he continued. 'Free fish, peat and plenty of Upland Geese, for example, helped to compensate for the low wages – roughly equating standards man for man to the rural parts of Devon.'

The current peat problem is just one of the many in the Aftermath which will ensure that life for the Falkland Islanders will never be quite the same again. I am told by some of them, however, that a changed life-style would not, in fact, be unacceptable.

11 | THE ROYAL AIR FORCE

5 August, 1982

Group Captain Bill Wratten, Commanding the Royal Air Force in the Falklands and also the first RAF Station Commander at Stanley, himself a Phantom pilot, stressed to me that the RAF's most urgent concern is to get Stanley Airfield developed as soon as possible to accommodate fast land-based air-defence jet fighters, most likely Phantoms. These, together with all the associated radars and the already permanently manned Rapier missile sites, will provide the vital air defence which the Falkland Islands require. During the period of the Royal Engineer work necessary to make Stanley operational for Phantoms, however, it was important that there was no degradation whatever of the current high state of readiness of the Falklands' air defence. [*The first Phantom eventually arrived on 17 October, 1982.*]

Assessment of the total hostile Argentinian threat to the Islands, and what is required to meet it, will decide the overall future Falklands force levels. Only then, in respect of air-defence forces in particular and taking into account the RAF's improved capability resulting from the developed airfield in general, can judgement be made on what embarked Royal Navy fixed-wing air contribution must be retained at sea in the South Atlantic.

The biggest problem now faced by the RAF in the Falklands, according to the Group Captain, is the changeable weather. It can change from snow to sun to driving rain to fog, not within days, but literally within the hour. Add to this the airfield cross-winds which average thirty mph, but at times can gust up to seventy mph, and the hazard of snow and ice on the runway, and you begin to appreciate the sort of problem he has in operating aircraft.

RAF Stanley is an exceptionally busy airfield. Its Air Traffic Controllers, working in difficult conditions, handle 'intense rates' of daily aircraft movements. These include Hercules transports flying to and from Ascension, countless Royal Navy, Army and RAF helicopters, and the air-defence Harriers. I have watched many of 24 Squadron's Hercules pilots working wonders 'well at the operating limits' to put their aircraft down safely. Their enforced angling of the aircraft on take-off, to counteract the cross-wind, is remarkable to watch.

The Harriers remain operational and need a short take-off run to get airborne with the heavy fuel and live weapons load required for their combat air patrols. These excellent and proven aircraft are necessarily maintained for the continued deterrent defence of the Falklands. The wind can give them a little trouble too, but does not affect their vertical landing which can be done facing any point of the compass.

'The helicopters are not really affected by the wind so long as they can see where they're going,' the Group Captain said: 'They're really all right'. What they have to watch out for, however, particularly the big twin-rotored Chinooks, is what the RAF call 'FOD'. These are all the loose bits and pieces of débris on the ground which the downdraught of the rotors can either cause to fly up to damage the helicopter itself or send scurrying at speed to cause damage or injury to man or machine elsewhere. With the airfield still surrounded by the litter of so many half-opened Argentine stores, quite apart from any British items, this can be a very real risk.

Inter-Service co-operation was excellent in the early Aftermath days, but not without its moments! Regimental Quartermaster Sergeant Andy Andrews of 36 Engineer Regiment Headquarters in Stanley decided to widen the range of the men's meat ration from 'compo' to 'fresh' and so, suitably briefed, hitched his way with the Regiment's Chief Clerk, Warrant Officer Class 2 Jim Saunderson, and a small team over to Ajax Bay by Wessex helicopter and thence, by assault boat, to San Carlos Settlement.

Making contact there with Brian May, from the Settlement, the party set off with packs and a Land-Rover, expertly coaxed through the bogs by Brian, for Third Corral Shanty on the slopes of Bombilla Hill. Searching for wild cattle the following day near Sandpass Brook they shot eight bulls and fifteen brace of Upland Geese. Leaving Jim Saunderson guarding the Regiment's share of the 'bag' at Third Corral Shanty, the RQMS headed back to San Carlos Settlement where the skilful and versatile RAF 'Chinook' helicopter No 18 Squadron was based. Fast talking brought him a hitching ride heading for Stanley, but it needed even faster talking to get the pilot to divert to pick up what the RQMS described as his 'freight' en route. After even greater persuasive efforts, the astonished RAF crew agreed to lift the carcasses by underslung net load and all was set well.

On arriving back over Stanley, however, the mood in the helicopter suddenly changed. The RQMS told me that with the aircraft held at the hover out over the water, the RAF Air Load Master put his hand on the net release hook, looked up and asked quietly 'And how many of these are for us?' The message was all too clear, the RQMS said. It was 'Give us half or we'll jettison the lot.' In the end the price for the ride was agreed at one bull and everyone was happy! The Regiment enjoyed its first fresh meat for many weeks. 'The steaks were delicious' was everyone's verdict.

The airfield at Stanley had been built by British contractors in the late Seventies to cater for the short-haul Fokker aircraft operated by Argentina, in fact by the Argentine Air Force, flying between the Falklands and

Argentina. Its runway was 4,100 feet long and 150 feet wide and designed to Load Classification Number (LCN) 16 but was subsequently estimated, with an increased pavement thickness, to be of LCN 30 standard.

During the campaign the runway had been cratered by the Vulcan bomber and Harrier raids, and had suffered over 1,000 'scabs' or shallow scuffs in its surface. The Argentinians had temporarily back-filled the five large craters, enabling them to continue to fly in C130 Hercules transports right up to the end. They had also arranged rings of earth on the runway to show up as craters on British air reconnaissance photographs.

By properly re-repairing three craters and dealing with about 500 'scabs', No 1 Troop of 59 Commando Squadron RE had the northern half of the runway ready to accept the first British Hercules on 24 June. The craters had compacted 'fill' and were topped by sheets of aluminium airfield AM2 matting, secured by four-feet-long steel pins, taken from a conveniently placed abandoned stockpile brought to the Island in the early Seventies by Argentinians in connection with a runway which was never finished. The 'scabs' were effectively repaired with Bostik 276, which is a magnesium phosphate cement/fine aggregate mixture.

The focus now turned on the southern part of the runway which included one huge crater made by the RAF Vulcan's 1,000 pound bomb. This alone took more than 1,000 square metres of the old Argentine AM2 matting to repair: 'We were in fact really very relieved that only one Vulcan bomb had actually hit the runway,' said a weary Sapper.

By 1 July No 3 Troop of 11 Field Squadron had completed the repairs and the whole runway was again usable, but both the crater and 'scab' repair areas called for constant monitoring and maintenance. Nevertheless the reopened runway withstood a further seventy-seven Hercules and several hundred Harrier landings, operationally vital to the Garrison, before it was closed for extension and complete re-surfacing on the evening of 15 August.

The priority of providing land-based RAF Phantoms at Stanley to reduce the Garrison's dependency on air cover provided by a Royal Navy carrier, retained for the purpose in South Atlantic waters, was recognized very early on. Planning for the extension and development of Stanley airfield after the cessation of hostilities started as early as April, 1982, a long time before the San Carlos landings. Considering the lead times required for obtaining and shipping the necessary stores, in the event it was only just early enough.

In May, 1982, 50 Field Squadron, even while it was still in Britain, was given the task of constructing an airfield to expeditionary standards using the existing Stanley site and based on American aluminium (AM2) matting. The principal requirements, dictated largely by the Phantom aircraft which were to use it, were for an extension of the existing runway to 6,100 feet at LCN 45 standard, five rotary hydraulic arrester gear installations, an aircraft apron five times larger than the existing one and three aircraft dispersal areas with associated hangars. There had also to be a proper road system around the airfield, power for runway lighting and other necessary facilities, dispersed fuel storage with a ship-to-shore pipeline and an aircraft engineering complex to include five working hangars.

Critical to the future of the whole post-campaign survival of the Falklands, the execution of this huge engineering project – 8,000 miles from Britain and where local resources were minimal – was a remarkable feat. The complications of design and planning, the urgency, let alone the acquisition, earmarking, training, assembly, movement and co-ordination of the necessary men, engineer plant and stores whilst the campaign was still in progress, were indeed formidable. For instance enough AM2 matting to surface the extended airfield had to be bought in America, shipped over and cross-loaded, and a team of instructors had to be sent over to the United States for a 'crash course' to learn the AM2 secrets, all while the war was still in progress.

Some 9,000 tons of airfield construction stores and engineer plant were sent down to the Falklands in the merchantmen *Strathewe* and *Cedar Bank* which anchored offshore in Port William Sound. The mammoth scale of the unloading task, the likely problems to be encountered, and previous experience derived from work in San Carlos Water led Lieutenant-Colonel Geoff Field to devote a complete unit to the execution of this very critical task. Overall responsibility was therefore given to Major Bruce Hawken and his 11 Field Squadron who, despite losing all their kit and stores when the *Atlantic Conveyor* was sunk, had nevertheless done sterling work earlier on constructing airstrips for Harrier aircraft above Port San Carlos and later at Stanley.

By working twenty-four hours a day for two weeks using only the ship's derricks, Royal Corps of Transport 'Mexeflote' lighters and landing craft, and relays of trucks, the bulk of this unloading was completed before the unit, which had been all through the campaign, returned to Britain.

Because of the speed at which everything had had to be loaded in Britain, inevitably some urgently required stores were trapped in the ships' holds behind or underneath other less important stores. I will never forget looking down into the deep holds of the *Cedar Bank* watching soldier stevedores, ankle-deep in powdered cement spilled out from broken sacks, and masked as a protection against inhaling the dust, struggling to sort out the many and often huge items into the required sequence.

The RCT's heavily loaded 'Mexeflote' lighters taxed the skills of their coxswains to the full, as the huge banded pallets of solid AM2 matting topped their narrow craft, tempting the side-winds to do their worst and reducing freeboard to so many inches. Often the sea state would suddenly blow up in typical Falklands fashion and then all work would have to stop until the winds abated.

Perhaps the greatest feat of delivery was of an enormous stone crusher which literally towered above its 'Mexeflote'. On 31 July, after being gingerly unloaded onto 3 Field Squadron's Class 60 slipway, a recovery vehicle and a Combat Engineer Tractor together slowly pulled and pushed it along Ross Road East and up the steep hill of Hebe Street en route to the airfield. Progress was at a snail's pace. I watched fascinated as the escort party on foot, carrying long poles, carefully pushed up and over the top of the crusher the many successive overhead cables which sagged into its path and which would otherwise have been cut by its enormous high steel frame.

Stanley airfield was the scene of intensive activity throughout July and early August. Obviously the existing runway would have to be closed whilst it received its new AM2 matting surface 'coat', which meant that during this period the Falkland Islands would be cut off by air from the umbilical cord 'air bridge' from Ascension, except for the delivery by air-drop of vital stores, and thus be at increased risk from the Argentine threat.

No transport aircraft or air defence fighter could use the runway during the period of its enforced closure, a situation of which the Argentinians might well be tempted to take advantage. Even if offset by increased Royal Navy carrier aircraft readiness, it would still be a time of greatly increased operational risk which just had to be accepted. Information regarding the projected dates of closure was therefore kept classified, but in the event was disclosed in advance by a media source.

Planning the developed airfield task was therefore geared to a minimum runway closure time, with as much preliminary work as possible being done beforehand. The rate of unloading the AM2 matting from the merchant ships, with all the uncertainties of delays from weather, became a critical factor. The CRE's Works' drawing office back in Stanley and 50 Field Squadron's planning room at the airfield were continuous hives of activity. In the Portakabin site office there was a marvellous scale model which clearly demonstrated all the different stages and complications of the airfield task.

Major Jeremy Harrison was undoubtedly the driving force behind the whole critical operation [he was subsequently awarded the MBE for his efforts], working very closely with Major David Reid who commanded the technical Specialist Team, Royal Engineers. Major Harrison's 50 Field Squadron (Construction) got ahead with the aircraft aprons and dispersals, prepared the anchorages for the arrester gear and experimented to find the best design for the runway extension part. The really difficult problem was how to build up the extension area into a solid enough base to match the existing runway at the join, so that when the AM2 matting was laid it fitted flush as a continuous surface throughout the whole 6,100-foot length. Certainly, modern membranes such as Terram and Trevira played their valuable part in the final pavement design. Peat, sand, no existing surface water drainage, a very high water table and a falling natural gradient added to the difficulties. But it was the eternal wind from the Antarctic and the icy 'angled' sleet that will characterize the site for ever in the memories of those that worked there.

After squelching round with Major Harrison, never was the temporary relief of escaping the biting wind and entering a tent shelter for a cup of hot Army tea more welcome.

In the meanwhile Major Mike Brooke's 3 Field Squadron, assisted by 60 Field Support Squadron, were 'winning' the first of the estimated requirements of 25,000 tons of rock 'fill' from a convenient quarry at the edge of the airfield. This turned out to be the hardest quartz granite, which initially created problems with the rock drills and extracted a worryingly excessive rate of wear on the stone-crushers' jaws.

Trials went on to determine the fastest efficient technique of laying the AM2 matting, what size of working party was best, and what was the optimum number of them that could be supported by the flow of delivered stores. Private bets were being made on the number of days 'Operation Tin Lion' would take. The joker in the pack, however, was the cruel, sleeting Falklands weather.

Training of the 'Squads' intensified after the last Hercules had taken off for Ascension on 15 August. The 'air bridge' was thus closed, and the whole of the Falklands Garrison was now entirely dependent on the air-dropping of vital stores by Ascension-based RAF Hercules. By 19 August everything was set to go. Eight 'Tin Troops' of twenty-six men – Sappers, Infantrymen from the 1st Battalion The Queen's Own Highlanders, some Royal Air Force men, and even some Royal Navy sailors – then swung into action laying the thousands of interlocking aluminium sheets on top of the existing runway and its extension. With two Tin Troops deployed at any one time, they worked non-stop day and night as a continuous 'work-belt' – three hours on and nine hours off (including travelling time). One dangerous aspect was that if a real Falkland gust of wind 'took' a loosely held sheet sideways on, it could be wrenched from one's grasp and be sent whipping lethally away like an enormous razor-blade.

Keen competition soon built up between the 'gangs' over the square footage of sheeting laid in a shift, and the men, well aware of the urgency, became totally committed to the task. At times, despite the weather, it was difficult to get them to stop work at the end of the shift. On one particularly dreadful night, in a slashing blizzard, having failed to halt them by persuasion, Major-General David Thorne had to give the 'Tin Troops' a direct order to stop work as the conditions were so appalling.

Even with enforced delays of thirty hours due to the weather, the task was finished late on 27 August, two days ahead of the planners' fourteen-day target, a truly magnificent effort by all concerned. The Argentinians had not reacted, and the British garrison could relax again, just a little. The 'air bridge' from Ascension was re-opened amid cheers, when the first Hercules landed safely on the new AM2 runway on 28 August.

The sheeting did not even bow-wave or ripple under the heavily-laden Hercules' landing load, as some Doubting Thomases had feared. Its rigid behaviour will thus provide a thoroughly satisfactory runway surface for the next two to four years, by which time a new permanent airfield at the Mount Pleasant site should be in operation.

The Army staff's codeword for Sappers is 'Holdfast'. Weary but exhilarated, the Royal Engineers instantly erected a large sign smartly painted in the Corps' colours on the front of the control tower designating their new creation 'Holdfast Airport'. This did not go down well with the RAF, however, who immediately took it down and replaced it with 'RAF Stanley'.

No air record of the Aftermath would be complete without mention of a unique incident which occurred a week before the airfield closed. On 8 August an RAF Hercules landed at Stanley airfield without a mid-air refuelling probe fitted above the cockpit. This was noticed by a very observant member of the media who just happened to be at the airfield at the time and asked an officer on duty in the control tower about it. He was told that the Hercules in question was based at Stanley which, being patently untrue, angered him considerably. Determined to get to the bottom of the story, he later repaired to the bar of the Upland Goose Hotel where he knew he would eventually find the Hercules crew.

A bottle or two later that night, he had his story. It was one which, in the current highly delicate South American post-Falklands political climate, was in fact very sensitive. The Hercules had been undertaking a classified proving trial, flying first from Ascension to Brazil, where it had refuelled, before flying on to the Falklands, thus eliminating the great expense and complication of the normal mid-air refuellings. The flight had gone well and proved the alternative route to be satisfactory.

The alert media member concerned passed the story to a fellow journalist belonging to a national newspaper, which duly became the only one to publish the story, on its front page.

It so happened, unfortunately, that at this very time Mr Cranley Onslow, Foreign Office Minister of State, was in Brazil conducting some delicate post-Falklands talks with the Brazilian Government, and the question of re-routeing RAF aircraft via Brazil to the Falklands was obviously one of his agenda items. At this particular moment the sensitivities of South American neighbour governments vis-à-vis Argentina were especially acute, which made the publicity even more unwelcome to the British Government.

The immediate upshot was – and sources say that this 'premature and unhelpful' publicity was a major factor in the Brazilian decision – that the RAF Hercules trial, together with any further question of 'via Brazil' flights to the Falklands, was terminated forthwith. The extremely expensive 'air bridge' system of two mid-air refuellings thus continues, costing the British taxpayer some £20 million a year.

[This situation continued until the new Mount Pleasant airfield opened in May, 1985. It is, of course, an open question whether any inter-governmental arrangement would ever have been achieved with Brazil without the 'blowing' of the story or not. But if it had, many millions of pounds would have been saved over the three-year-long period of the 'air bridge'. The incident was a clear case of a very keen-eyed media man's nose for a news story, a fair one in circumstances which had been badly handled by the MOD, being unfortunately and expensively at odds with national interests. Had the media man been handled more tactfully, told the truth and given something of the appropriate background 'off the record' at the time, then he might well not have been so angry at what had happened and might not have passed on the story.

What still upsets him is that, following publication of the story, he was somewhat cold-shouldered by the military and rather quickly sent out of the Islands on a Hercules just before Stanley airport closed. Perhaps the last word goes to someone very senior in the Foreign Office at the time who later commented to me, 'Why did the MOD not send down on this sensitive trial a Hercules fitted with a fuel probe, even though it was not going to be used? Then no one would have noticed anything different on arrival at Stanley.']

12 | THE ROYAL NAVY

I was in excellent Royal hands yesterday as Prince Andrew, piloting the Sea King helicopter which had flown into Stanley airfield to collect me and the Naval Task Force's mail, headed out to sea. I thought his face had looked rather familiar, even under his 'bone dome' flying helmet, when I had climbed aboard. After take-off I had shown the crewman my scribbled 'HRH?' on the back of an envelope, to which, in the roaring noise, he had nodded affirmatively. Later on in the flight I was standing just at the back of the flight deck when the Prince leant forward from the left-hand pilot's seat revealing the large letters 'HRH' stencilled onto the back of his orange-glow flying waistcoat. [*The helicopter was from 820 Naval Air Squadron on board HMS* Invincible.]

'Somewhere in the South Atlantic,' a while later, we made our rendezvous with HMS *Avenger* (3,250 tons), a Type 21 frigate. The Prince brought the machine into the hover, turned and gave me the thumbs-up sign to leave. Acknowledging it similarly, I put on the simple harness loop and, helped by the crewman and still wearing my all-enveloping red survival suit and lifejacket, swung out of the helicopter's starboard door and was winched down onto *Avenger*'s heavily pitching and rolling deck. Reviving me with a large mug of coffee, Captain Hugh White RN told me his ship had arrived in the Total Exclusion Zone on 25 May after a record fourteen and a half days' voyage south. As a General Purpose Frigate – she was a sister ship to HMS *Antelope* – *Avenger* had been involved in doing almost everything during the campaign.

She had fired 1,000 shells in eight bombardments, in particular on Fox Bay, Stanley and Pebble Island, and had been bombarding nearby when HMS *Glamorgan* was hit by a land-launched Exocet. Luckily the stricken vessel still had power, he said, and was able to keep up her speed, thus saving herself from any further Exocet or Mirage attack the next morning, or endangering other ships going to her assistance.

Avenger had also been in San Carlos Water, in Falkland Sound, and had actually taken shelter during the campaign in Albemarle Harbour in West Falkland. She had done escort work to HMS *Fearless* and *Intrepid*, had been off Fitzroy, and had undertaken other special work. In all she had changed from 'defence stations' to 'action stations' fifty-five times.

The ship's worst moment was in early June [*6 June*] when she picked up two Argentine Super-Entendards on her radar some thirty to forty miles out.

Chief Petty Officer Mike Child, in the operations room, told me how he saw two radar blips suddenly give birth to two further blips – Exocets. *Avenger* was the outermost ship of the screen and those on the bridge suddenly saw the Exocet coming towards them. But a 4.5-inch shell fired from the ship hit and exploded one Exocet. The second one was never seen again, the thought being that the first one exploding had set it off too, or else it had been decoyed away.

The whole sequence from blip to burst had taken a little under two and a half minutes. 'Better than a wardroom movie any day,' Captain White had signalled at the time. The accompanying wave of Skyhawks had then attacked the ship at bridge height, straddling it with bombs, but all missed.

One of *Avenger*'s best moments was taking the Argentine surrender at Fox Bay on the morning of 15 June. She had anchored there on the night of General Menendez's surrender whilst looking for an Argentine cargo vessel. An initial party of six all ranks under Lieutenant-Commander Tony Bollingbroke, the ship's First Lieutenant, landed by ship's Lynx helicopter, armed only with pistols, to receive it. Colonel Ernesto Repossi, thirty-one officers and 940 heavily armed men from 86 Infantry Regiment and a company of Engineers gave themselves up. It really was a tearful ceremony for them, the Commander told me. The Argentinians there were very moved, but behaved correctly. At the time the *Avenger* was lying so exposed at anchor in a force nine gale 'that green seas were coming over her bows,' I was told.

The *Avenger*'s sailors, who spent two days ashore, found skilfully concealed Argentine ammunition, fuel and weapon dumps, also cleverly faked artillery positions. The radar site had miraculously survived all the bombardments. The very young Argentinian soldiers had been sleeping back to back in long lines in the sheep sheds for warmth. In the bitter cold, they had no bedding and hardly any food left, but apparently had not ill-treated the local population. 'Generally,' the Commander said, 'they were pathetically keen to leave and never return.'

Commander Bollingbroke was later having dinner with the Fox Settlement Manager when an Argentinian Major knocked on the door and entered. 'You remember,' he said, 'I promised you a bottle of champagne when victory was complete. Well,' he continued, handing a bottle to the Settlement Manager, 'victory is now complete, but it is not ours. Anyway, here is your champagne.'

Avenger's mission, while keeping up her guard operationally, is now to help get the Islands back on their feet by 'inshore work' – visiting Settlements, delivering food and supplies and generally undertaking a 'hearts and minds' role.

The British presence in the South Atlantic is now that of 'a non-aggressive but determinedly effective force to deter any Argentine attempt to take hostile action against British interests.' This was how it was described to me by Rear-Admiral Derek Reffell who took over command of the Naval Task Force from Rear-Admiral Sandy Woodward in June.

We were 'somewhere in the South Atlantic' on board his flagship HMS *Bristol* (6,750 tons), the only Type 82 destroyer ever built, to which I had been flown earlier by Wasp helicopter, and to which the Admiral had also kindly invited the indomitable Captain Jeremy Black of the carrier *Invincible*, and the Captains of the frigate HMS *Penelope* (Commander Peter Rickard), the Royal Fleet Auxiliary *Olna* (Captain J. A. Bailey RFA) and of course HMS *Bristol* (Captain Alan Grose), for me to meet later at lunch. From them I learnt much of the naval war, and of the behaviour and outlook of the embarked press. 'There was I trying to fight the war with the press demanding the use of seventy per cent of my already overworked operational communications for sending their stories,' said one.

The Admiral reminded me that the declared 200-mile Total Exclusion Zone around the Falklands was no longer being enforced. 'One effect of this has been that Polish fishing trawlers are now already very much back in business in the Zone's waters,' he said. They had also penetrated into the 'FIPZ' or Falkland Islands Protection Zone of 150 miles radius which the British Government had warned Argentine ships not to enter for the time being.

The Admiral considered that neither the British nor the Argentine Governments now wished to pursue any form of hostilities. But the really important question was whether the Argentine Government now had all its armed forces under really tight control. There remained the threat of some breakaway group or maverick possibly taking 'some highly independent offensive action under, on or over the surface on his own acount,' he warned. If anyone had any of these three possible modes of attack in mind, there were recent historical and 'honour' reasons which might make one think the submarine mode was the more likely.

All the Naval Task Force ships have therefore to remain fully vigilant at present, taking anti-submarine and other precautions, with ships' companies closed up to 'defence stations' ready for anything which might happen. One simply cannot take chances. 'As a result, the sailors are still working hours similar to those in the war in order to be alert, and keep up their proven high state of training.'

'The most difficult problem in this situation,' the Admiral continued, 'is to keep up this necessary state of vigilance in the face of boredom rather than of imminent danger. It is one thing to be watching a radar screen every moment of your shift when you know that something is very likely to appear on it very suddenly. Being human, it is another thing to keep up this pitch if such an event is really much less likely. Training programmes have to go on, even though the sailors, as a result of the war, are already better trained than they were before.'

There were many other valuable things which the Royal Navy had to do as its on-going contribution to what the Admiral stressed very strongly was 'the fully Tri-Service operation of defending the Falklands'. In saying this, he paid particular tribute both to the Royal Fleet Auxiliaries and to the Merchant Navy for their excellent work as part of this one totally integrated team.

The Naval Task Force is now helping with the considerable logistical programme of getting things ashore at Stanley and elsewhere in East and West Falklands where normal facilities are virtually non-existent. For instance, the frigate HMS *Avenger*, which I recently visited, has spent a lot of time of late on inshore work, visiting the Settlements and delivering food and supplies to isolated areas. It was all part of the important process of helping the Islands 'get back on their feet'. The Navy also has the continuing responsibility for protecting the long sea lanes stretching back to Ascension and beyond.

In the longer term, Royal Navy ships and submarines must form part of British force levels for the Falklands, the Admiral stressed, but developments now in hand, he said, [*in fact referring to the development of the airfield*] would make it possible to dispense with the large Royal Navy fixed-wing carrier presence. 'Morale,' the Admiral said, 'is not a problem.' Certainly, talking to sailors during my visits to the Naval Task Force, I would agree with him completely. The men I met currently at sea, in the murk, mist and heavy seas of the South Atlantic, are both cheerful and impressive, and a formidable deterrent to anyone.

4 August, 1982

Helicoptering over the Royal Navy Task Force in the South Atlantic is a unique experience. It gave me the distinct impression that here was an area of ocean which had become a temporary extension of Great Britain. Warships and their supporting merchantmen were spread out over a wide area. They were alert and aggressively ready to defend it, if necessary, as determinedly as if it really was a part of Britain.

The 'envelope' of ocean the Task Force covers is, of course, always moving. Within it there is constant activity, as in any built-up area at home. The Sea King helicopters come and go, and I saw others hovering to do 'their anti-submarine thing'. The Wasp helicopters buzzed about their business from ship to ship like workers from any hive.

Suffering from suspected contaminated fuel and seeking help, my pilot flew through a very heavy sea mist and, in a luckily well-timed clear patch, landed on the elusive HMS *Invincible* (19,500 tons). Two things about her in particular struck me very forcibly. First, used to old-fashioned aircraft carriers, I was astonished at how small was her flight deck, with its Harrier 'ski jump' ramp end. It brought home to me the intricate control which must have been necessary to keep up her continuous record of flying operations on the way down to, and throughout, the war.

Second, down below in the darkened operations room, I felt I had intruded into some enormous electronic brain – which indeed I had. It was clearly divided up, like any human brain, into separate functional cells. Each one pulsated with its own electronic displays and coloured buttons, watched by keen-eyed shadowy sailors. This, I said to myself, is modern naval warfare, but I noted the Captain's chair, sited by itself, still occupying its traditional dominant position from which to command the brain.

5 August, 1982

Having sailed 11,000 miles and after first working hard in South Georgia, the oil rig support vessel MV *Stena Inspector* is now in Falkland waters. In Grytviken she carried out much-needed repairs to the jetties and the local 'real estate', as well as helping to salvage the captured Argentine submarine *Santa Fe*.

Acting as a mini-dockyard, the vessel is now busy repairing and carrying out deep maintenance on the Task Force's frigates and other ships. It is a role which could have important relevance to future Royal Navy operations both here and elsewhere.

Operating a Naval Task Force 8,000 miles away from home waters without any heavy repair capability would have been plain crazy. With no alternative friendly-nation facilities available in the area, and there being nothing else suitable in the Royal Navy, the oil rig support ship *Stena Seaspread*, belonging to Stena UK Ltd, was taken up from trade. She was given a Fleet Maintenance Unit containing various trades, including divers, increased machine shops, special stores and a large heavy-duty crane. The ship's saturation diving fitment with diving bell and pressurized accommodation, and its extensive fire-fighting capability, added yet other important operational dimensions to the Force.

As the Falklands campaign force levels built up and ships suffered both war and heavy seas damage, so the ship maintenance and repair load increased. The MV *Stena Inspector*, a Swedish sister ship then working in the Gulf of Mexico, had therefore also to be acquired, transferred to the British flag, refitted (and modified in the American shipyard of Charleston) and sailed to the South Atlantic under her Merchant Navy Master, Captain David Ede, whom I met on board. The *Stena Seaspread* has now gone home.

A quite remarkable feature of the ship, I discovered, was her ability to hold her sea station extremely accurately – essential in modern deep diving work – without any form of anchor. This 'dynamic positioning' is achieved by four 'azimuth thrusters', or inboard water jets, which can be independently rotated to any angle. Any shift from the desired holding position is automatically restored through changes in the thrusters' power and angle, worked out by a computer. The *Stena Inspector*, having once pinpointed her desired position by taut wire, acoustic transponder or shore radio beacon, can then hold it to plus or minus two metres in winds upwards of sixty knots without an anchor.

'This marvellous facility,' as the Senior RN officer on board, Captain Peter Stickland, put it, 'means the vessel is a very secure platform. It allows a ship to be repaired alongside on both sides at once in up to a fifty knot wind, with no risk of any vessel "going walkabout".' The Royal Navy tradesmen on board with whom I spoke all commended the ship's very modern machine tools of which they were making full use. 'Tremendous kit,' said one shipwright jealously. The vessel is self-sufficient in water; her 'reverse osmosis' plant can produce fifty tons per day.

At the time of my visit, a frigate was being repaired alongside to port, and a locally acquired vessel was being worked on alongside to starboard. 'She has shown she can go out with the Fleet on deployment and carry out heavy repairs,' said Captain Stickland. 'She can provide almost everything the Royal Navy needs.'

As I dodged under a spare submarine periscope in the well deck, two 4.5-inch Naval gun barrels, sixteen tons worth, were being inched skywards aft like matchsticks by an RAF Chinook helicopter's winch. With Fleet Support facilities overseas becoming less and less available for uncontrollable political reasons, it struck me how a ship on the lines of the *Stena Inspector*'s capability appeared to have a great future with the Royal Navy. Certainly in support of the Falkland Islands Task Force it has proved not only invaluable but essential.

Plucked from the *Stena Inspector*'s deck by a Royal Navy Sea King, in seconds I was landing at Navy Point, or 'The Camber' as it is called, which lies across the Sound from Stanley.

The Royal Navy's helicopter squadrons ashore are based here in this ageing Naval property. There are helicopters and stores and pipelines and flying crews and briefing rooms spread around and between these greying pensionable buildings in an apparently haphazard fashion.

This outward clutter belies the enviable reputation for aggressive foul-weather flying, split-second timing, and impeccable navigation richly earned by this stimulating band of cheerful pirates.

14 February, 1983

Diverted directly from a naval exercise off Gibraltar, the nuclear-powered (SSN) submarine HMS *Spartan*, under Commander James Taylor RN, quickly topped up with stores and was the first submarine to reach Falkland waters following last year's Argentine invasion. The boat was never 'on the roof' (surfaced) throughout the whole of the campaign.

Spartan was enforcing the Maritime Exclusion Zone around the Islands for two weeks before the first surface units arrived. Observing, without being seen, she made a number of useful contacts. Later, a total of five SSNs and one diesel-electric SSK boats were deployed to ensure that no Argentine ships left the twelve-mile-limit offshore zone or were in a position to attack the Task Force. In the intelligence-gathering role, the submarines were engaged in a variety of tasks including the monitoring of Argentine air, surface and sub-surface activities. On 2 May *Conqueror* sank the Argentine cruiser *General Belgrano*.

By the time *Spartan* returned to England, she had been away for twenty-three weeks, of which thirteen had been spent continuously submerged in the South Atlantic campaign. This long spell underwater was eventually broken when she had to come up to put a sick crew member ashore at Ascension. Her reward for so doing was to receive an RAF helicopter-delivered load of exceptionally welcome strawberries: 'Unbelievable, they were,' said Able Seaman Trevor Herbert, from Ivybridge in Devon, doing 'lookout' duty with me on the bridge. However, on return to Britain, I was told, someone in NAAFI had had the nerve to try and bill the submarine £75 for them, an invitation very firmly declined in true Naval parlance!

Probably the Falklands experience caused less upheaval in the Submarine Branch than in any other part of the Armed Services, Commander Neil Robertson, now in command of *Spartan*, and whose guest on board I was for a few days, told me. The Command and Control system for the boats was already in existence at Fleet Headquarters at Norwood during peacetime; the sailors were well used to long operational-type patrols and the boats kept their 'two-watch' system, equivalent to 'defence stations', throughout. 'Not enough targets,' was how Able Seaman Graham Wrigley, from Prestatyn in North Wales, summed up his view of the Falklands tour.

SSN submarines cost over £125 million each, are capital ships in their own right and are the main striking power of today's British Fleet. 'Very dangerous to an enemy,' commented Commander Robertson. Their array of sonar-based detection devices and other sensors certainly give them great potential in the grim game of underwater 'hide and seek' demanded by their key role of hunting and killing enemy submarines.

Targets generally are engaged, as appropriate, by the wire-guided Tigerfish homing torpedo, soon to be improved, and by the underwater-launched sea-skimming Sub-Harpoon anti-ship missile system now being fitted. The boats will eventually be equipped with the new British heavyweight torpedo Spear-fish.

The Captain and his Executive Officer, Lieutenant-Commander Dai Morgan, explained that the essential difference in operation between a Polaris missile-carrying SSBN and a Hunter-Killer SSN is that, whereas the former submarine avoids a contact, the latter seeks a contact and, on making one, will turn and 'start stalking its prey'. The smaller diesel-electric SSK submarines are still very much needed because, although if in the right place at the right time they can do some of the SSN's tasks, they can also fulfil some other shallower water tasks with which the SSNs might have some difficulty or do not normally undertake.

The Falklands conflict highlighted the nuclear-powered SSNs, and also invested them with a very strong political dimension; they seem to make politicians feel much safer. The requirement for their continued presence in the South Atlantic Aftermath is therefore bound to be prolonged. Such deployment, however, detracts from the submarine effort available for executing their 'No. 1' priority task in the North Atlantic, helping to keep the West ahead of the threat posed by the Soviet submarines, a dimension of war potential into which the Soviet Union is currently pouring huge resources.

Here, then, is yet another very important and difficult Falklands Aftermath problem of conflicting deployment priorities, which requires an early compromise solution. Until it is sorted out, the existing limited SSN resources will remain considerably strained.

13 | ROY COVE

7 August, 1982

The gold of the furze glowing in the sun against the soft hills and blue sea loch of Roy Cove made an idyllic setting. Out in King George Bay glistened Rabbit Island. We were on the far west coast of West Falkland, away for once from the sleet of Stanley. The Settlement has a total of 80,000 acres and 20,000 sheep, split up into six farms. The Argentinians never occupied it, although they gave its population of fourteen men, women and children some nasty frights. Moira McGee, whose husband Tom farms, told me how they used to see the Argentine planes, further inland, flying east at speed on their bombing missions, keeping very low in the valleys in order to escape the British air-defence radars.

Once there was great activity for three days whilst the Argentinians searched the nearby beaches and cliffs with helicopters, obviously thinking some British Special Forces had come ashore there. 'A big white helicopter landed in the paddock, some Argies got out, but soon got back in again and flew off. That's the only time we actually saw any,' she said. 'Their other trick – really it was just showing off, I think – was to make dummy bombing attacks on the Settlement.'

The McGees did have a very worrying time, however, when, although their radio telephone had been disconnected as the Argentinians had ordered, a small Argentine plane spotted their forbidden aerial still fitted to the farm-house roof. It circled slowly round and round the house for ages. 'We thought that was it,' she smiled, 'but eventually it flew away. As time went on,' she said, 'we just felt the Argentinians were coming nearer and nearer.'

Luckily the McGees had enough supplies on the farm to last them out.

We were sitting in Moira's cosy warm kitchen, being thawed out with tea and a deliciously fresh-baked fruit cake, and I had just learnt that you can run an Aga on peat. But now, after a total of fifteen years in West Falkland, and leaving a grown-up son and a daughter working on nearby Saunders Island, the McGees are off at the end of the month to farm a mere 1,200 acres in the Dumfries area. 'Its time we settled down,' said Moira.

Their neighbours, New Zealanders Ian Butler and his wife, bought their farm through an advertisement. They only took over their 9,000 acres and 3,000 sheep at Christmas. The Butlers were caught in Stanley at the time of the invasion, but were flown back to Roy Cove by the Argentinians in a Falkland Islands Government Air Service (FIGAS) 'Islander'. At the Argentine

HQ in Stanley, whilst waiting for the flight, they saw big operational maps of the Islands with all the Settlements marked up with a system of squares and circles. Roy Cove was the only one marked with a squiggle, and they wondered why! Answering my question as to why he had moved from New Zealand to West Falkland, Ian laughingly replied, 'Well, the children were grown up: and we must have been crazy.'

14 | THE QUEEN'S OWN HIGHLANDERS

The Queen's Own Highlanders, who had been on stand-by for the Falklands campaign since April, and who had trained so hard for it, only arrived when the fighting was over. Naturally, they were very disappointed to have missed the action. They are certainly one of the finest trained battalions in the Army today. With so many men from the Highlands and Islands, they were ideally suited to come to the Falklands which bears such a resemblance to Britain's far north. Now, having done a Herculean task in clearing up so much of the Aftermath of war in Stanley and out in the Settlements both of East and West Falkland, they are looking forward to their next more conventional tasks. [*To this day, many cannot understand why this battalion was not sent with 5 Infantry Brigade to participate in the Campaign.*]

'Planning for my operational role is number one priority,' said Lieutenant-Colonel Nicholas Ridley, the Commanding Officer: 'Taking into account the nature of the threat, and relating this to the actual geography and distances in my area, makes this a most interesting and challenging task.' He has, of course, help from an attached company of The Queen's Lancashire Regiment. Already the battalion is gearing itself up to make maximum use of what Colonel Ridley describes as 'a fabulous training area' which has been made available, thanks to the tremendous co-operation he has had from the local farmers. 'Of course you may use this hunk of twenty square miles of land' is the sort of thing he is being offered.

The opportunity for hard, realistic infantry training here in the Falklands is unrivalled. First, by the quirk of war, there is any amount of live ammunition for training. Second, there are Gunners and Sappers directly available for 'All Arms' working. Third, there are Royal Navy ships only too ready to join in with naval gunfire support, and RAF Harriers anxious to practise their air strikes. Fourth, there are plenty of Navy, Army and Air Force helicopters for troop movement or for close fire support with rockets and missiles. Fifth, there is no restriction either on full live use of the Battalion's own supporting mortars or Milan anti-tank missiles. Sixth, the sheer harshness of operating in the 'yomping' terrain will bring any battalion up to a peak of fitness and self-reliance. Finally, in some areas, battle alertness 'for real' is still required against Argentine mines.

As Colonel Ridley put it to me, 'The whole place can be just one monumental live firing exercise.' Captured Argentine equipment, like their damaged

Panhard armoured cars, for instance, would make good 'hard' targets. His plans include two twenty-four hour exercises a week for every platoon, and one forty-eight hour one a week per company, leading up to a four-day Battalion exercise. 'The secret,' confided Major Colin Gilmour, commanding D Company, 'is to be fit with a pack on your back, and walk everywhere. The tufty grass makes for very strong ankles.'

Lieutenant Murdo MacDonald, from Strathpeffer, has just established a Training Battle Camp based on a remote bothie in the wilds of West Falkland [*Black Hill House*] where he shares the rough tufted, rock-outcropped moorland with flocks of Upland Geese. 'It's just like Scotland,' he told me. Outlining his plans for a very demanding 3-week Corporals' course as we walked round his remotely beautiful camp area, not for nothing, I thought, has he been an Outward Bound instructor and taught at the Army's tough training school in the wild Brecon hills.

I toured the Battalion's locations in both East and West Falkland [*including an attractive proposed site for Battalion Tactical HQ at Shag Cove*] with burly Major Mike Crowe, Officer Commanding Headquarter Company. Many are at existing Settlements, where relationships with the civilians are good, and 'to our mutual benefit', I was told by both parties. Second-Lieutenant Alasdair Ogilvy's platoon of D Company had just finished cleaning up and renovating his Settlement's Community Centre [*at Fox Bay West*] and, the night before I called, had re-christened it with a bonanza party for the seven families (thirty-three souls all told) who live there. His Platoon Sergeant, Steven Byers, is from Edey in the North Orkneys, an island almost as treeless and windswept as the Falklands. In another of his D Company's locations, Major Colin Gilmour told me, literally thousands of fresh mussels were available, and duck and Upland Goose figure regularly on the menu.

Private John Mackay who grew up in Wick, a town in the very north of Scotland, showed me the room in the sheep-shearers' bunkhouse he shared with three others. 'The weather is much better than I ever expected – not so cold as at my home,' he said. Others told me they had expected to be living out in their 'bivvies' (bivouacs). Among the Jocks living in the bunkhouse I was surprised to meet Able Seaman Grant Donovan from Winchester. He explained that he was on an exchange scheme between his ship, HMS *Birmingham* (4,100 tons), and the Battalion, which gave him the chance of a few days ashore: 'really good' was his verdict. HMS *Birmingham* and the Battalion have links that go back a long time.

Lance-Corporal Donald MacKenzie operates a 'Gemini' inflatable craft as a ferry across a sea loch in West Falkland [*between Fox Bay West and Fox Bay East*]. From Stornoway, he is a tailor by trade. 'I'd like to settle out here,' he told me, 'It's the same as at home and there's plenty of opportunity to set up a small business wherever you look. Now take their clothes for instance . . .' he started. He had got it all worked out.

Major Gilmour's D Company Headquarters was in an adjoining Settlement [*Fox Bay East*] which had eight families, including five children, making a total population of thirty people. He is responsible for the defence of the very large West Falkland area stretching out to Weddell and Beaver Islands, and Dunnose Head, over in the far west. 'We have to record and get to know all the local people in our area,' he said. 'Then we know who is who. Obviously we have to rely largely on them to tell us if there are strangers about, supplementing our own patrolling'.

'With the size and nature of the area we have to cover, we need helicopters to deploy patrols very quickly to investigate any possible operational incidents. The only alternative is foot patrols and, in the hard tufted grass terrain, they would have to be going very well indeed to cover even three miles in an hour, which is an awfully slow reaction time. Obviously the better our initial information, the more effectively we can react, and this is where the locals' "eyes and ears" come in.'

The Argentinians had stationed an infantry battalion in Fox Bay West, and their Headquarters and an engineer unit in Fox Bay East. They had a large fuel dump and a big stock of ammunition there, including SAM 7s. Mines had been laid on the coast, facing seaward, around the airstrip and near the dug-in positions; much clearance work had still to be done. 'A reasonable bunch of Argies' had been the local verdict, but most of the civilians, with the exception of Richard Cockwell, the Settlement Manager, and his family, had moved out during the occupation.

There had been no fighting at Fox Bay, but Royal Navy Harriers had destroyed the white Argentine HQ Building, tucked in behind the promontory, with cluster bombs. They had also bombed Dunnose Head.

An example of current military relationships at Fox Bay East, the Jocks told me, was how one of the more elderly Falkland Islanders in the Settlement regularly called in to Company Headquarters at seven am, expecting his first beer! He was beginning to be a bit of a problem!

Snow-covered hills overlooked The Queen's Lancashire Regiment's Company Camp [*at Port Howard*]. The Company had only recently moved in, having taken over from a Scots Guards Company, but the sun was out and Lieutenant Vernon Meeson, the Advance Party Commander, from Grimsargh near Preston, told me he was looking forward to their tour. He felt his Lancashire soldiers 'were naturally good at getting on with people' and so would fit in well. 'There are even two Land Girls in the Settlement,' he added optimistically. He also told me that there were 120 horses in the Settlement in need of exercise. I can see some mounted infantry patrolling around here before too long, a sight which would gladden the hearts of many of 'The Old and Bold' back in Britain.

Port Howard is an attractive red-roofed Settlement with a population of forty. Robin Lee, from New Zealand, is Manager of the farm of 20,000 acres which carries 40,000 sheep. The Argentinians did not arrive until two weeks after their invasion; they eventually had about 780 men in the area. There are still mines about, especially up the gulley to the rear of the settlement, and reports say that a Royal Marine lost a limb on a floating mine by the beach.

Lieutenant Meeson showed me the hole in the floor in the corner of the room in the house his Detachment were occupying; it was where the Argentinians had kept prisoner a member of the SAS whom they had captured nearby.

[*In early June, Captain Gavin Hamilton and a Lance-Corporal, operating the radio, part of a four-man SAS patrol observing Port Howard, found themselves surrounded by Argentinians. Captain Hamilton, although wounded in the fire fight which he himself had initiated in order to cover his radio operator's withdrawal, nevertheless continued to hold the Argentinians off by fire until he himself was killed. The Lance-Corporal managed to survive the completely exposed route from the position, but was subsequently captured. Strangely, the Argentinians did not show much interest in their SAS prisoner, maybe because of the colour of his skin, but perhaps because, he said later, 'I told them I was only the batman who had to hump the radio around.' Captain Hamilton, who had distinguished himself earlier in the campaign, was later awarded a posthumous Military Cross.*]

The flight back was typically Falklands. After taking off from Fox Bay, we cut across Falklands Sound to Goose Green. We then flew along to the immediate south of, and below the crestline of, the Wickham Heights which run from west to east like a great backbone.

We passed low over some of the enormous boulder runs. These are 'rivers' of huge boulders that 'flow' down from the mountains towards the sea, dating from the Ice Age. Lieutenant-Colonel Geoffrey Field and I had walked up to one soon after my arrival. The sheer quantity and size of the boulders make the runs very formidable obstacles indeed which even sheep cannot penetrate. One can therefore appreciate why the ecology of the patches of vegetation inside a run have been preserved to this day.

But, as we flew on, the weather deteriorated and suddenly we were in dangerous white-out conditions. Our Army Air Corps pilot immediately dropped the helicopter to virtually ground level and, by dodging to and fro around the alternative blodges of cloud and bits of mountain that suddenly came into our view, we literally tunnelled our way through to the north side of the mountain ridges, dodged behind Mount Kent and flew back home through the few feet of gap left between the very low-hugging cloud and the sodden-looking peat.

I came back from my tour very heartened. As with so many other places, to be in the capital, Stanley, is not to see the real nature of the country. Soldiers need to get out and about, train hard, get to know the locals and every part of their wide operational area. Only then are they doing the job they were sent here for – first to deter aggression and then, if that fails, to defend the Falkland Islands.

It was a stroke of someone's genius for the Queen's Own Highlanders to be the first post-war unit here. They are without doubt a first-class Battalion. Even in the local chat around Stanley I have heard civilians openly remark on the discipline and alert smartness of these Jocks, even when doing scruffy cleaning-up jobs like sweeping the streets of Stanley. Perhaps, as the first Infantry Battalion in the Aftermath, rubbing shoulders with many who fought in the battle here, and now moving on to hard training, they have had the best of both worlds. Maybe this is some compensation for their omission from the campaign, and for the loss of their planned tour in Cyprus. Others who follow will not be so lucky.

15 | LIEUTENANT-GENERAL SIR PAUL TRAVERS

Lieutenant-General Sir Paul Travers, the Army's Quartermaster General, left the Falklands yesterday after a four day visit. He is the first member of the Army's top hierarchy to have made the trip.

In particular, General Travers was seeing for himself the problems of present and future accommodation for the troops, and of logistic support for the force. He made an extensive tour of the Islands, visiting troop locations in remote areas as well as in Stanley itself. It is understood that he is to make a report to the Army Board at its meeting on Friday.

The burly, engaging Paul Travers is an old friend and, incredibly, but to his eternal credit, the first really senior person from the Ministry of Defence, the Government or any other Whitehall Department to visit the Falklands since the campaign ended some eight weeks ago. We had passed on the road and met when visiting units, but it was not until we spent a long late evening in his room at the Upland Goose, sinking most of a whisky bottle, that we could really talk.

I told him I was delighted that at last an Army General was visiting the Falklands Aftermath to see things for himself; for until someone did so, the real flavour of the situation and its tremendous problems, aggravated by the appalling weather and by the virtually negative existence of any infrastructure of any kind (both of which contrived to make everything that had to be done more than doubly hard, slow and difficult), could not be reflected as it should be in the relevant corridors of Whitehall.

Furthermore, although not his problem, the Falkland Islanders I had spoken to felt let down that no major British political figure – ideally Mrs Thatcher herself but if not her, then at least her Foreign or Defence Minister – had yet been down to see them in the immediate Aftermath. Many of the British garrison had been expecting an earlier morale-raising visit by some very senior military or political figure, but I appreciated that maybe other considerations had been dominant at home.

Agreeing, and saying how anxious he had been to 'come South', he said, 'You've no conception of what little idea any of them have back there of what it's like out here, and I'll certainly tell them when I get home. I've had a marvellous, comprehensive and stimulating tour, and I'm tremendously impressed with how hard and how cheerfully everyone is working. Of course we must improve the conditions as much and as soon as we can, but morale everywhere is absolutely sky high.'

The Army is indeed lucky to have such a popular, conscientious and competent man as its Quartermaster General. [Tragically Paul Travers, still QMG, died of a sudden heart attack on 10 June, 1983.]

16 | THE ATOs

6 August, 1982

What Captain Dick Gill, one of the two Royal Army Ordnance Corps Ammunition Technical Officers with the Logistic Battalion, called 'a quite unbelievable amount' of British and Argentine ammunition is still dispersed around the Falkland Islands.

Large stocks of British ammunition were brought into the San Carlos bridgehead at Ajax Bay and, later, into forward areas such as Teal Inlet and Fitzroy, to support the advancing troops. Much of it now remains, unused from the war.

An estimated 1,000 tons of Argentine bombs, explosives and ammunition of every kind has been collected to date into dumps in the Stanley area alone, representing several million pounds' worth. More stocks are being found all the time – for instance the stables at Stanley Racecourse were recently discovered to be stacked high with 105 mm shells, 120 mm and other rockets and mortar bombs. This figure does not take into account Argentinian stocks dumped in the mountain battle grounds, or in the gun positions around Stanley beyond the minefields and which are currently flooded, or the nasty-looking piles out by Moody Brook. Surprise being the name of this particular game, the total tonnage of Argentinian ammunition is expected to rise considerably.

The task of collecting, inspecting, storing and ultimately disposing of it all, one way or the other, currently falls to Captains Dick Gill and Geoff Cox from Carlisle and Deepcut respectively. I toured the dumps with them, as they kept up a running commentary on the enormously wide technical span of their 'collection'. 'It's just as if you'd tipped a whole ammunition depot down on the ground,' laughed Dick Gill. Working on ammunition out here for six months, they told me, would be equivalent to at least five years' worth of practical experience for the young Army ammunition specialist NCOs coming out from Britain. They would have to make decisions and carry responsibility for their rank far in excess of that normally undertaken in peacetime Britain. In similar previous situations this freedom had sometimes subsequently produced a 'frustration syndrome' when the men went home; it was a point to watch.

A large quantity of Argentine ammunition is still boxed and in pristine condition. Since there is a degree of commonality between Argentine and British weapons, much of this can be useful to Britain; for example, several million rounds of rifle ammunition. All loose small items – like that so far collected into 170 large oil drums each containing 40,000 rounds – will have to be got rid of. There are some items which even the experienced officers cannot yet identify.

Bulk explosive, shells, detonators and detonating cord, rockets, grenades, mortar and other bombs, either of no possible use to Britain or unsafe, are destroyed by controlled explosions. Out along the Darwin Road, near Mount William, where it is remote, still heavily mined and therefore where no one can go freely, makes an ideal place in which to set off the necessary series of really good bangs.

We set off two real 'cocktails' there yesterday – 1,200 pounds worth of mixed explosive content in all – creating a lovely 'mushroom' cloud and a forty-foot-wide crater. ('Blow 1' contained 110 × 105 mm RCL rounds, nine US Mark 6 anti-tank mines, thirty-four assorted grenades and a quantity of cordite bagged charges. 'Blow 2' comprised 108 × 105 mm RCL rounds, two × 105 mm pack howitzer shells, twenty-four × 3.5 inch rockets and ten anti-tank mines.) The skill lies in arranging matters so that everything actually detonates at once, so that some items are not just scattered as a result of the explosion to make a new area clearance task. One problem is that many Argentine stocks are either still in mined areas or in places too soft to approach by vehicle. The Argentinians got them there in fine weather when the peat was very dry. As a result, where it is safe to do so, these stocks are blown up in situ. Items containing white phosphorous are always very difficult to dispose of.

The Argentinians showed considerable ingenuity with some of their ammunition. The rocket for their 105 mm recoilless gun, for instance, was the most home-made bit of Heath Robinson work I have ever seen: the explosive head was attached to an improvised long metal basket containing cordite. 'You'd have to be a brave man to fire that lot,' said Captain Cox. Another devilish touch was an improvised guide-tube launcher for up to nineteen SNEB 68 mm rockets. In Fox Bay East, just before surrendering, the Argentinians had decided to hide the fact that they had Soviet SAM 7 infra-red 'fire and forget' anti-aircraft missiles. They had loaded the tubes with stones and hurled them into an inlet. The hoard was only discovered later when one missile, insufficiently weighted, was spotted, luckily for everyone, sticking upright out of the water.

One major EOD problem yet to be tackled is the Argentine ammunition ship *Bahia Buen Suceso*. She is an Argentine Navy supply ship and was one of the original scrap metal dealers' ships that went into South Georgia in March, 1982. Now in San Carlos Water, to where she had been towed in late June after the surrender, having earlier run aground by Fox Bay East, she has a list of eight degrees and has a good load of ammunition still on board, much of which is reported to be 'in a very dodgy condition'. [*The* Bahia Buen Suceso *was eventually towed out to deep water east and well clear of Stanley, where she was sunk by rockets and cannon fire by Sea Harriers of 809 Naval Air Squadron from HMS* Illustrious.]

In addition to sorting out the Argentine problem, the Royal Army Ordnance Corps has also to co-ordinate, check, inspect, classify and re-deploy all the large British ammunition stocks still widely deployed at Ajax Bay, Teal Inlet and elsewhere. This is a task impossible to complete until the final force levels and deployment plans for the future British garrison are known, and one which in itself could easily take at least six months – requiring ammunition technicians, helicopters, shipping and much manpower. Indeed, a special Composite Ammunition Company RAOC has now been formed to deal with the whole extensive Falklands ammunition problem in the foreseeable future. It is going to be busy for a long, long time to come.

Captain Dick Gill's first impression of what he saw in Stanley was one of 'absolute horror'. The streets were coated in small arms ammunition. Every garden had piles of grenades and there were anti-tank rockets everywhere.

In Callaghan Road he had literally stumbled over forty Blowpipe missiles, and in Rock Road there were more than thirty large shipping containers full of small arms ammunition. There were piles of Panhard armoured-car 90 mm shells parked next to Falkland Islanders' homes. Exocet anti-ship missiles were stacked in a trailer on the eastern edge of town, with Roland anti-air missiles near them. Tigercat missiles were piled at the back of the Hospital. Just off the jetty was an ammunition mix which, he told me, 'defied description'.

The RAOC Ammunition Team to cope with all this was initially just himself, Captain Ken Moules, a watchkeeper on HMS *Fearless*, Warrant Officer Class 1 Kevin Callaghan and three Ammunition Technicians from the Commando Logistic Squadron, 81 Ordnance Company and the Army Air Corps Squadron respectively.

The first priority was obviously to make a quick assessment of what the situation was, and then start to clear the streets and gardens, the peat sheds and the garages, gradually working through the whole town. But some of the team then went home and had to be replaced.

Dick Gill's prime concern was, and still is, for the local Falkland Islanders, and especially for their children. Neither the former, wanting to get out and about again, nor the latter, wanting to go out and play, would appreciate the potentially lethal material with which they are surrounded. It is certainly a miracle that there has been no serious accident to date.

[Reporting his findings following a visit to the Falklands in July, 1982, Brigadier Charles Smith, Director of Land Services Ammunition, described the ammunition-clearing task as 'presenting quite the worst case imaginable of any battle Aftermath'. He proposed the immediate formation of a Composite Ammunition Company, whose sole task 'would be to bring order into the ammunition chaos'. The unit was rapidly formed and arrived in the Falklands on 8 August, 1982. By the time it returned to Britain for disbandment on 31 January, 1983 'it had virtually completed the massive task which faced it on arrival,' the Brigadier wrote later.

In statistical terms the Company had cleared all the dumps of ammunition scattered around the Falklands, about 3,000 tons' worth, together with forty-seven battlefield sites. Over a million rounds of small arms ammunition had been disposed of and 45,000 unexploded ordnance items of all kinds had been explosively demolished. Four and a half million more items of Argentinian ammunition of all kinds, worth some £8 million and with a weight of about 1,000 tons, had been checked over, found serviceable and are now earmarked for use by Britain's Armed Forces.]

17 | THE ARGENTINIANS

The Argentine garrison here had good equipment. From what I have seen in the Falklands, contrary to many reports both during the occupation and since, it was well equipped and was certainly never short of ammunition, food or supplies, although distribution was often a different story.

The Argentinians believed in putting down the heaviest weight of fire possible in any situation – and did so, to which the British Commandos and Battalions who suffered and bravely overcame it will bear witness. Much of what the Argentinians left behind has now been collected in, but much remains visible in the as yet uncleared minefields and other outlying battle areas.

Particulary successful was the Argentinians' extensive range of modern night-fighting and surveillance aids. Their passive infra-red viewers, image intensifiers and thermal imagers were excellent and were used at significant range to great effect during British infantry attacks. One of their Surveillance Scopes had an effective range of three kilometres. Three American 'Probeye' viewers were captured in Stanley, and the Argentinians used infra-red beams which were directly linked to heavy machine guns so that they fired automatically on targets interrupting the beam. One device consisted of a TV camera zoom with a four-times magnification lens clipped over an image intensifier tube connected to a pair of binoculars.

They appreciated the value of snipers, perhaps a little old-fashioned to some, using machine guns as well as rifles, and equipped theirs suitably and well. The constantly accurate fire brought down at night, for example, even by heavy machine guns, as during the Battle for Tumbledown, was evidence of thoughtful application of sophisticated techniques.

The Argentinians' electronic warfare and jamming equipment was also good, and they had a number of excellent radars, as well as the older Skyguard and Super Fledermaus. Many will remember the pictures on TV, soon after the invasion, of large amphibious and other troop-carrying vehicles trundling through Stanley; perhaps because these were found unsuitable for the very soft Falklands terrain, they were withdrawn again quite quickly. The only armoured vehicles the garrison possessed were Panhard ERV 90s, but even these were never properly deployed.

By contrast, there were modern land-rover type Mercedes and Volkswagen vehicles, Dodge, Ford, Chevrolet and Unimog light trucks, and heavy Mercedes lorries aplenty. 'It seems the Argentinians filled the place up with transport, but there was nowhere for it to go,' said Major Tony Ball, Officer Commanding 10 Field Workshops, who had landed at San Carlos on 3 June and part of whose recent job has been to sort out all the captured Argentine equipment, and whose guest I was for the day.

For field gunnery I was shown the 105 mm pack howitzers the Argentinians used and also the 155 mm towed guns they employed when greater range and weight of shell was required. Some of their use of artillery was different from ours. For example they often fired haphazardly on chosen lines of arc rather than on proper information and observation. There were several occasions when a British infantry company, immediately it came under shell-fire, moved sideways 200–300 yards and was then perfectly safe because the Argentinians' fire was not directed or adjusted to follow.

The shrapnel effect of exploding artillery shells fitted with impact fuses was curtailed by the fact that they often penetrated the peat before exploding and thus suffered from a masking effect – a Falklands dimension experienced by both sides. Air defence had obviously been taken very seriously. I saw the Argentine Oerlikon 35 mm twin-barrelled guns which, linked to their Skyguard radars, are excellent. They also had the Rheinmetall 20 mm cannon, together with the French 'Roland', British 'Tigercat' and Russian SAM 7 missiles.

About 10,000 small arms of every type were captured. These were mainly FN rifles of different types, but there were also infantry mortars of various calibres, .50 and .30 heavy machine guns, various sizes and makes of hand guns, and even the odd vintage Mauser and shotgun. Many rifles had a picture of the Virgin Mary or other Patron Saint taped to the butt. Strangely, in some areas which had been occupied by Argentinian conscripts, some rifles were recovered loaded with blank ammunition!

Drill rounds and inert drill mortar bombs were found too. For anti-armour defence there were 120 mm recoilless rifles, with seemingly unlimited ammunition, and the old German Cobra wire-guided missiles. The land-based Exocets, suspected but even so something of a surprise, were anti-ship, and it was one of these which hit the County Class Destroyer HMS *Glamorgan* (6,200 tons). The range of Argentinian mines was modern, sophisticated and lethal.

Many weapons and equipment in good condition, of use or of interest to the British Army, are being shipped home. Others, useless or rusted beyond economic repair, are sea-dumped. [*Detail of the Argentine military equipment collected as at 26 July, 1982, is given in Annex C.*]

The Pucara was the Argentinian Garrison's dangerous 'indigenous' ground attack aircraft, of which I have seen a number still 'nose-down tail-up' around the Falklands. But they also had a fair number of good helicopters for troop movement and logistic re-supply. These included the Italian 'Augusta 109', the American 'Huey', the familiar twin-rotored 'Chinook' and the 'Puma'.

All in all the Argentinians had a good array of modern battleworthy equipment with which to support their well-dug and well-prepared defensive positions. It was professionally deployed and the interlocking arcs of fire had clearly been properly thought out. They used deception to useful effect. The 'spoof' craters on Stanley airfield runway and the well-made camouflage-netted mock-ups representing gun positions, for instance on the approach to Stanley from Fitzroy and at Fox Bay, were good efforts to fool air photo-graphy. They were good improvisers – as witness the home-made Sned rocket launchers which were ranged by a system of string knots.

The Argentinians certainly did not lose the war because of bad equipment.

One senior officer in the Falkland Islands was very concerned at the quantity of Argentine documentary material valuable to the British which had been lost in the immediate Aftermath because no one had been specifically briefed or had assumed responsibility to lay hands on it at once. 'In 1944/45 we learnt how to be victorious – we had Intelligence-trained troops well forward to gather in quickly everything of value. We did not billet troops in towns which had just been liberated, who would have either deliberately or inadvertently destroyed important documents, maps or sensitive important equipment. We recovered much extremely useful material,' he said. 'In the climax of victory here, everyone had been too knackered immediately to home in on the vital source of defeated enemy information and, as a result, much was simply burnt or destroyed. It was four days before an Intelligence "grip" was taken, but by then it was too late to get the bonus we should have done. It was a terrible mistake.'

Similarly, huge numbers of Argentinian personal weapons in good condition, taken off the prisoners-of-war, were left for several weeks to deteriorate and rust in the open at the mercy of the weather, rather than being quickly gathered up and put under some form of protective cover for future use.

I was shown old ships' containers crammed with thousands of the better of these rifles, light and heavy machine guns which, having been sorted through, had a chance of being refurbished into usefulness for certain types of units back home. The rest were beyond salvage and only fit for dumping at sea.

Touring round Argentinian artillery pieces in the abandoned gun lines of Stanley Common, the Darwin Road edge of town and elsewhere, one found several valuable gunsights apparently deliberately smashed. I was told this had been done either maliciously or exuberantly after the fighting was over, as part of the process of relieving the high tension understandably aroused by the fighting. Similarly, up at Stanley airfield, I was told of five Argentinian Pucara aircraft in good condition at the time of surrender which were subsequently ruined because an exuberant Flight Lieutenant had allegedly gone round them pulling the ejection seat handles.

1. South Atlantic rendezvous with the RAF Victor Tanker.

2. The Hercules's probe enters the Victor's fuel pipe's basket end.

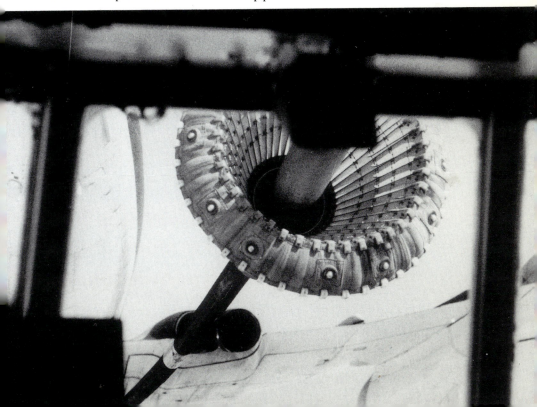

3. An 'Aladdin's Cave' array of captured Argentinian ammunition.

4. Argentinian 155-mm howitzer beside the Darwin Road.

5. Argentinian Panhard armoured cars near Moody Brook.

6. Argentinian ammunition and weaponry at Goose Green.

7. Major Guy Lucas RE astride an unexploded 1,000 lb Argentine bomb which had been dropped on 3 Commando Brigade Headquarters behind Mount Kent on 13 June, 1982.

8. An uncleared Argentine position on Mount Longdon.

9. Lieutenant-Colonel Geoff Field RE with an Argentinian Pucara on Goose Green airfield.

10. Captain Richard Gill QGM, RAOC.

11. A cocktail of collected ordnance ready for blowing up near the Darwin Road.

12. Spanish P4B anti-personnel mine. (approx diameter 3 inches)

13. Italian SB33 anti-personnel mine. (approx diameter 3 inches)

14. Argentinian FMK1 anti-personnel mine. (approx diameter 3 inches)

15. Argentinian minelaying line used for laying mines to a set pattern in a minefield.

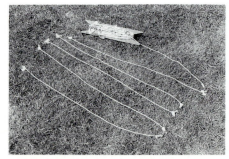

Spanish C3B anti-tank mine. (approx diameter 11 ˙hes)

17. Italian SP81 anti-tank mine. (approx diameter $9\frac{1}{2}$ inches)

Argentinian FMK3 anti-tank mine. (approx diam-˙r $9\frac{1}{2}$ inches)

19. Israeli No. 4 anti-personnel mine. (approx $5\frac{1}{2}$ inches long)

Israeli No. 6 anti-tank mine. (approx diameter 12 ˙˙˙es)

21. American M1 anti-tank mine. (diameter nearly 12 inches)

22. Area of Stanley airfield west of the Control Tower.

23. Sappers putting in the arrester gear anchorages beside the new AM2 runway at Stanley airfield.

Many sources have confirmed the bravery and sheer guts of the Argentine Air Force pilots who repeatedly attacked the British Task Force's vessels. It is said that many were drawn from the cream of the Argentinian polo-playing aristocracy, and had nerve, honour and the traditional macho image to maintain to the full.

Contrary to some reports, a number of Argentinian officers stayed in their trenches fighting with their men during the final battles for Stanley. Their field ration was far superior to that of their men, and many soldiers out in the defensive positions went hungry while those in Stanley, particularly the officers, had plenty to eat.

A senior officer concerned with repatriating Argentinian prisoners-of-war told me of a number of incidents, related to him by soldier POWs, of their bad officer–man relationship. He quoted the incident on board a repatriation boat of the officer who insisted that he wanted to visit his men below. Eventually he was taken down, but it immediately transpired that he had only gone down to demand one of his soldiers' sleeping bags for himself. He spoke of another group who, while defending Mount Longdon, had had to live only on tinned tomatoes for their last week.

Many of the Argentinian officers had brought their 'fancy uniforms' over to 'Las Malvinas', he said. Asked for their views on the Falkland experience, 'It was all a nonsense by our two Foreign Offices' was the reply of several. Nevertheless their faith in their cause, that 'Las Malvinas' were theirs, was deeply founded.

Fourteen-year-olds were common among the Argentine troops, the officer said. One young POW had related how he had been happily spending an evening at a disco in Buenos Aires when the lights had suddenly gone out. When they came on again a little later, the place was full of police. Anyone (he was one of them) who could not prove he was in employment was taken away, and the next thing they were in the Falklands.

Spotting an obviously older unmilitary-looking officer in the POW compound, the senior officer has asked him why he was in the Army and in the Falklands. It turned out that the man was a schoolmaster who had personally taken his Sixth Form on a day's 'interest visit' to the local military barracks. All had gone well to start with, but suddenly he and his whole form were told they were being enlisted there and then into the Army, and were not going home. Within three days he and his boys were in Las Malvinas.

Many of the young Argentinian conscript POWs said they had thought, on arriving in the Falklands, that they were actually in Chile, or defending a part of Argentina against the Chileans. For them, they said, Goose Green was the turning point. They didn't want to die and the weather was appalling anyway.

They said they had feared the reputation of the Commandos and 'The

Paras', and had been scared that the Queen of England had actually sent down her own private Guards to teach them a lesson. And as for the Gurkhas, they knew them to be cannibals!

18 | REX HUNT AND THE FALKLAND ISLANDERS

Mr Rex Hunt, the Civil Commissioner, is a real character. Lively, small in stature but with a big warm heart for the Islands and the Islanders, at the moment he almost *is* the Falklands. He has no false airs or graces, but an obvious and genuine concern to get the place back on its feet again, despite the immense problems.

The way Mr Hunt operates is quite unlike any other senior Foreign Office official with whom I have worked in other parts of the world. He is very popular with all the Falkland Islanders with whom I have spoken, especially because they feel he understands them and their strange, distant environment. 'We are different, you know.' They trust him to do his best for them in what they see as a very difficult Aftermath in which all sorts of pressures back in Britain, in the United Nations and elsewhere will be exerted on them – and decisions made about them and their future – by people and governments who, they feel, may not know them, their feelings or their way of life.

The loathing of many of the Islanders for the Foreign Office, which they feel has let them down and only wants to get rid of them, is ill-disguised. They would not have accepted any Foreign Office official other than 'Our Governor' back again in the Islands as Civil Commissioner, and they are determined now to hang on to him as long as they possibly can. It was not difficult to see why the reports say that he is not popular with the traditionalists in the Foreign Office.

I entered the back of the public counter at the office of Cable and Wireless early yesterday morning from the telex room to speak to the girl clerk on duty. There was a queue of eight Falkland Islanders waiting at her counter. I suddenly recognized a familiar small figure patiently waiting his turn as No 6 in line – it was Rex Hunt. He was chatting away to everyone else in the queue – he clearly knew them all – asking about Mrs A's niece, Mrs B's water problem, Mr C's ill grandchild, John, and answering as many questions as he asked of them. In those few minutes I learnt what Rex Hunt is to the Falkland Islanders.

Discussing the immediate future of the Falklands with a new acquaintance, I was told I had to appreciate that Stanley was very like a small West Highland coastal village in Scotland. Its 'Parish' Council, used to dealing with a smaller scale of problems, had suddenly been thrust into the limelight of the world stage – a role for which, naturally, it was entirely unprepared, untrained and inexperienced. It had been forced to make the quantum jump from mini to macro which events had forced upon it, and this was one of the biggest of the civilian problems of the Aftermath. 'Tragically, the old kelpers' world has gone for ever, the implications of which will only dawn on everyone during the coming year, during which everyone will be concentrating on pushing the Falklands into the 20th century,' he said.

One not-unconnected aspect of this change was the fact that initially the military controlled all the means of nearly everything, including movement, and hence so many aspects of Aftermath life both in Stanley and out in the 'camp' Settlements. Hitching helicopter rides was the norm, for example, and some Islanders began to accept the constant military assistance as not only the 'norm' but as theirs by right.

As things began to return to more normal conditions, some civil–military stresses and strains began to arise. This was inevitable, especially following the arrival in Stanley of Jack Morgan, the Military Commissioner's Command Secretary (or Civil Servant MOD financial adviser). Well-chosen, a large, cheerful extrovert with wide military operational experience, nevertheless he had a strict brief from Sir Frank Cooper, Permanent Under-Secretary of the MOD in London, to start tightening things up and getting back to peacetime financial economy and practice, a task that, in the circumstances of any campaign Aftermath, is always a difficult and unpopular one with military and civilians alike. Particular practices and 'mutual benefit' arrangements built up and considered important during and immediately following a campaign's operational phases, for instance, are regarded as costing money and being an unacceptable diversion of economic resources in peacetime.

In the Aftermath, the Falkland Islanders invited 'the military' into their homes and could not do enough for them. The Government never charged any rent for any of the public buildings which 'the military' took over or shared, such as the Hospital, the Post Office and the Town Hall.

[Two years later the troops' nickname for the 'locals' was 'Bennies', taken from a popular British TV programme. The locals took exception to this, and the Falklands Garrison was ordered to refrain from using it. Shortly afterwards it emerged that the troops were using the new nickname of 'Stills'. In explanation, the men said of the locals that 'they are still Bennies!' Later a number of troops changed the nickname again to 'FUBS', an acronym standing for an 'earthy' military description of a group of ungrateful people.]

Prior to the Argentine invasion, the Head of Government of the Falkland Islands was constitutionally appointed by the British Government and he was supported by an Executive ('Exco') and Legislative Council ('Legco'). The former comprised two appointed and two elected members, and two civil servants. The Councils administered and ran the Falkland Islands, and their dependencies of South Georgia and the South Sandwich Islands, in all matters except for defence and external affairs.

During the time of the Argentine occupation Mr Harold Rowlands, the Financial Secretary and a Falkland Islander, carried on as the Officer Administering the Falkland Islands Government. With the Governor and the Chief Secretary, Mr Richard Baker, having both been evacuated by the Argentinians, he was the most senior officer of the Government still left in the Islands.

Circumstances were very difficult for him and taxed his ingenuity to the utmost. For example, when the Argentinians ordered the Falklands to change their currency from pounds to pesos, Mr Rowlands immediately refused, saying he was 'far too old to learn about all those noughts. I couldn't possibly change.'

A Joint Civil-Military Committee was established as soon as Rex Hunt returned. Meeting once a week in Government House, it was an essential forum in which 'the military', in the person of Major-General Jeremy Moore and his principal staff officers, briefed 'the civil', in the person of Rex Hunt and his senior aides, on progress in sorting out the Aftermath. In turn, the Civil Commissioner's team raised with 'the military' any problems of the civil community – such as fuel, accommodation and so on – which needed urgent action.

As it was, only the Army had the resources with which to try and restore the situation – in the prevailing circumstances one could hardly say 'to normality', only 'in the direction of a normal state of affairs'.

There were, however, one or two senior officers there at the time who considered that the Services could and should have done more in those very early Aftermath days to help the Falkland Islanders. Their understandable view was a very simple one: 'What was the campaign all about, after all?'

On 28 July 'Legco' met in the Town Hall for the first time since the campaign. Two matters were of great importance for the Islanders. First, Major-General David Thorne was present by direct order from Britain as the Military Commissioner and as the ninth but non-voting member of 'Legco'.

Second, Mr Hunt made it clear to the Legislative Councillors that his change in title to Civil Commissioner did not affect the manner in which the Islands and their Dependencies were governed; this remained exactly the same as before the Argentine occupation. He would be executing all his duties as in the former appointment of Governor, except that he would now have the Military Commissioner as his defence adviser whose word on defence and internal security matters, but excluding the Police, would be mandatory. As Civil Commissioner, Mr Hunt told the Councillors, he was no longer Commander-in-Chief.

The highlight of this important first meeting of 'Legco' was an historic speech by the Civil Commissioner, the key extracts of which were:

'I am sure that honourable members would wish me first and foremost to pay tribute and to express the everlasting thanks of this Council to the Prime Minister of Great Britain, Mrs Margaret Thatcher; the Commander-in-Chief, Sir John Fieldhouse and his staff; the Commander of the Task Force, Admiral Woodward; and the Commander Land Forces, General Moore, and all the members of the Armed Forces and Merchant Marine who took part in the magnificent campaign in the South Atlantic that led to the liberation of these Islands and their Dependencies in the incredibly short time of ten and a half weeks. It was a feat not only of outstanding courage and professionalism on the part of the fighting forces but also a remarkable effort of logistics in keeping them supplied from a base 8,000 miles away. This Council salutes all those thousands of men and women who took part in the planning and execution of what will surely go down in history as one of the most successful military operations of all time. If I may paraphrase Churchill's immortal words: "Never in the field of human conflict was so much owed by so few to so many".

'Alas, victory was not achieved without casualties, and I know that Honourable Members would wish me to take this opportunity to express Legislative Council's deepest condolences to all those who suffered loss or injury during the conflict. They may rest assured that we *shall* remember them and we accept it as our bounden duty to ensure that this sacrifice shall not have been in vain. It is up to us now to see that out of their sacrifice and suffering we build a better, brighter and more secure future for the Falkland Islands and their Dependencies.

'As a constant reminder of those who laid down their lives so that Falkland Islanders could be free, it is proposed to erect a monument in Stanley to their everlasting glory, and to commemorate the 14th of June every year from henceforth.

'For the present, however, all our energies and efforts are concerned with getting back to normal as quickly as possible. By this I do not mean a return to the way of life that we had before the 2nd of April. I am not naïve enough to think that this is possible, even if it were desirable. By this I mean restoring the civil administration, repairing the damage of war, clearing up the mess of war, providing reliable and adequate essential services and, last but not least, bringing some fun and laughter back into the lives of the ordinary people of these Islands.

'As I have said before, I am optimistic about the future of these Islands. The Argentines tried to grab them by military might. They failed. Doubtless they will try to carry on the battle by diplomatic means in the various bodies of the United Nations. They may try to get Britain back to the negotiating table. But Honourable Members can take comfort from the Prime Minister's firm and clear statement to the UN Secretary-General a week or two ago that there was nothing to negotiate with the Argentines. The future of these Islands is concerned with the type of association we have with Britain, not with Argentina.

'Finally, may I, as one who was not allowed to share your ordeal, pay tribute to all the people of these Islands who endured those ten and a half long weeks of agony under Argentine occupation. You all deserve a medal. Unfortunately only Servicemen qualify for a campaign medal. Doubtless some of those whose stirring deeds have attracted attention will be recognized in due course, but, as in all wars, there will be many unsung heroes whose feats of courage will be unrecognized. It is to them that I pay my last tribute and humble thanks.'

19 | CHRISTCHURCH CATHEDRAL: CLAIMS

Christchurch Cathedral

As the fighting in the Falklands Campaign closed in around Stanley, the International Committee of the Red Cross proposed, and both sides agreed, the establishment of a protected neutralized zone (provided for in Article 15 of the Fourth Geneva Convention) within which members of the civilian non-combatant population, and also wounded and sick civilians and Servicemen alike, would find a safe sanctuary away from the ragings of battle.

The area selected was a rectangle of some five acres centred around Stanley's Anglican Cathedral, an easily identifiable large and prominent red-brick building bounded by John Street, Dean Street, Philomel Street and Ross Road. In the event, however, the final stages of the battle moved even quicker than expected and the early Argentine surrender made the establishment of this neutralized zone unnecessary.

The present Christchurch Cathedral, constructed of brick and timber, took two years to build. The size of a large parish church, it was completed in 1894. It has stained glass windows and carved choir stalls, and the large west window is dedicated to the memory of George Markham, Dean of Stanley, who died on 1 April, 1888. Nearby are the St Mary's Roman Catholic Church and the United Free Church Tabernacle.

Numerous tablets look down from the northern and southern interior walls on the Cathedral's rows of dark, polished wooden pews. They record the memory not only of Falkland Islanders but of British Servicemen who died in Falkland waters. They record, for instance, Captain and Officer Commanding the Falkland Island Volunteers Frederick Craigie-Halkett who died in 1899, casualties from the naval engagement fought by HMS *Good Hope* and HMS *Monmouth* on 1 November, 1914, and Falkland Islander pilots who were killed flying with the Royal Naval Air Service in 1918 and in the Battle of Britain.

The congregation today, Sunday 8 August, at the familiar service of Matins – the same, even 8,000 miles away – comprises forty all ranks in uniform from the three Services, two Merchant Navy officers and three Falkland Islanders. Their many heavy outer garments which the Falklands winter weather makes essential, even for coming to church, lie strewn over an impressively large area of the rear pews. The choir is multi-Service, the organist a soldier, and a woman Falkland Islander is both sidesman and lesson reader.

Claims

In July the British Government announced it would entertain claims for compensation from Falkland Islanders who had suffered loss as a result of the Argentinian invasion and the subsequent campaign.

The MOD Civil Servant selected in Britain to fly down and take on the very difficult task of sorting out, going through and subsequently visiting all the claimants, and investigating and assessing their actual losses for himself against what had been claimed, was Barry Neale.

Barry, from the Claims Branch of the Ministry of Defence Lands Department, flew down at short notice in early August with Jack Morgan, the first Command Secretary to be appointed to the Falklands. They both joined me with the Davidson family. The selection at home had produced a good choice. For one thing, Barry had to grasp the Falklands level of prices and costs very quickly, and they were very different from those in Britain. He was not only experienced, painstaking and thorough, but also had a good instinct for when the odd claimant inflated his claim against Her Majesty's purse. Although he was working to a directive from London, nevertheless he was a humane person with a quick sense of fairness and a sense of humour, who had genuine sympathy with the Islanders for what they had gone through during the Argentine occupation. His was a very important Aftermath task.

20 | THE ANIMALS

The look on the brown-and-white speckled calf's face was bewildered, lost and pathetic, as it nuzzled its suddenly inexplicably still mother's body. She was one of fifteen cattle and one horse which had just been shot dead by a Queen's Own Highlander marksman, all having lost legs on Argentine anti-personnel mines. It was one of the most distressing afternoons I have ever spent.

The shots came from the Army Gazelle helicopter piloted by Staff Sergeant Bill Cooper. It also contained Major Brian Thompson, Royal Army Veterinary Corps, the Force Vet, from Melton Mowbray, Warrant Officer Class 2 Ronnie Hardie, from Caithness, with his sniper's 7.62 mm L 42 A1 rifle, and the farmer, Claude Molkenbuhr, from Murrell. I was in an accompanying Gazelle piloted by Major Anthony Stansfield, OC 657 Squadron Army Air Corps.

The beautiful, sandy Kidney Cove, and others below Mount Low on the Murrell Peninsula, together with the better pasture edging them, had been callously and quite indiscriminately sown with unmarked mines by the Argentinians, quite contrary to all international conventions. Although the mines had been individually buried, there was no perimeter wire to identify the area or restrict the animals. Naturally, most of the mines had been sown near the beaches to which area the animals, knowing it to be the best grazing, were drawn. Their plight was only discovered when someone, observing from the air, saw the dead and injured animals. We had tried to get to them the previous day, but dangerous low mist had come in to blanket out everything and our pilot, Major Stansfield, had had to abandon the sortie.

Our helicopter's job was twofold. First we acted as scout, flying at very low level around the Murrell Peninsula and coming slowly up to each cow and horse we could find to see if it was sound of limb. Time and again, a pathetically maimed animal tried to hobble away from us on its three legs, the other stump infected, puffed and swollen, or with the raw bone showing. A few had set off anti-personnel mines while grazing, and had had their jaws blown off. In a magnificent herd of ten semi-wild horses, galloping along with and below us, but showing no fear, one lovely roan with flowing mane – his front right hoof, pastern and the lower part of his fetlock missing – gallantly tried to keep up. We reported our finds over the radio for the other helicopter to take action.

Our second task was to act as aerial cowboy and, by twisting and turning, sweeping around and hovering quite still, drive the animals back inland away from the mined beach area. One calf, obviously miserable, kept slipping back again and again to suckle its dead mother. Luckily we found a length of partly flattened fence – the Argentinians had taken the wooden posts for firewood – and then, just like at any Lakeland Fell sheepdog trials, by skilful 'Collie' flying at almost zero feet, Major Stansfield carefully edged an assorted herd through a clear narrow gap.

Sheep, being so low on the ground, were of course killed instantly when they set off an anti-personnel mine. It literally blew them to pieces, as witness some freshly dead on the ground which the circling Turkey Vultures had yet to pick clean. More cheering to see were two sea lions flopping around the low rocks, and the two King Penguins, all aflap with panic waddle at our approach, but instantly changing into sleek Olympic swimmers as soon as they made the water.

'A necessary evil – it's a job that just has to be done,' said the Vet. Because the presence of mines made it too dangerous to land, the wounded animals had to be shot humanely from a helicopter. The only and unacceptable alternative would be to leave them to endure a slow and painful death on the wild hillsides as their festering infections gradually spread. The actual shooting demands very close teamwork.

First the Vet, using his binoculars from the helicopter, has to examine the animals and decide which ones have to be shot. The farmer, sitting alongside him, has to agree. Then Warrant Officer Class 2 Hardie, six times Army champion shot and his Battalion's Signals Sergeant-Major, has to work very closely with the pilot to get into the right position to fire. The pilot has to keep the aircraft steady, despite wind problems. The sniper has to allow for rotor downdraught, the inevitable aircraft shake, the power of his bullet to pass right through the animal, angle, range and also the possibility of his target moving at the last minute. Nevertheless, I watched Hardie fell cattle time after time with a single shot straight through the heart. He reluctantly admitted to me afterwards he was 'an unofficial stalker' at home.

Claude and Judy Molkenbuhr – he had been a head shepherd at Port Howard on West Falkland for twenty-six years – had been thrilled at last to buy their own farm at Murrell two years ago, coincidentally on 2 April, 1980. (The Argentinians invaded on 2 April, 1982.) They had 10,800 acres, 3,054 sheep, seventy-one head of cattle, fifteen horses and nine pigs. With their children, they had had to leave the farm on 24 May when the Argentinians made it too difficult for them to stay, but took their tractor and trailer with them. Many have told me of the wonderful work Claude then did, with others, hauling men and supplies right up into the mountains behind the British front line.

The Molkenbuhrs returned after the surrender to find thir farmhouse spattered with bullet holes, with forty-eight shell craters within close walking distance, and their old sow cruelly locked up in the pantry. Upstairs, in what had been the bedroom, Claude showed me the words 'ENGLISH

WHORE' written in Spanish in huge letters on the walls. He told me his floors were covered in filth and excreta; he had to burn all his carpets. The Molkenbuhrs lost everything of value from their house, including Judy's engagement ring, but the competition trophy they had won with their dog was subsequently found in an Argentinian trench after the surrender. 'We never thought they'd got what it took,' they said, 'and we never doubted for a moment that the British would come.' From the Argentinians' slaughter of his stock, and from mines, he reckons he has lost about 1,000 sheep, plus, of course, the 500 or so lambs which they would have produced in October. His old sow had rushed out of the pantry, when released, desperate to drink, but was dead within forty-eight hours. Much of his land is now mined – no one yet knows to what extent – although the holes made by those which have exploded give some indication. 'Two years' wasted work,' he reflected sadly.

Back in the spotless kitchen and warmed by tea from an enormous teapot and currant rock cakes hot from the oven, we discussed the future. The Molkenbuhrs want to stay in the Falklands and farm their own land. They had a compensation claim already lodged for £48,000 – to fix the house alone will cost £10,000 – but at the moment future prospects look bleak. The family are incredibly philosophical and stoic. They have no wish to move to Stanley. 'What's Stanley got that I haven't?' said Judy. 'From Port Howard, we only visited it about once every four years.' She then told me she had had to go to London for an operation last year. 'I was staying near Regent's Park,' she said. 'I went there quite a lot and also looked at the shops.' But, back in the Falklands, she certainly doesn't hanker for, or miss, either the shops or the bright lights.

'Sickening,' said Claude to me at the end of our harrowing day, 'just sickening. It made me feel like crying every time one went down.' We all felt the same way. In wars many brave men die, but it is the innocent who also suffer and whose lives are forfeit too, even in the animal kingdom, and, tragically, more may yet have to die before those wantonly sown Argentinian mines by the beaches can be properly – if ever – rendered safe. [*Judy died of cancer in 1985. Claude has rebuilt his home and is staying on alone.*]

Major Brian Thompson, RAVC, the Force Vet, has many responsibilities. A key Aftermath task is to minimize any danger or damage to 'the fantastic and unique' Falklands wildlife resulting from the presence of the British Garrison. This includes knowing where the various penguin colonies breed, and ensuring that low-flying helicopter or training activities do not interfere with them. King Penguins, for instance, only lay one egg every eighteen months, which they incubate with their feet, so not disturbing them is very important. He is working on this with Mr Ian Strange, a local civilian wildlife expert. One recent task was to de-oil some King Penguins on Pebble Island. 'It's a wonderful experience and a very real challenge,' he told me.

Quite apart from his military duties, Major Thompson is also acting as vet to the local farmers, taking over the responsibilities of the civilian vet who is in Britain on leave. He has been instrumental in instituting a veterinary educational programme aimed at improving animal husbandry and the control and eradication of disease. There are many other day-to-day problems which arise from the Islands' huge animal population, for instance aircraft frightening them, and moving big flocks near dangerous mined areas. Calls come in for him over the Islanders' own radio network. Some he can deal with over the air, but often he goes off in the next available helicopter. There is even a herd of guanaco (small llamas) for him to keep an eye on over in tiny Staats Island which lies off the south-west of West Falkland.

Major Thompson also has to locate and then supervise the slaughter of sheep and cattle, certify them as fit fresh meat for the population of Stanley, and then arrange for the carcasses to be flown into Stanley by RAF Chinook helicopter.

It was and still is vital to prevent any new disease being introduced into the Falklands. An urgent and essential task therefore was to destroy the piles of rotting Argentinian meat left lying about. He has since had to keep an eagle eye out for any sign of foot and mouth disease which might unwittingly have been introduced by a Service or Merchant Navy source. The important export procedures for animals (including birds) and the animal quarantine rules had also to be re-established quickly.

With fences broken down and burnt for firewood by the Argentinians, thus allowing rams freedom to roam, breeding schemes went all awry and will take years to get right again.

One big veterinary problem in Stanley on re-occupation by the British was the eradication of rats; and not just the big grey ones, sharing their sheds, about which the Supply Company's Ration Platoon had told me hair-raising stories. A new type of black 'super-rat' was found at Fox Bay, thought to have disembarked from an Argentine supply ship: 'There were rats as big as pussy cats,' Major Thompson told me. The war against the Falkland rats continues.

The civil community of Stanley are still living claustrophobic and very restricted lives, principally due to the presence of so many mines and unexploded items in and around the area, but also aggravated by the traumatic shock of what they have lived through. They cannot follow their normal outdoor pursuits, or visit beaches at weekends. The result is, Major Thompson said, that pets have become a very important factor for morale – dogs and cats mean more to their owners now than ever before, and so he spends a lot of time going round visiting and treating them, carrying a rucksack of drugs. Another animal preventive measure is to ensure the continuity of the statutory dosing every six weeks of all Falkland Islander dogs against Hydatid disease, which can be transmitted to humans.

21 | SOUTH GEORGIA

18 August, 1982

Take the highest sections of the Alps, cream them thickly with deep snow, and then immerse them in water until only their upper parts still show – and you have South Georgia.

After the grey overcast of our passage from the Falklands in the converted Leander Class frigate HMS *Andromeda* (3,100 tons), we entered Cumberland Bay to a dawn breaking on a pure white abundance of sunlit snow peaks, rising sheer from the calm water, backed by a brilliantly clear blue sky.

The larger connecting valleys were filled with enormous glaciers whose jagged, fissured cliffs of ice glowed with eerie blues, greys and greens against the still water's edge. Even the Duty Watch on the bridge, hardened by four continuous months of South Atlantic sea duty, was awed by this unexpectedly striking revelation. 'It's just beautiful,' said the tough Leading Hand beside me. Carefully skirting a towering green, iced wedding cake of an iceberg, complete with snow-piped decoration, we turned and slowly edged our way up to the mooring in King Edward Cove.

Piper Alasdair Gillies, from Ullapool, piped a welcome from on board the small British Antarctic Survey's motor boat *Albatross* circling us. A few minutes later we were put ashore at the jetty and were soon being briefed in his Headquarters at nearby Shackleton House by Captain Greg Luton of The Queen's Own Highlanders, currently in command of Grytviken Garrison. Captain Luton, from Brantford, Ontario, was previously an officer in the Canadian Army. He then resigned his commission in order to enlist as a private in the British Army and achieve his ambition of becoming an officer in a Highland Regiment. He is currently Administrator, Customs and Immigration Officer, and Postmaster, as well as being Garrison Commander of South Georgia.

In the meanwhile the mail we had brought, the first to reach South Georgia for well over a month, was being distributed to eager hands. Although many of the men received between twenty and thirty letters, the record went to Private Mark Jones, from St Albans, an Army Catering Corps cook. Proudly embarrassed, he told me he had received forty-nine!

The majority of the soldiers live in the large green-painted Shackleton House on King Edward Point, owned by the British Antarctic Survey (BAS), and originally due for demolition. This area of King Edward Cove was also the administrative centre of South Georgia, complete with Post Office, customs

Bird Is

Prince Olav Harbour
Possession Bay

Fortuna Glacier

Murray
Snowfield

Leith

Stromness

King Haakon Bay

Trident
Ridge

Husvik — Cumberland Bay

Grytviken

Godthul

▲ Mount Paget
2915m

South

Atlantic

Ocean

SOUTH GEORGIA

0   5   10   20 miles 25

0   10   20   kms

and a jail. It lies under a mile away, and quite separate from, the abandoned whaling station of Grytviken sited on the small ledge of shore at the head of the Cove. King Edward Point was also the scene of the original defensive action against the Argentinians by Lieutenant Keith Mills and his party of Royal Marines on 3 April.

The soldiers' accommodation is in warm and spacious rooms. 'Much better than anywhere in the Falklands,' I was told, and I would agree. The Medical Officer and the cooks also have excellent facilities, even though these were originally designed to cater for fewer numbers.

'After arriving, the men had to spend three weeks clearing up the filth of the months of Argentine occupation – and I mean filth, including excreta. It was disgusting,' the Doctor said. There are still unexploded shells and some mortar bombs in the water, and there is also a minefield which remains to be rendered safe, now buried deep under the snow. Well marked, however, it cannot be dealt with until the Antarctic summer returns and the snow melts.

There are plenty of rats in Grytviken, but King Edward Point boasts a huge mythical cat, said to have been put ashore there some years ago by the Russians. Its size grows with the telling by the sentries on night duty, but everyone assumes that the batteries for its Soviet transmitting 'bugs' are long since well and truly flat!

The Garrison necessarily lives in what Captain Luton calls 'an encapsulated environment. Unless you are aware of its potential dangers, you could well

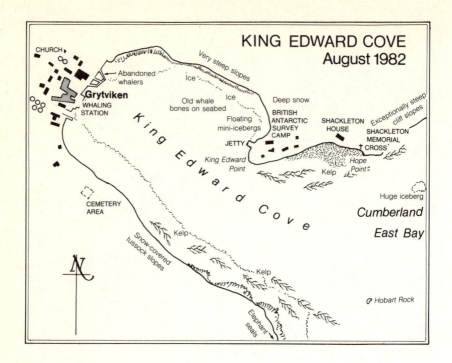

be deceived as to the natural hostility of the climate. It is dangerous – and without heat, light and food, you die,' he said. The soldiers' routine is a regular one, but their remote Antarctic life demands that a high proportion of it is necessarily spent on self-maintenance. Every day starts with an inspection of their 'fighting order equipment' which includes snow shoes, for, at the time of my visit, the snow was between eight and ten feet deep.

In general the mornings are spent on practical training or lectures, and the afternoon on the constant vital maintenance of the Garrison's defensive dispositions, its accommodation, stores, facilities and its few 'Snocat' tracked vehicles. Snow clearing is a daily chore. It snows every night at the moment, and to this are added large drifts which the local 'katabatic' wind effect deposits in different, unlikely and unpredictable places each night as if by magic. 'At least,' said Captain Malcolm Willis of Ewshot, Surrey, the Garrison's Medical Officer from 16 Field Ambulance of 1 Infantry Brigade but attached to 5 Infantry Brigade for the Campaign, 'shovelling it away keeps the soldiers fit.' Many of the Jocks I spoke with said they really enjoyed their life in South Georgia and would rather be there than in the Falklands.

Small reconnaissance patrols radiate from the base, either on snow shoes, skis or by boat. Sometimes they stay out overnight. Daily, however, in camp before supper, everyone attends an Antarctic-type lecture on, for example, survival or the building of snow houses. But by evening, such are the conditions, everyone is tired and, despite the attraction of a film or the little unit canteen, early abed.

The BAS's facilities were good, and many of them now support the military Garrison's very existence. Royal Engineers run the small power station, the real key to survival, and also do essential maintenance work using the well-equipped trade workshops. Lance-Corporal Kevin Louis, a 'chippie' from Grimsby, showed me the excellent wood-working machines; mending broken windows and frames had been his main task. Plumber Sapper Gary Gates of Bexley Heath had been kept busy renewing pipes, but, curiously for this climate, was without any lagging for them.

The nearby Post Office, still stocked with fascinating forms dealing with whales, was like some nineteenth-century film set. It now serves as the Garrison Office, but I was able to have some stamps locally postmarked nevertheless. Corporal Michael Evans, Royal Signals, was running the Communications Centre shift on duty, he is from Colchester. 'No problems at all,' he grinned. 'We are through to Headquarters in the Falklands clearly by voice every day. We only use morse occasionally, just to keep up our speeds!'

In a place like South Georgia all the men of the Garrison have to muck in together to do everything required to support their communal existence in the relentless, harsh reality of Antarctic life. Nearly everyone has to double-up his normal military usefulness by either learning new skills or applying his hobby interests for the common good.

Obviously the Queen's Own Highlanders cannot replace the many specialized skills of the BAS's scientists, but, centred on their now inevitably 'disturbed' laboratories, the Battalion has already re-started taking simple meteorological records. Corporal Graham Bonnyman, from Elgin, is the 'Met Officer' and records his daily readings of air and sea temperatures, wind and barometric pressure. 'As far as the Jocks are concerned,' he chuckled, 'there are only three temperatures out here: cold, bloody cold and ****** freezing!' – a very apt summary, I thought.

One of the more unusual extra jobs of Section Corporal Alan Henderson, from Forres, is that of 'Chicken Major'. He is responsible for an assorted batch of eighteen chickens who in some incredible way survived ending up in either an Argentinian or British cooking pot. Egg production is currently low – only three a day. The reason, he told me, is that his charges had not yet recovered from the previous unit's firing of their 81 mm mortars from immediately behind the henhouse. [M Company of 42 Commando.]

A boat is essential both militarily and domestically, and thanks to much skilled maintenance work on her engine, the BAS's sturdy Albatross is back in commission and doing sterling work. Her new crew is Corporal David Squibb of the Royal Signals, from Bristol, who is 'used to messing about in boats', and Lance-Corporal Archibald MacDonald of the Battalion who previously worked a sixty-five-foot lobster boat out of Barra. Life jackets are, of course, de rigueur, even though in practice one would probably not survive in these water temperatures for more than about a minute and a half anyway.

Second-Lieutenant Hugh Macnally, once a stalker from near Forres, walked me over the squeaking snow to the Shackleton Memorial at Hope Point. It is a simple white cross, topped with red paint. 'We hold our regular Sunday service here,' he said, 'out in the open.' From this southernmost military outpost in the world, it seemed only fitting and moving that this should include a one-minute silence and the added poignancy of a piper's lament carried by the wind across the small ice floes to the distant glaciers, the high peaks and the listening snows.

[*On my return from the South Atlantic I found a letter awaiting me from Mr Ted Shipsey of Peacehaven in Sussex. A Royal Marine mate of his, stationed at Grytviken, had met the mysterious cat which I mentioned in the above piece and had sent him the following comment in a letter:*

'*I was on patrol over by the slipway, I suppose it was around 2000 hours when this bloody great thing approached me in the gloom. At first I thought it were a dog. Then I saw it was some sort of cat thing. I say that, because it were **** huge, mate.*

'*It looked like a smalley leopard. But it were a cat alright, because it had its tail up in the air. I were a bit wary at first, and was going to shoot it out of hand, but it were friendly. Bloody amazing. I suppose it belongs to them scientist chaps. Anyway, it has plenty of scoff round here, what with penguins and hoards of festering rats.*'

Other witnesses had variously written about the cat as follows:

*1. '*We were on patrol when we witnessed something quite extraordinary. Before I go any further, may I add that we hadn't been near the canteen – it being about 1030 in the forenoon. This bloody great thing leaped out of the 'oggin with a fish in its gob. It looked like a big moggy – we couldn't believe it. Fred was for shooting the ****** but I stopped him. It disappeared in the rocks. It was huge, mate, nigh on as big as one of those cougars from America.*'

*2. '*I saw this thing like a small scruffy North American cat. It was big, though, too big to be a cat. There are a load of rats in Grytviken, and this thing seems to subsist on them. Whilst I was watching it, it managed to grab one. But instead of playing with it like a cat would, this thing flung it into the air – same as I've seen leopard seals perform with penguins. The skin etc., went one way, and the cat was left with the body. It was an extraordinary sight. It was very good at catching those rats.*'

*3. '*We'd been out on patrol from the base. There were lots of patrols at first, 'cause of the chance of the Argies trying to re-take the place. Late one afternoon when we were coming back we saw something unbelievable. Right up on this rock we sighted this huge thing which looked like a cat. It was curled up there, and appeared to be impervious to storm and cold. I've never seen anything like it.*']

18 August, 1982

With Second-Lieutenant Hugh Macnally at the wheel, we left King Edward Cove on board the British Antarctic Survey's motor boat *Albatross*. First nosing our way out through the easily-crackable thin sheet of surface ice, and from then on carefully avoiding the 'growlers' (small icebergs), we headed out on our short patrol into Cumberland Bay.

This time we passed much nearer to the towering iceberg in the Cove entrance than we had done on our arrival in the frigate HMS *Andromeda*. Not only were its translucent greens even more varied and striking at close quarters, but below water level the iceberg was circumscribed by an extraordinarily beautiful ring of the most intense vivid pale blue, glowing like some monster fluorescent tube around its base.

The sea was calm as we chugged parallel to the huge cliff faces which rose straight out of the water nearby. It is certainly not a trip to do in anything other than a quiet sea state! Twice the tell-tale radar warned of a submerged rock in time for Hugh to throw the engine into high reverse and keep clear. To go too near the cliff face is also an invitation to attract the heavy kelp seaweed around the propeller. Flying patrols of Blue-eyed Cormorants, on the sheer rock faces, kept us under constant observation.

We rounded Sappho Point – there are some very nasty black rocks there upon which you and your boat would be instant mincemeat in an angry sea – in company with a Giant Petrel. These birds are an unattractive brown, are three feet long and have a wingspan of seven feet. The ridge of feathers shrouding their eyes give a disconcerting, frowning look. They sweep very low indeed over the waves with apparently effortless power.

We reached our destination, a small beach at Maiviken, after about half an hour. It is quite a difficult navigational approach in between the rocks, but we had a reception committee from the colony of fur seals living there. I counted eighty-five of all sizes. The older bull 'grandads' were just lying doggo either on the beach or in the tussock grass just above it. The highly active 'young uns', however, swam out to greet us. From under the water, they popped up their quizzical little heads and then in an instant were magically flapping a tail above the water where their heads had just been.

As we headed out of Maiviken, an Arctic Tern flew alongside for a while, displaying its beautiful fork-tail. Then a Yellow-Billed Sheathbill, a pure white, soft, cuddly doll of a bird the size of a large pigeon, came out to pay us what was obviously just a social call. Very tame, it couldn't get close enough to us! They are only normally found in this small area of the South Atlantic.

Although we had only been out for just over an hour, already the sun had moved quickly. The cliff faces had suddenly turned hard and black and cold, and their shadow radiated an evil chill. Across Cumberland Bay East, as we turned starboard to re-enter King Edward Cove, the high snows were already glowing red from the falling sun. The evening was still crystal clear, and the glassy water edged the shore line with a narrow bank of the purest pale blue.

The waters to our front, right across to the distant glaciers, were now glowing bright red as well. Was this, I thought, some very rare and vividly supernatural phenomenon being shown to me as a reminder of the blood shed by the many tens of thousands of whales once slaughtered here in Cumberland Bay? But even as I watched, transfixed, the sun's red glow faded from the distant high snows, and its mirrored reflection in the glassy water – for that is what I had seen – faded too, and the grip of the instant, penetrating cold of the Antarctic winter's night was upon us.

Looking across King Edward Cove from outside the British Garrison's Shackleton House base, the captured Argentine submarine *Santa Fe* lies half-submerged, having been re-beached over by the rocks on the opposite shore. Her black conning tower and forward deck are above water, and much of her lethal ordnance is still on board. But her man-made regular lines intrude obscenely among the adjacent wet rocks and kelp, and especially so against the soft white curves of the high snow-cliff backdrop. Even the twelve huge Elephant Seals I could see nearby, grotesquely splayed across the beach like enormous barrel-like slugs, had turned their backs on it.

Further round to the right, the Argentine helicopter downed by fire from Lieutenant Keith Mill's Royal Marines during their original defensive action, lies embedded in the snow, its bullet-ridden hulk looking like a kitchen colander. In the water to my front are the rocks which the Royal Navy pounded with 4.5-inch shells under the noses of the Argentine Grytviken Garrison in a successful move to induce its surrender. The rocks are now noticeably lower than they were before the barrage!

Captain Malcolm Willis, RAMC, from Ewshot in Surrey, is the South Georgia Garrison's Medical Officer. Earlier in the Falklands campaign, with 16 Field Ambulance, he had been at Fitzroy and had watched the bombing of the LSLs *Sir Galahad* and *Sir Tristram*. Thereafter, as he told me, he had worked on the seemingly endless procession of casualties – burns, amputations, everything. Even professionally it had obviously been a traumatic experience; after all that, he said, the stark quiet beauty of South Georgia had been a marvellous therapy. He volunteered to take me to Grytviken proper.

Stepping down by the King Edward jetty on to the four-foot-wide little beach that encircled the Cove, and thus edging round the minefield, we walked the 1,000 yards to Grytviken. Much of the water had a thin layer of sheet ice and in places small ice floes had congregated. From time to time we met whale bones, remaining symbols of the carnage of not so long ago. Nearing the far jetty, in order not to sink helplessly, we put on our snow shoes, like handleless tennis racquets, climbed up the snow bank and entered the old factory area.

Originally said to have been discovered by Amerigo Vespuci in 1502, and followed later by a British expedition in 1675, formal possession of South Georgia was taken by Captain Cook on 17 January, 1775, in Possession Bay. International sealers were active from 1790, and by 1820 it had become the sealing centre of the region. In 1880, for instance, one American sealer, Edmund Fanning, made a record catch of 57,000 Fur Seals. In 1825, estimates of the total output from South Georgia to date were not less than 1,200,000 seal skins and 20,000 tons of elephant seal oil.

The principal development of the great 20th century whaling industry took place in 1903 when C. A. Larsen's company established six processing factories, of which Grytviken was one. Albion Star Ltd ceased its operations there in 1963, but a Japanese consortium took over until it, in turn, closed down after the 1964 season. Since then, the only living occupants of Grytviken have been rats.

Grytviken is a deserted, eerie, derelict factory, brown with rust and age. Captain Willis pointed out the huge whale oil storage tanks, probably still half full, he said. We walked into abandoned sheds housing vast boilers which once helped to render down the blubber. Similar huge sheds were for processing the whale meat, and other giant configurations of pipes and vats dealt with other parts of the whales. Within twenty minutes of being dragged ashore, apparently, nothing remained of the great beast except the entrails which were thrown to the birds.

We clambered round the ghostly buildings, many still containing rusting stores, half-split bales of wool, old piping and other factory dross. I was amazed to find one place full of good quality rope cordage of differing heavy diameters. Many roofs were rent, corners cracked and shed walls had gaped to engorge the constant snow drifts. I found it an unpleasant world, its silence broken only by the pattered scurry of the hurrying rats, and the constant low hiss of the water uncannily still ebbing and flowing in the main feed pipes.

Leaning at seventy degrees against the jetty was an old whaler, with another one outboard of her, dejection and decay staring at me from a long-forgotten heyday. Half-closing my eyes, I tried to imagine them once streaking in pursuit through the water, with the harpoon man poised to follow the alerting cry of 'whale'. A seaman from one of the Task Force's accompanying merchantmen, which had called at Grytviken earlier, told Captain Willis he well remembered his whaling days here when 'the waters of the Cove were red with blood'.

We snow-shoed our way to the little white wooden church at the back of the factory, built by the Norwegians in 1913. Beside it is the now derelict gymnasium and cinema hall, built in 1930, and what was obviously once some accommodation. Further round the Cove, a little way out of Grytviken itself, is the cemetery in which Chief Petty Officer Artuso, an Argentine prisoner-of-war shot because of an unfortunate incident which occurred whilst the captured Argentine submarine *Santa Fe* was being moved, was buried with full military honours.

Seeing me looking up at what seemed like a ski jump, 'Yes' said Captain Willis, 'you're right. It is said a young Norwegian priest was once sent down here on disciplinary transfer. A keen sportsman, nothing daunted, he built a ski jump and a football pitch and everyone was happy.' Beyond the cinema I could see the tips of some goal posts peeping through the snow.

Inside the attractive little church the altar hangings are still in place, and the hymn boards are headed in Norwegian. For me, the austere, hard wooden pews reflected the image of the rough, unpolished life of the place around me, and the fierce basicness of the religious message by which the bygone men

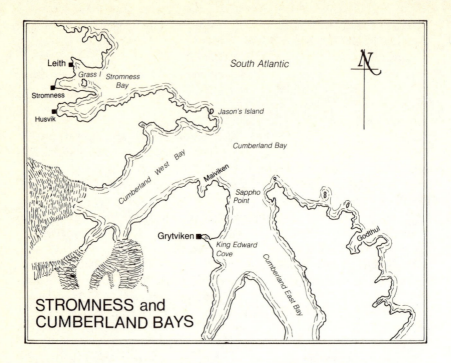

STROMNESS and
CUMBERLAND BAYS

must have surely lived. Having removed my snow shoes, I climbed to the little organ loft above the church door to find a quite modern harmonium. The foot-pedal pumps produced instant wind, and I delightedly found it 'fully operational'. In that empty silent place, beside where the great Shackleton himself lies buried, what else could I play for my invisible congregation but 'He who would true valour see, let him come hither'?

19 August, 1982

Our task was to set out from the British Garrison's Headquarters on King Edward Point, near Grytviken, to visit the other abandoned whaling stations at Leith, Stromness and Husvik which form an important part of the British Garrison's military parish. They can of course be reached by helicopter or even on skis, following a carefully reconnoitred but difficult trail over the mountains and glaciers, with a few strategically positioned survival huts en route. But we were going round by sea in HMS *Andromeda*.

The three ex-whaling stations lie at the heads of three adjacent natural harbours leading off Stromness Bay, which is further along the coast to the west of Grytviken. Leith is by far the largest. By my eye reckoning, it looked at least twice the size of Stromness, and six times the size of Grytviken, which in turn seemed roughly comparable with Husvik, the smallest.

Early in the century some 2,000 Norwegians reputedly lived in the whaling stations of South Georgia, which then also included Godthul and Prince Olav Harbour. Even in 1958 there was a population of 1,265, which included seven women. Today there is only the British military presence, but with numbers sufficiently strong to defend the territory against any Argentine attack or raid.

South Georgia lies about 700 miles east-south-east of the Falkland Islands. About 100 miles long by an average of twenty miles wide – at times only three – it is steeply mountainous and seventy per cent of its surface is covered with glaciers. Mount Paget, its highest point, is just on 9,000 feet. With a deeply indented coastline, there is hardly any flat land at all and, except for tussock grass, it is virtually barren.

South Georgia's south-west side is always ice-covered, and permanent snow lies between about 900 feet on its southern part and about 1,400 feet in the north. In summer the snow-free lower hills reveal tussock and moss. At this time, also, the heat causes calving of the glaciers' ice cliffs, creating huge icebergs which then float out to sea to endanger the unwary mariner. It either snows or rains on an average of 304 days per year; clear days, such as we had on the day of our arrival here, are rare.

Sadly our earlier brilliant weather vanished as quickly as it had come, and we headed into the South Atlantic from Cumberland Bay in very low cloud and sea mist. Gone were our gorgeous snow peaks and glaciers. It was now only the occasional glimpse of Jason's Island's sombre cliffs that showed we were near land at all. Stromness Bay is the next large one west of Cumberland, and we turned into it through the murk to reach Leith.

I had never realized just how big Leith was relative to Grytviken. Little wonder this was where the whole affair started. Again, no wonder the Argentinian scrap merchants, landed by the Argentine Navy in the first place, had started work here, where there was so much valuable, readily available 'booty' to carry away. There is even a whole line of ship's mooring buoys off the jetties, on one of which was a row of good lathes all ready for loading. Captain Malcolm Willis, who knew the area well, told me the scrap merchants had bought up the rights and stock in the place relatively cheaply – a figure of £5,000 for the rights and £100,000 for the actual scrap was mentioned – but they had reckoned to clear £2–£3 million profit on the deal. Well fitted out with accommodation, workshops and a vast quantity of very valuable easily marketable stores, the place had been abandoned in December, 1965, by the whaling company then operating it.

I also never appreciated that the notorious Argentinian Captain Astiz had held sway at their Leith Garrison, nor that it had been well laid out defensively with mines and defensive charges. I was told that the expert who did this was not an Argentinian sapper, as one might have expected, but their Garrison's own medical officer!

This layout apparently caused a little problem later by restricting the options as to where Captain Barker of HMS *Endurance* (2,640 tons) could land to arrange the surrender. Although big and ugly, sprawling and brown, as I had now learnt to expect old whaling stations to be, I was delighted to see the

Union Jack rightly flying over Leith once again.

We then moved on to Stromness, a smaller station, which apparently was never occupied by the Argentinians. Again my informant, Captain Willis, provided a running commentary. He pointed out the large quantities of valuable stores such as steel plate and timber, which lay abandoned in the characteristically brown sheds, alongside the whale-oil tanks and the knitwork of enormous rusting pipes.

East of Stromness, as you pull away towards Grass Island, uncomfortably familiar to certain members of Her Majesty's Forces during the campaign [the SAS], you sail parallel with a high, very steep snow-covered mountain face that drops away into the water. By some freak of wind conditions, however, much of its lower snow has been blown clear to reveal the tussock grass underneath. Suddenly, looking like some primitive man's enormous cave mural, we saw reindeer all along the cliff with their antlers and delicate legs exquisitely etched against the snow. Quite relaxed on the near-vertical slope, some were lying down in groups, their unusual grey-tinted fur camouflaging well against the tussock. Others grazed; I counted ninety-five in all. Then, high up on his own, I saw a huge magnificently-antlered stag. The cloud was down and one could not distinguish where snow, cloud or sky started or ended. He seemed to be suspended in air as he turned to look down at us – strikingly dominant, proud, totally wild and free.

We took in Husvik, a similar but much smaller station than Stromness, from a little way offshore, since the weather was fast closing in and the inner approach to it is much rock-strewn.

Even as we sailed out of Stromness Bay back into the South Atlantic to return to Grytviken, Storm Petrels had joined the Giant Petrels and the Cape Gulls off the coast, and the sea state had begun to change, as it can do so quickly in these latitudes. Rightly the Captain of *Andromeda* began to be itchy to get his frigate back out into the open sea. These inlet harbours, especially with icebergs about, are certainly no place in which to be caught out by an angry ocean.

[A report which came to me much later quoted the scrap dealer Mr Constantino Davidoff of Buenos Aires as having originally negotiated to pay £10,000 for the option to purchase scrap from the abandoned whaling stations, with a further £105,000 payable if the option was taken up within the deadline of 31 March, 1980, later extended to 31 March, 1983.

It also quoted an estimate of the likely outcome of the deal as netting a £4.5 million profit provided market prices for scrap held up. This figure derived from a valuation of £7.5 million for the available scrap, less salvaging and other costs of £3.0 million.

The surrender of the Argentine Garrison at Leith, on the day following that at Grytviken, was in fact effected by the ice-patrol vessel HMS Endurance (with its famous red-painted hull) and the frigate HMS Plymouth (2,800 tons), commanded by Captains Nick Barker and David Pentreath respectively. Moving to Leith from off Grytviken, Captain Barker used his ship's radio to call on the Argentinians to surrender.

The Military Commander ashore replied by asking for safe refuge for the civilians, but refused to surrender the Garrison's military component. The civilians were then told to walk along to nearby Stromness, and the Royal Navy started planning for a military assault.

About an hour later, however, at dusk, the Argentine Garrison Commander, now identified as Captain Alfredo Astiz, agreed to surrender and was ordered to muster his men on the football field just west of Leith. But this he refused to do because the pitch was not only heavily mined, but also the helicopter landing point there had a very large explosive charge buried just underneath its large 'H' sign.

Rightly wary of his men landing and entering Leith in the dark of night, Captain Barker told the Argentinians to stay where they were overnight and muster instead at dawn on a nearby hill. The Captain's wariness was justified when it later transpired that, had anyone entered Leith that night after a surrender, the Argentinians had planned to welcome them by triggering off a number of suitably placed explosive charges.

The official surrender was signed by Captain Astiz on board HMS Plymouth on 26 April, 1982, and the total of Argentinian military prisoners and civilian detainees taken was nearly 200. HMS Endurance's ship's company then spent some two weeks making the Leith area 'safe', and clearing up after its occupation. During this time a total of 2,750 pounds of explosives was recovered from Leith's beaches, foreshore and buildings and destroyed.

In late May HMS Endurance returned to Stromness Bay, deploying working parties ashore to recover steel plate and angle-iron from the old but excellently preserved stocks still lying in Leith, Stromness and Husvik. These stores were loaded onto the cable ship Iris which delivered them to the MV Stena Seaspread to be used for the repair of vessels in the battle zone.]

22 | HMS ANDROMEDA

I had never looked up at a forty-foot-plus wave from below before as its towering wall of sheer white-flecked omnipotence bore down upon us. Some unknown hand then hurled our bows bodily upwards to meet its crest. Just topping it in a cascade of spray, which smacked back to white-out the windows of the bridge, they then plunged forty-feet-plus straight down again like an instant lift to cleave full depth into the angry foam of the next trough bottom. The next monster was now looming ahead, and so the deep yo-yo game continued, hour after hour.

I was on board HMS *Andromeda*, the first Sea Wolf conversion of the Batch Three Leander Class frigates, and we were in a Force Eleven storm. It was the worst weather, I was told, experienced by any Task Force ship since the Falklands campaign started, although they had had some pretty bad seas. Having ridden out two 'lows' the previous day – and even the Commanding Officer, Captain Jim Weatherall, had described them as 'quite spectacular' – we had been hit by a sneaky unknown third 'low' shortly before midnight.

I couldn't find anyone who had slept at all that night; even the Captain had been hurled from his bunk twice whilst briefly resting. Apart from pitching, the *Andromeda* was also rolling over to more than twenty degrees each side. I spent the night hours alternately climbing up one side or the other of my bunk, often weightless like an astronaut, or else being alternately pushed down by some invisible overpowering press, first to imprint my outline like a mould on the mattress, and then, factory-like, being expelled upwards out of my casting.

All cooking was 'out'; only a half-filled cup and a bacon roll was practicable in the circumstances. Walking about the ship, or rather staggering around it for us soldiers, meant successive hurlings from side to steel side of a passage equipped with all sorts of protruding handles and coloured knobs. The worry was to grab any one in reach and hope it was not setting off some frightening alarm bell. Ladders between decks were just a test of faith. I swear I saw one Chief Petty Officer ahead of me, calmly walking by alternately diagonalling the passageway at forty-five degrees, with no hands! Brilliant, but maybe just showing off to a 'brown job'.

Near the upper deck, though, the seeping damp turned the metal deck into a skating-rink disaster area for my inexperienced rubber soles. One great wave hurled the entire Bridge Watch across the bridge as, to a man, they grabbed at anything they could find. Not so lucky, or experienced, my feet shot from under me at the back of the Bridge, and I landed heavily on my back, some hard projections having caught me, and particularly my elbow, in the process.

In the ship's sick bay, the 'Doc' (Surgeon Lieutenant John Hall RN) agreed it was not the best time for darning, and said normally he would have invited the Captain to find some calm bit of sea and to reduce to a slow steady speed. Then, with me prostrately horizontal, and with his Leading Medical Assistant spreadeagled like a strut between the bulkhead and Doc's back to steady him, out came the needle and thread, and into my elbow went the large even stitches.

But back on the Bridge was the only place to be, witnessing this uncontrollable rage of awesome majesty, this terrifying display of the absolute power of the deep. The sea was like an endless cauldron of molten dark blue and white-streaked marble at full boil. There were huge swirls and twirls of blue and green spirals and suds, imposed on the humping, heaving mountains of very angry water.

It was not a running sea, but a totally confused one. This meant the wave walls were disorientated, and often clashed into each other all around us. It became almost a game in one's mind to guess which would dominate the other, and how the ship would react. Where one followed closely behind the other, the bows would come smacking down on the second one, having ridden the first. This would produce a bomb-burst effect forward, lined with the dreaded 'green water'.

'White water is safe,' the Officer of the Watch Sub-Lieutenant Mark White told me. 'Everything just gets drenched and is temporarily obscured. It's the green water which can be dangerous.' 'You can't avoid them all in these conditions,' the Captain said. 'There's always the odd one that will catch you.' Once in the night, and again at seven am, one did catch us, with a tremendous crash that resounded through the ship and double-shuddered her from bows to stern.

The forward deck was permanently awash and the momentarily lingering white smack of spray over the Bridge obscured all vision with determined regularity. The scurries and eddies from each dousing had hardly cleared before the next one sent new white-ringed wavelets swamping around the 'forward' missile bases in angry, searching abandon. It was the fifty to sixty knot whip behind the spray that really powered it horizontally, searing across the deck. A pump broke loose at one moment, but a seaman on a lifeline, repeatedly thumped and enveloped by the resentful white water, quickly secured it.

We were virtually hove-to for some twelve hours, 'making perhaps two knots, but backwards or forwards I couldn't really say,' the Duty Watchkeeper told me. Not until late in the afternoon had the sea state slackened enough for the Captain to judge it right to turn and put the sea on our port beam. 'It's a fine subjective judgement,' he told me, 'the moment when to turn, and you have to get it right.' On went the power – eighteen knots – a very quick turn to starboard and we were at last on our way heading for the Falklands.

I learnt many things from that Force Eleven. First, how tiring and difficult such conditions are for a Royal Navy ship's company just going about their normal 'defence watch' duties – for that is what they were all doing – let alone 'action stations', and the problems of trying to sleep off watch, especially so for the Captain who has to be ever alert on or by the Bridge. Second, the effect of heavy seas on the fighting efficiency of a warship, and on her many weapon systems. Perhaps the 'Cod War' was our last real taste of this.

Third, the physical damage heavy seas can do to necessarily exposed parts of modern weapon systems, aerials and even helicopter hangar doors. This comes not only from the sheer destructive weight of falling water, but also from the strain on key water-proofing of the continuous pounding of heavy spray. Fourth, the marvellous resilience, cheerfulness, humour and morale of the British sailor, especially in this case after four months continuously at sea on South Atlantic operations.

Fifthly, that I was not seasick. But lastly, and most important, my supreme confidence throughout the experience in a superb Royal Navy crew and their Leander frigate to weather any storm.

Forever now, every time I sing 'For those in peril on the Sea' my stitch scars will twinge, and I will vividly remember those towering forty-foot waves of the distant South Atlantic and pray that those in peril are in as equally good hands as I was proud to be.

22 August, 1982

The last three Royal Navy frigates in the Task Force which took part in the Falklands campaign, having been replaced on station, are now sailing for Devonport and home. They are HMS *Andromeda* (3,100 tons), a Batch Three 'Seawolf' conversion Leander, HMS *Penelope* (3,200 tons), a Leander 'Exocet' conversion, and HMS *Avenger* (3,250 tons), a Type 21. Their Commanding Officers are Captain Jim Weatherall, Commander Peter Rickard and Captain Hugo White respectively.

This leaves down here only two other ships from the war: the carrier HMS *Invincible* (19,500 tons) commanded by Captain Jeremy Black, and Rear-Admiral Derek Reffell's flagship HMS *Bristol* (7,100 tons) commanded by Captain Alan Grose. In due course the carrier HMS *Illustrious* (19,500 tons), fitted as a flagship, is expected to relieve both of them.

I have just spent a week at sea on board HMS *Andromeda*, which sailed from Devonport on 7 May. On her return home, she will have been continuously at sea a little over four months. Many of her ship's company, however, were on her previous deployment to American waters in early January. The necessarily fast operational turnround in Devonport meant that some of *Andromeda*'s men have only had six days' leave this year.

Having flown out to Berkeley Sound by helicopter to land on her deck, I was made welcome on board by Captain Jim Weatherall, and soon fixed up with my anti-flash gear and briefed on the safety drills by Lieutenant-Commander Roger Parkes, the First Lieutenant. I received my 'Guide to the Wildlife of South Georgia' written by the ship's Penguin Officer, Midshipman Lee Jensen. Supervised by Lieutenant-Commanders David Watson, from Purbrook, and Mike Cowley, from Plymouth, the Senior Weapons Officer and the Ship's Engineer respectively, I covered every part of the ship during my stay. I was taken from the anchor chains by the bows, via the Sea Wolfs, the Exocets and torpedoes and decoys, to the stern. I watched from the Bridge, and crawled around checking the size of boiler flames and inspecting the bilge pumps. One minute I was being briefed on the ship's Exocet and Sea Wolf missiles, followed by a descent into the missile replenishment lockers; the next I was working a visual missile tracker in the operations room and then dealing with anti-submarine warfare, inspecting the Lynx helicopter armament or chatting in the communications centre which handled 1,000 signals a day during the war.

After four months of continuous 'defence stations', punctuated by a dozen 'action stations', I found *Andromeda*'s complement of 214 sailors in remarkably cheerful form, despite an understandable deeper tiredness in some. I found myself lost in admiration of men who, for instance, twelve-hour watch and twelve-hour watch about, had spent their whole four months' Falklands conflict stint deep down among the engine room's catwalks, or hourly checking the many temperature gauges in the boiler room. I found myself climbing their vertical ladders' route to safety, had disaster struck, with humble footsteps.

Down in what I thought was aptly called 'The Devil's Kitchen' the walls ran with condensation. Because it had been impossible, with such a long continuous operational deployment, to shut down and do normal planned maintenance, steam glands leaked and rust had to be tolerated. Ingenious improvisations had been made where electric pumps had failed, or when kelp had been sucked in. For instance, I found half the fresh water distillation system happily working the cycle back to front.

The Chief Petty Officer 'steam pioneers' sang the praises of their older power system, saying, 'There is a greater expectancy of living with trouble with steam.'

In support of this they proudly quoted the fact that *Andromeda* had sailed all the way south at full speed ahead 'day after day' instead of the normal maximum number of hours, 'and we can mend just about anything,' they said.

Andromeda's principal task during the war had been to act in the demanding role of 'goalkeeper' to HMS *Invincible*. This excellent modern naval tactic involves constant movement and alertness, combined with close station-keeping at night. From time to time she was 'let off the leash' to act as escort into San Carlos Water, for example, and, actually see the Falkland Islands.

I had a drink down in 'Three Echo Alfa' Mess Deck, whose 'Killick' (or senior in charge of the mess deck) was Leading Weapons Engineer Mechanic (WEM) Philip Mulliner from Plymouth. They were changing over watches and there was little room to spare, but the video was showing an exotic Caribbean colour film of beachcombers, gorgeous girls and sharks and everyone was very relaxed.

For both WEM Chris Gray of Redruth, and WEM Jim Manday of Chatterin, this had been their first trip to sea after training. Chris had enjoyed it, but Jim had been 'a bit bored'; he's off to box for the Royal Navy in Portugal in September – anything but boring then – and was more worried about his fitness. All the Mess Deck had now been ashore in Stanley at some stage. Leading WEM Tom Salt, from Hereford, thought the whole place 'unreal, like some war movie, with landrovers all over the place'. The others had thought it small, depressing, offering little, and described it as 'a town hanging on'. By contrast they thought South Georgia 'a beautiful place – so quiet and with clean air – a place where you could hear distant voices'.

The four months had been tiring, they said, understandably, but they had always been kept informed about what was happening in the war. But now they, with Weapons Engineer Artificer (WEA) Graham Armstrong from Preston, and Leading WEMs Andy Palmer from Coventry and Steve Dale from Barnsley, had their eyes fixed on their forthcoming leave.

Later I was invited into the Chief Petty Officers' Mess by the Chief Bosun's Mate, CPO Alan Cooper from Chatham, popularly known as 'The Buffer', for a pint. They told me there that for them the whole Falklands scene had changed the moment HMS *Sheffield* was hit.

'That was the turning point. We then knew it was for real,' they said.

They were all very interested in the various forthcoming Falklands inquiries, and rightly cross that so much operationally useful information had been put out in Britain during the campaign. They followed to a surprisingly close degree everything currently being written and broadcast about the Navy and the Falklands, and did not hold back with their interesting ideas about both. Naturally they held strong views, with which I sympathized, about the different financial treatments now being applied to various other elements associated with the Task Force.

My time at sea was invaluable in making me re-appreciate the fundamentally different roles 'at the coal face' of the three Services. Whereas the higher levels of the nation's defence command and management must think and work in overall Joint Service defence terms, never must they or their political masters ever forget that the working level job to be done requires the co-ordinated efforts of three very different and distinct breeds of men.

Of course there is overlap and fringe areas of commonality to be exploited for economy, but of necessity the training, outlook and even the rank structures of the three Services cannot be, and do not need to be, properly equated. Those responsible for the nation's defence overlook or misunderstand these basic facts of Service life at their peril.

I left HMS *Andromeda*, sadly, back in Berkeley Sound, being winched up from the deck into a Sea King helicopter early in the morning. But I left with a wide impression of the highly professional and articulate modern sailor, and of a very experienced humane Captain who ran an efficient, happy and very sensible ship. He too, like all on board, now very much deserves his home leave at Bishop's Waltham with his wife, five children and sixteen animals – including two llamas.

23 | LAFONIA

'The Triangle' is the established helicopter pick-up and set-down point for Stanley. Near the Headquarters and the Memorial, it is a small triangular-shaped field in the grounds of Government House adjoining the road which runs along the edge of Port Stanley towards Moody Brook.

With the winter nights in July and August being long, everyone, especially helicopter passengers, has to get up early to make the best use of the daylight. Because of the time-zone difference and Fleet Street's hours of working, a correspondent's norm here has to be to get up in the dark and fight his way through a pre-dawn blizzard to telex his stories to London from the Cable and Wireless building. If the circuits there are 'out', the alternative is to walk back through Stanley to the LSL *Sir Bedevere*, moored alongside, and send your piece via the ship's Radio Officer. The ship also has a Chinese crewman who, for a consideration, will operate as a barber. The practical advantage of all this is that one is very soon wide awake enough to make the early helicopter rendezvous without difficulty. Punctuality is important because the pilots only fly in to 'The Triangle' from their own separate bases elsewhere and, because of their tightly scheduled multi-task missions and the problems of air traffic control in the tiny little field, can only allow two to three minutes 'put down' at the RV – engines on, rotors turning – before they lift off and are away.

Today, off with the Queen's Own Highlanders again, accompanying Captain Martin Strong, the Battalion Paymaster, on his rounds, I was lifted off by courtesy of a No 847 Squadron Royal Navy Wessex. After a brief put-down at Goose Green, we flew on to visit B Company [then deployed at North Arm, in the South of Lafonia in East Falkland, and said to have the reputation of housing the hardest drinkers in the Islands].

Major Peter Grant-Peterkin, the Company Commander, walked me round, and lively Lynn, wife of the New Zealander Settlement Manager Tony Blake, who was passing by in her landrover, stopped to welcome me with a brief chat. The Settlement had been intermittently visited by, but never occupied by, the Argentinians. A remote place in an attractive setting, it nevertheless has all the features which I have learned to expect of a Settlement. Near the centre of the neat group of white houses with their coloured roofs are the huge mounds of cut peat sods. A little way out is the solid timbered frame which, at first sight, looks like a French

24. Sappers working on the undershoot area at the end of the extended runway at Stanley airfield.

25. RAF Chinook helicopter lifting a cabin near the Control Tower at Stanley airfield.

26. The Memorial Cross to the Scots Guards, in wood, looks down over Stanley from the peak of Mount Tumbledown.

27. Approaching Stanley from the Darwin Road. The Hospital is to the left: Navy Point is across the water.

28. A mountain-top Rapier detachment sited to defend Stanley airfield.

29. The burnt and distorted superstructure of the RFA *Sir Tristram*, moored by Navy Point.

30. The first Falklands War Cemetery at Ajax Bay.

31. A bewildered animal in the Argentinian mined area of Mount Murrell.

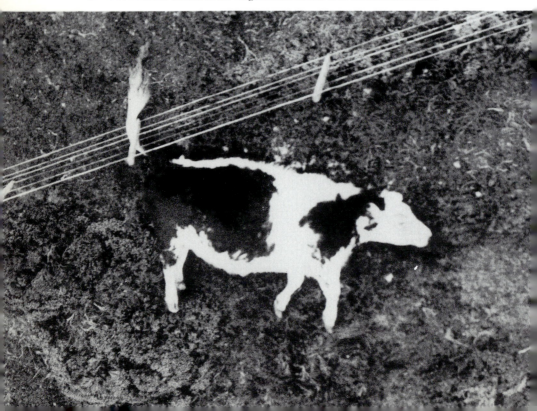

32. Piper Alasdair Gillies of the Queen's Own Highlanders in South Georgia.

33. HMS *Andromeda* at Grytviken, South Georgia, with the British Antarctic Survey's motor boat, the *Albatross*, at the BAS jetty.

34. The author, on snowshoes, by the abandoned pier at Grytviken.

35. 'An endless cauldron of molten, dark blue marble' – HMS *Andromeda* caught by a Force Eleven in the South Atlantic.

36. Sir Rex Hunt, Governor of the Falkland Islands and their Dependencies and High Commissioner for the British Antarctic Territory.

37. Major-General (now Sir) David Thorne, the first Military Commissioner and Commander British Forces Falkland Islands, with Mrs Thatcher during her visit in January 1983.

38. Rear-Admiral (now Vice-Admiral Sir) Derek Reffell, Commander of the Royal Navy Task Force in the South Atlantic in the early Aftermath.

40. Group Captain (now Air Commodore) Bill Wratten, CBE, AFC, Senior RAF Officer and Station Commander Stanley in the early Aftermath.

39. Captain (now Commodore) Jimmy James RN, Senior Naval Officer Falkland Islands (SNOFI) in the early Aftermath.

41. Lieutenant-Colonel Nicholas Ridley, Commanding Officer of 1st Battalion The Queen's Own Highlanders, the first infantry battalion to serve in the Falklands Aftermath.

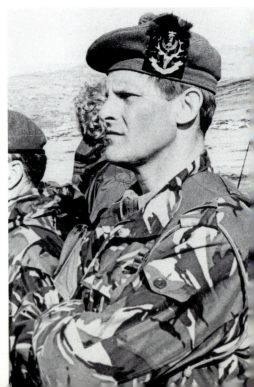

Revolution guillotine. It is occupied by a strung-up de-fleeced sheep's carcass, off which the Settlement's sheep dogs will live for about five days until it is replaced by another one.

Company Sergeant-Major Donald Munro, from Inverness and with fifteen years' service, told me the local population of sixty had been very friendly and generous to the soldiers. The Settlement 'was massive big with 65,000 sheep and 125,000 acres stretching across the great plain of Lafonia. It's a grand place for horsemen.'

A cheery young man, crossing a sheep paddock behind the Settlement, waved to us from his tractor. 'Yes, a very friendly type, he's only eighteen – but an alcoholic already,' the Company Commander said quietly as he passed us. 'They do have their problems out here, even in normal times. For a start, the Island's population is so small, and with the Settlements so spread out and communication overland so tenuous, think of their difficulties of just finding and then keeping a girlfriend in another Settlement.'

We toured the sheep-shearing sheds, so hectic in October but empty now save for the scraps of fleece and wool caught up on the many timber pen frames. It was a world of locks, pellies, skirts, pieces and necks. Many such sheds in other Settlements had been used by the Argentinians as soldiers' accommodation; some had later been used by the British as initial 'round-ups' for Argentinian prisoners. In the immediate Aftermath some sheds, temporarily lived in by British soldiers, were found to have been scattered with hidden grenades under the floor-boards and even fixed with the odd booby-trap by the Argentinians. A single small-gauge rail track led from the shearing sheds out along the small jetty, the only outward and visible sign of any communication with the outside world, at which the pre-war boat from Stanley would periodically call on its rounds of the Settlements.

B Company was well-housed by Falklands standards; the friendliness and 'give and take' between the two communities made for a mutually advantageous relationship between them. Some of the men, when not on other duties, often helped out on horseback with the Settlement's sheep. But the Company is soon to be redeployed to another more permanent station in accordance with the Commander British Forces' longer term plan.

26 August, 1982

Scottish girls have certainly not forgotten the soldiers in the Falklands, and answering their letters is a new compelling occupation for men of B Company, The Queen's Own Highlanders. This is especially so when on night guard, but not on actual sentry duty, and for them, of course, postage is free.

It is all due to Lance-Corporal Gordon Girdwood, from Livingstone, near Edinburgh. The Company is stationed in a remote Settlement in East Falkland.

[*North Arm, in the South of Lafonia*]. Three weeks ago he had a letter published in the Scottish *Sunday Mail* asking readers to write. By the first bag he had 235 replies; by the second he had a further 200. The letters are still coming in – there were 570 when I last saw him – but now at a reducing rate.

All the letters are addressed to him personally and come from people aged six to eighty-seven. Most are from girls of around nineteen to twenty years of age, who enclose photographs. Lance-Corporal Girdwood told me most of the correspondents very much want to know what life is really like in the Falklands, what the conditions are and how the soldiers are faring. Some people send poems. The eighty-seven year old sent in a marvellous one about the Falklands campaign. Others have sent newspapers and even food parcels.

'No,' he said, 'no offers of marriage have come in yet, but anyway I'm engaged and will get married on my return home.' He met his fiancée, Kathy Lane from Maidstone, whilst serving with the Battalion in Hong Kong last year. She has now returned to Britain, and he has his own letters from her, three or four a week, anyway. By the end of his tour in the Falklands he expects to have saved £2,000 towards his start in married life.

Having first read every letter himself, and assessed its writer, Gordon said, he then has to decide which soldier in the Company is the most suitable to answer it. 'I know everybody and their tastes and home town,' he told me, 'I just do my best to match them all up together, especially those from the same home area of Scotland.' The readers' response to Lance-Corporal Girdwood's original letter was a marvellous one, and much appreciated by the Jocks. They now hope that the resulting contacts which have been established will keep going and flourish.

Some at home in Britain may be beginning to forget the victorious campaign that at the time welded together the nation's support. Others may be losing interest in the men, still down here 8,000 miles from home, on whom the Herculean task of dealing with the extremely difficult Aftermath now falls. But thank God for those Scottish girls, and others, who still have the time, the interest, and a soft spot to spare for Highlanders on remote detachments in the Falklands. Of course there are other equally deserving Servicemen out here too, but long may warm and generous thoughts from home continue for them all.

Exactly on time, our helicopter returned from its other tasks, picked us up and deposited us with A Company at Goose Green, commanded by Major David Watson. Even in the month I had been away much had been done in clearing up the Settlement and disposing of its resultant wartime rash of unexploded or unused ammunition.

I was taken down to the still uncleared Argentine minefield which lay across the narrow point at the east of the Settlement, and shown the cleared minefield gap through which the Company's two-man 'rubbish detail' took their daily load to the tip at the extremity of the point. Earlier in the month one of the Company drivers had turned his vehicle around there, before backing his 'acquired' Argentine Mercedes jeep into the tip area as he had done every day before. But this time his rear wheel had travelled a little further in than usual and onto an Argentine anti-tank mine.

Looking at the carcass of the wrecked vehicle I felt it almost beyond belief that anyone could have got out alive. But the fact that, unusually, it has been the rear wheel that had activated the mine instead of the front one had made all the difference. Piper Graham Marr and Private John Catto had at once been helicoptered back to the Military Hospital in Stanley where, apart from shock, they were found not to be seriously injured. They were very lucky to be alive, but the incident highlighted yet again, not only the still ever-present danger of known Argentine minefields, but also the hazard of coming across unknown mines literally anywhere in areas lately occupied by the Argentinians.

The possibility of some mines and booby-traps having been hurriedly but intelligently laid by uncompromising individual Argentinians during the actual process of being ordered to surrender, in order to cause a few extra British casualties thereafter, cannot be excluded. Apart from the Goose Green rubbish-tip incident, there were other instances in the abandoned Argentine trenches and in a few sheep-shearing sheds.

After touring 'A' Company's area, and lunch, we drove along the track to the tiny Darwin Settlement where Lieutenant Angus Duncan's platoon was now stationed. Once again I looked with astonishment and admiration on 2 PARA's world-famous battlefield – the blackened furze-fringed cleft in the hill, the bare slopes, the successive lines of Argentine trenches and the forward slopes where earlier I had seen the bloated dead cattle lying, rigid in death, with their legs pointing skywards like quadruple gun barrels.

24 | THE FIPZ

It is late August and the Argentinians have still not formally ended hostilities. They are very unlikely to do so anyway for a very long time yet, since they have nothing to lose but a lot to gain by not ending them. But now they have recovered sufficiently from their defeat in the Falklands to start taking a form of provocatively offensive action against the British, who continue to prevent them from entering the circumscribing 150-mile-radius Falkland Islands Protection Zone (the FIPZ).

The use of Argentine vessels to probe the circumference of the FIPZ serves two purposes. First, for very little outlay of effort, it forces the British on to a high level of continuous patrolling of the FIPZ in order to be able to react quickly against any potentially successful infringements which, in the world context, could be politically embarrassing. This level, in turn, obviously relates to the size of the forces which Britain must then necessarily retain in the South Atlantic to maintain the integrity of the FIPZ, and hence directly to the peacetime costs of the Falklands garrison forces. Obviously the Argentinians would wish to see these made as high as they can. Secondly, by monitoring the British reactions to their probes, the Argentinians obtain a very useful continuous flow of information regarding the speed and type of reaction, the tactics, the communications, the state of the defences and the general operational efficiency of the British Garrison.

26 August, 1982

The Royal Navy Task Force continues to patrol the Protection Zone around the Falkland Islands and make its presence noticeable. It is very keen on identifying any contacts, usually by using naval aircraft. It is extremely careful to be precise in all these cases, and not exceed the well-publicised terms regulating the Zone. 'We know them, and the Argentinians know them – and when they know that we know that they are trying to probe it, they call it a day,' said a Royal Navy spokesman yesterday.

Argentina's tentative attempts to try and enter the Zone occur now on a routine basis. These are all detected and subsequently investigated. Once spotted, the probe attempt is usually cheerfully acknowledged by the Argentinians, often with a wave! They then turn away. It is all very low key.

'There is currently nothing about the activity which could be termed tension or a problem,' the spokesman said. 'So far nothing has happened which could be described as an incident per se. At present the contacts are essentially very amicable and not sensitive as such.'

The idea apparently being put out by Buenos Aires that the contacts are being made by British Army helicopters is of course erroneous. What are known here as 'Teeny Weeny Airways' could not possibly have the range to do it! All contacts are made by the Royal Navy, normally with their Sea King or Lynx helicopters.

25 | 'TEENY WEENY AIRWAYS'

Flying one day in a Gazelle helicopter near the Murrell Peninsula, I innocently asked my Army Air Corps Pilot how easily visible were the Argentine mines laid in the sand on the beaches. 'I'll show you,' he replied, grinning from under his enveloping 'bone dome' helmet.

In a matter of minutes we were down to about three to four feet clear above a sea-slapped small sandy cove south of Kidney Island, nose pointing in to the rockface and flying very slowly sideways along the beach.

He did not need to point, for just below me as we crabbed along I saw for myself with awesome clarity and fascinating proximity the successive rows of variously wholly or partially exposed anti-tank mines being playfully washed by the sea.

I wondered casually about the downward pressure exerted by our rotors, and felt it was not exactly the time to hit an air pocket or have a sudden 'flame-out'. As we pulled away, my thoughts turned to another Army Air Corps pilot I had flown with who, rather more peaceably, always flew with his fishing rod on board, ready to touch down for a few minutes to take the large trout which lurked north of Teal Inlet.

The Army Air Corps 657 Squadron is based just outside Stanley by the road leading north to Moody Brook, and uses the old Falkland Islands Government Air Service seaplane hangar whose slipway reaches down to the icy water. Its Scout and Gazelle aircraft are parked in the open on the other side of the road, edging the peat.

Safety is especially important when flying small helicopters in this wild country with its dangerously changing weather conditions. Fuel levels are constantly checked, and, if flying to West Falkland, one first touches down at the aluminium-matting Harrier airstrip above Port San Carlos Settlement, alongside the RAF's No 18 Chinook Squadron, to top up from the Emergency Fuel Handling Equipment's storage pillow tanks. Already wearing a life jacket, on taking off one nevertheless climbs up to sufficient altitude before crossing the intervening Falkland Sound so that, should anything untoward happen in flight, one has a chance of making landfall rather than ditching into the unwelcoming chilly water.

Flying over such bleak, starkly beautiful but inhospitable country, constant touch is maintained throughout all flights with bases and with other helicopters flying in the area. Actual departure and estimated arrival times, destinations and any other relevant details of the flight's successive ports of call are invariably broadcast over the radio. This is a very necessary check, and on two occasions my helicopter was diverted from its mission to look for another one. The first had failed to show up at the expected time and place, and the other had been out of radio contact for a worryingly long period of time. In the event we found both, and all was well.

Occasionally we fly with a Junior NCO Observer occupying the front left-hand seat. Because he has to acquire enough basic flying skills to be able to take over and land the machine should anything disastrous happen to the pilot, he sometimes takes over in distant West Falkland: Observers are very good at this and I am sure will eventually graduate to proper pilot training, but there were the odd 'interesting' moments!

But what I will never forget is the tremendous thrill of flying fast and very low with a highly skilled pilot over mile upon mile of the subtly changing greens of the tufted grass and peat, interspersed with bouts of brilliant angled weaving in and out along the contours of the small low hillocks – a truly memorable experience.

26 | UNSUNG HEROES

There are many unsung heroes in any campaign and its aftermath, and the Falklands is no exception – for instance the doctors and stretcher bearers, the helicopter pilots and those in the vital business of logistic support.

All the 'big name' participating units have long since gone home, and many men from the sub-units of the Logistic Battalion, now commanded by Lieutenant-Colonel Roger Hurles, have been replaced. Nevertheless, a surprising number of individual campaigners still remain. Some, unforgiveably, have had their original return home dates put back. Others daily just cross off the dates on their 'chuff' calendar.

I am thinking especially of men like Sergeant 'Ginger' Clayton, Royal Corps of Transport, from Hythe near Southampton, who belongs to 17 Port Regiment, Marchwood. He operated a Mexeflote powered raft discharging cargo in San Carlos Water at the time of the initial landings, one of the several endlessly plying from ship to shore with loads of ammunition and other stores. Sometimes their craft were minus six inches of freeboard as, with decks awash, they surged shorewards carrying 250 tons at a time, more than double the normally permitted load. Clearly it was not the healthiest of deck cargo to live with under the incessant Argentinian air attacks, and of course there was no way they could take cover!

I asked Sergeant Clayton where he had lived throughout that time. 'At the back of my Mexeflote,' he said, 'where I'd rigged up my bivvie. It seemed the best place to be.'

These big narrow rafts had been brought down in sections as deck cargo on the Landing Ships Logistic (LSLs) and assembled in the water immediately alongside on arrival in San Carlos Water. One was being put together alongside the *Sir Tristram* as the first Argentine air attacks developed. 'Bums escaping up a ship's rope ladders, rather than down them, was a unique sight,' I was told. Luckily not one Mexeflote was ever hit.

Sergeant Derek Boultby, from Marchwood, had just taken his craft inshore at Fitzroy when the *Sir Galahad* (5,674 tons) and *Sir Tristram* were bombed. He at once took it out again to pick up survivors and dived overboard himself to rescue one of the Chinese crew.

'Without Mexeflote, it couldn't have been done,' said Major Mike Bowles, RCT, currently the Composite Port Squadron Commander and a Combined Services rugger player, commenting on the whole Falklands operation. 'We couldn't have had a stiffer test logistically than Operation Corporate (Code-name for the Falklands operation). All our equipment worked well and fully justified itself. The articulating-body 'Rough Terrain' fork-lift truck, for instance, has proved excellent.' His Headquarters is in the Falkland Islands Company building, where the shelves of the upper rooms are lined with beautifully bound tomes containing historic records of the Company's tradings and shipments.

Major Bowles's Squadron (from 17 Port Regiment, Marchwood) is tasked daily by the Joint Services Movements Staff, headed by Major Roger Latch-ford, RCT, for deploying its stevedores, operating its fleet of 250-ton Ramp Craft Logistic (RCL), and its Mexeflotes and Work Boats. All these are primarily engaged on ship-to-shore cargo discharge which, in the absence of proper dock or jetty facilities, is carried out over specially prepared slipways. The principal tasks to date have been the unloading of such items as American AM2 airfield runway matting, Portakabin accommodation, rations, stores and RAF Phantoms' support equipment. The Movements Staff are not only responsible for the unloading of all ships in the harbour, but also for all air movement of personnel and freight to Britain. It comprises officers from all three Services.

I went on board to watch one of the latest type of RCLs, skippered by Staff-Sergeant Alan Greenham from Eastleigh, discharging cargo alongside the old seaplane hangar on the road to Moody Brook. The Ship's Engineer was Sergeant Philip Thompson from Glastonbury, and its First Mate was Corporal Stephen White from Jersey. It was a mixed cargo from one of the stores ships, and, going 'forrard', I found another campaign veteran, Lance-Corporal Ian Kendrick from Birkenhead, still here and working on the load deck. He had been at San Carlos on D-Day. 'It was all right,' he told me cheerfully, 'and interesting; soon got used to it.' What a marvellous summary of the war, I thought, and it was people like you, thousands of you, who together won it. Ian is hoping to get home by mid-September.

27 August, 1982

The Army Logistic Battalion's new Bakery now being installed in Stanley has come straight out of the Army School of Mechanical Transport at Leconfield in Yorkshire. The ovens, which bake twenty-four ounce loaves, are of 1936 design and saw service during the Second World War and in many campaigns since. I well remember them in Borneo in 1966, and the Army last used them to help feed refugees at the time of the Turkish invasion of Cyprus in 1974.

Master Baker Warrant Officer Class 1 David Timms, from Versen in BAOR, and Staff Sergeant John Cummings from Aldershot, proudly showed me the kit – still all 'bulled up' to top display standard – and lovingly explained its workings. 'Old fashioned maybe,' they said, 'but still excellent. Baking good bread has not changed over the years, and with these ovens we can produce the ration of twelve ounces of bread for everyone ashore in one shift and thus save manpower.'

The Bakery is part of Major Stuart Hodge's Supply Company which is established in an old woodshed, until recently under six inches of water, and in a timber store the Argentinians had used as a hospital. The Army's hygienists having hopefully got rid of all the large grey rats and the Argentinians' unspeakable medical remains and other filth, the ration store is now getting shipshape under Warrant Officer Timms.

One stack of cabbages I saw had first been refrigerated for three weeks in a merchant ship, followed by four weeks in store ashore. The cold weather here has been such that, apart from the outer leaves, they are still edible. The current Army Ration Scale in operation is for about one-third to be fresh rations and two-thirds packed 'Compo' rations.

The Battalion's Stores Company were working mainly on board the anchored offshore vessels being used as floating storehouses, but up at Stanley Racecourse I watched men of Major Peter Courtney-Green's Royal Army Ordnance Corps Ammunition Company work in twelve huge pits, each one flooded and full of grey oozing mud, digging out boxes and boxes of Argentinian ammunition from the slosh. They were extracting about 1,000 boxes per hole, mainly of 105 mm gun ammunition. Their record was 500 boxes dug out in a day. The 450 tons recovered by the time of my visit has a value of around £2 million.

'It's the most expensive commodity any Army uses,' the Major said. Staff Sergeant Keith Durlton, an RAOC Ammunition Technician from Warrington, who was in charge, described the haul as 'being just unbelievable'.

After inspection, all boxed ammunition in good condition and of use to the British Army is being shipped back to Britain, for example, very large quantities of 105 mm gun ammunition. A great deal of small arms rounds, perhaps seven million, are being kept for use as training ammunition. Most unboxed or damaged items are blown up a few miles out along the Darwin Road near Mount William.

Men from Lieutenant Fred Curtis's Royal Pioneer Corps (RPC) Platoon, which is an integral part of the RAOC Ammunition Company, were humping hard. One pair, Corporal Ron Jaffray from Dundee, and Private Neil Davies from Merthyr Tydfil, were cheerfully heaving boxes out of the slime. 'It's an interesting end-product job for us Pioneers,' they told me, 'seeing all this different ammunition, and it's a job that just has to be done.'

Captain Carl Hewitt, from Verwood, Ringwood, runs the Supply Company's Petroleum Platoon. 'It's the only real one in the Army today,' he said proudly. He supplies liquid fuel to the Army, the Royal Air Force and the civilian community, using offshore dracone storage and the pipes and pumps of the Army's excellent Emergency Bulk Fuel Installation's equipment.

There is, however, a daily requirement to fill up about 500 jerricans for delivery by helicopter underslung load to inaccessible outlying detachments in the mountains manning Rapiers and other air defence systems. I was astonished to find Private Garry Fulton, from Manchester, slowly filling them up by hose one by one. Because the Army has now switched to so much bulk refuelling in BAOR, I was told, there has been a rundown of old-fashioned jerrican filling machines, but some should arrive down here soon. I hope so, for this is certainly one little aspect of the Falklands factor which could soon be rectified.

Aged fifty-three, Major Ian Winfield, from South Cerney, was one of the oldest officers in the Task Force. Commanding the Royal Engineers Forces Postal Unit (from 2nd Postal and Courier Communications Regiment), he came down on the *QE2* and trans-shipped to the *Canberra* in South Georgia. He landed with 5 Infantry Brigade at San Carlos on 1 June with his team of Staff Sergeant Alan Butler, from Liverpool, and three Sappers, and set up shop at Ajax Bay. He was joined there by Sergeant Willoughby, Corporal Hunter, Lance-Corporal Cooke and Sapper Gardner, all of whom he had earlier detached to come down with 3 Commando Brigade.

Receiving mail from home has always been one of the most important factors in keeping up troops' morale, and this was as true as ever both in the Falklands campaign and its Aftermath.

The 'Posties' sorted some 400 tons of incoming mail, re-bagged it into dustbin liners and distributed it as quickly as they could, using any means to which they could gain access, normally ship to ship or helicopter. Just after the surrender, mail was airdropped by RAF Hercules from Ascension, but some bags fell into the Argentinian minefields near Sapper Hill.

Moving fron Ajax Bay into the old civilian Post Office in Stanley, the unit's first task was to use high-pressure hoses to clean the Argentinian excreta off the floors; 500 POWs had just been occupying the building. The Post Office had remained open during the Argentine occupation, and in the future Argentine stamps used during that time will surely become collector's treasures.

The Post Office is now in business with both military counter-clerks operating normal British facilities and dealing with Forces' mail and classified material, and a Falkland Islander selling Falkland Island stamps and dealing with local mail and parcels. The spacious floor is filled by mail bags marked with unit or ships' names, and there is a steady flow each morning of 'reps' coming in to collect them. Nearly everyone uses 'blueies', the troops' name for the blue-coloured Forces Air Mail letter forms. On average letters from home now take three days to reach the British Forces Post Office in Stanley. The Garrison ceased to be 'on active service' in early August, but nevertheless postage home continues to be free.

Mail was air-dropped during the twelve days Stanley Airfield was closed for its extension and AM2 matting top, but one problem which was foreseen early on as a result of the impending airfield closure was that of how to get the troops' mail out during this period, because no RAF

Hercules from Ascension could land anywhere.

Rapid trials were therefore undertaken at the Joint Air Transport Establishment, Brize Norton, on variations of the old-fashioned and long disused 'snatch method' of collecting messages from the ground; the resultant technique proved successful at Stanley. In essence, two heavy, weighted, vertical poles, rather like high-jump posts, are spaced out on the ground. A large wire loop is hung between them, suspended from pegs fixed near their tops. The loop is free to be lifted off the pegs just as a high-jump bar is on a jumper's landing side if he hits it. A 100 lb mail bag is then fixed to the bottom of the loop by another wire.

The Air Drop Zone (DZ) used during the airfield closure period was at Seal Point, not far from Stanley, and this had to be correctly laid out each time by Captain Alan Batty and his team from 47 Air Despatch Squadron RCT. The bigger problem was the ever-changing weather because it could literally be sunshine and a thirty-knot wind one minute, and a violent snowstorm and a sixty-knot wind from a different direction the next. If it really closed in, the aircraft could not see to make the drop and with the limited time it could stay in the area – because of fuel limitations, about fifteen minutes – it would have to return direct to Ascension with its load.

The DZ was laid out with its marking lights and coloured panels in accordance with the latest estimate of the weather conditions. The RAF Liaison Officer with the team made radio contact with the incoming Hercules and kept up a running commentary on the weather, the approach and the DZ. Eventually a coloured flare was fired to indicate that all was ready to receive the drop. At about 500 feet, in three or four passes, the Army's Air Despatch crews pushed their in-bound load of parachuting containers out of the aircraft. Now it was time for the outgoing mail's 'snatch'. After a practice low run to test the approach, the RAF Hercules flew in straight and level only fifty feet up with a grappling hook trailing aft from its rear fuselage door. The hook engaged the wire loop and lifted it off the posts, taking the mailbag with it. As the aircraft flew on, the trailing wire and its new attachments, kept taut by the aircraft's 140-knot speed, were winched in and the mail bag recovered inboard for onward routing home by VC 10 from Ascension. Civilian mail was also taken out whenever possible on a 'fill-up' basis, in fact this was nearly always possible.

The age-old cry 'The mail must get through' had once again been fulfilled, and possibly the biggest potential threat to the Garrison's morale had been happily overcome.

The Falklands have always been renowned for their attractive stamps. Indeed for many years they have been a major source of revenue. A special room and counter in the Post Office is set aside for purchases of sets of earlier Falklands and South Georgia commemorative and other issues. The attractive local girl running it told me she was doing very good business

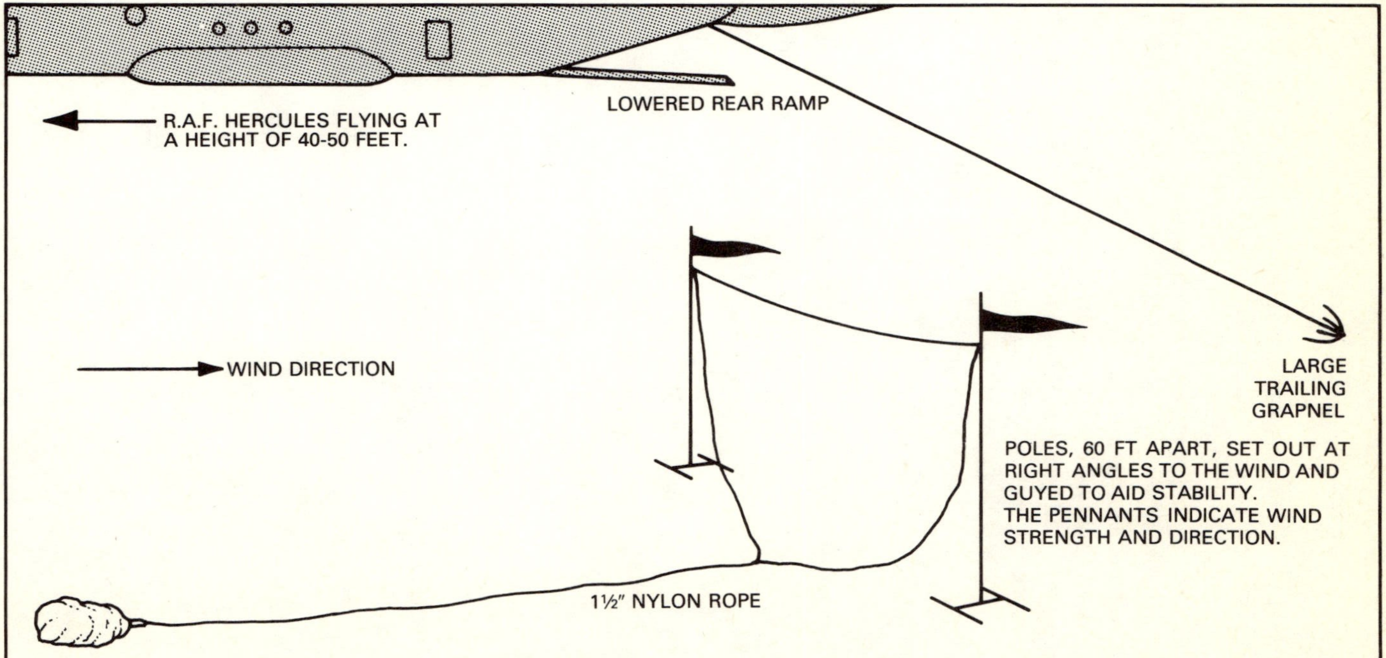

R.A.F. HERCULES FLYING AT A HEIGHT OF 40-50 FEET.

LOWERED REAR RAMP

LARGE TRAILING GRAPNEL

POLES, 60 FT APART, SET OUT AT RIGHT ANGLES TO THE WIND AND GUYED TO AID STABILITY. THE PENNANTS INDICATE WIND STRENGTH AND DIRECTION.

WIND DIRECTION

1½" NYLON ROPE

THE MAIL SNATCH

AS OPERATED AT SEAL POINT 16-27 AUGUST 1982 DURING THE CLOSURE OF STANLEY AIRFIELD FOR EXTENSION AND RESURFACING. A TOTAL OF 13 SNATCHES WERE MADE, LIFTING OUT 1,240 LBS OF MAIL AND DESPATCHES, THE ONE ON 20 AUGUST BEING MADE IN A 60-KNOT WIND.

ORANGE 'DAY GLO' PLASTIC BAG CONTAINING UP TO 100 LBS OF OUTGOING MAIL, LAID OUT UPWIND OF POSTS.

SKETCH BY P.C.S., HQ L.F.F.I., AUGUST, 1982

with the Garrison, especially with men going home. After all, there is very little else they can buy.

The Royal Military Police unit occupy a house opposite the Post Office, easily identifiable because a large corner of the roof is missing. Among their many duties is that of keeping strict traffic control of the huge amount of Army transport constantly powering through Stanley's overworked narrow streets with loads of heavy stores. For sheer 'flow' and safety reasons a one-way system had had to be introduced. Another very different temporary RMP responsibility is that of Immigration Control. As all the 'immigrants' are currently either Service or Service-sponsored individuals not requiring passport control, the duties are virtually non-existent. However, following up a friend's suggestion, I produced my passport at the RMP Duty Room desk where the Corporal on shift happily square-stamped it 'Immigration Department, Falklands', added his signature, backdated it to my date of arrival and handed it back – 'as a souvenir', he said.

British newspapers and magazines are sent down here in fair quantity for the Garrison, but as always the appetite for news from home would consume many more. The BBC World Service is avidly listened to as the main means of contact with the outside world, but nearly everyone, military and civilian alike (and especially the Intelligence services in Argentina itself), listens to the local Falkland Islands Broadcasting Service run by Patrick Watts, the Director [awarded an MBE in the Falklands Honours List]. Its programmes are relatively unsophisticated by West European standards, but it nevertheless serves a vital purpose by imparting local information not only to the immediate population of Stanley, but to the remainder of the population of 1,800 scattered throughout the Settlements and isolated farms of the 'camp'.

But today there are two additional publications of note, typed and duplicated on foolscap-size paper, which are an important reflection on current life in the Falklands. One is civilian and one is military.

The first is the lively weekly *The Penguin News*, edited by Graham Bound and subtitled 'The Falkland News Magazine'. A pre-war production, its wealth of information includes interesting items from the Legislative Council's business, eg a month's paid leave or a month's paid salary for Government employees who stayed at their post during the occupation and served beyond the call of duty; and the activities of prominent Falkland Islanders, eg 'Legco' Councillors John Cheek and Tony Blake to visit the United Nations and marksmen Gerald Cheek and Tony Petterson to shoot at the Commonwealth Games. It reports local sport – for example The Port Stanley 1982 Run, thirteen miles from Moody Brook to the Airport and back, organized by 266 Squadron, Royal Signals: and the latest minefield situation. There are advertisements, poems and correspondence.

The edition of 23 August carried a real world-scale scoop – a letter from Mrs Thatcher. The enterprising Editor had earlier written a letter to the Prime Minister, enclosing several copies of *The Penguin News*, 'hoping she might find them of interest'.

Mrs Thatcher's published reply, received on 19 August, was as follows:

10 Downing Street
29th July 1982

Graham L. Bound, Esq
Editor, The Penguin News.
Dear Mr Bound,

Thank you for your letter of 20th July.

I do indeed read the Penguin News. Please continue to send it to me. You convey so vividly the atmosphere and flavour of the Falkland Islands and the splendid qualities of its people which we have so much cause to admire.

This week I received Lord Shackleton's initial report on the economic future of the Islands. We are studying it carefully and shall be applying our minds with speed and energy to its recommendations in the coming weeks. Meanwhile I follow with the closest attention all the work which is being done on the immediate and urgent task of rehabilitation. I know how much damage and distress has been caused by the events of these last few months and how much there is to be done to repair it. But things can and will be put right just as quickly as we can manage it.

You ask whether I intend to visit the Islands. There is nothing I should like more and I shall try to do so one day when things have settled down.

Meanwhile, please convey to your readership my warm admiration for the courage and grit they have shown and my fervent hope and belief that the sacrifices that have been made will be demonstrated, by the future quality of life on the Islands, to have been worthwhile.

My best wishes to you all.

Yours sincerely,

MARGARET THATCHER

The second publication is *The Kelper Khronicle*. It is produced by an anonymous military source – allegedly concealed in the British Forces' Headquarters – and describes itself as 'An occasional disinformation sheet provided strictly for the amusement of British forces in the Falkland Islands'.

It is full of strictly Service, and of course Inter-Service, humour, flavoured with a very Falklands sauce, and, as is only to be expected, the Argentinians do not escape its penetrating beam. The amusing, the cynical, the plumb crazy and the earthy all come together in a cocktail production reflecting dashes of Monty Python, *Private Eye, Punch*, music hall comedy, and of course the historic tradition of British Forces humour down the centuries.

Apart from mentioning the report on the 1982 Trans-Antarctic Ice Floe Race, won by Sir Rupert ('Binky') Spottisway-Whistler-Spottisway, the 155 mm howitzer and Exocet souvenir trinkets taken off highly-spirited soldiers returning home, the Kite Club which has a requirement for 'a good wind and 8,000 miles of string', twenty exciting things to do with kelp, the spoof advertisements for jobs and accommodation, and some 'interesting' correspondence, I will close with a sample of what the Editor described as 'one of the very indifferent poems submitted'.

It is 'The Airfield' by Stanley, aged nine:

> 'I must go down to the airfield again
> To watch the tents fly by;
> I left my socks and vest there –
> I wonder if they're dry.'

28 | THE COMMUNICATORS

29 August, 1982

Here in the Falklands military job-satisfaction leads to high morale just as much as anywhere else. The communications business, for instance, is always 'for real' because either 'You are through or you are not'. 'The unique thing about my job,' beams Lance-Corporal Kevin Griffiths, Royal Corps of Signals, from Tewkesbury, 'is that I speak to the General every day.' He is one of the Headquarters telephone switchboard operators.

Signallers from 30 Signal Regiment, Blandford, were deployed right from the start of the Falklands Campaign, providing rear link radio detachments with 3 PARA and with all the Battalions of 5 Infantry Brigade. 'It was simply amazing,' the present Commanding Officer, Lieutenant-Colonel Roger Thompson, told me, 'how quickly our eighteen-year-old soldiers – often straight from their vehicle-bound training in England – instantly adapted to having to work on their feet humping manpack radio sets. For many of them, on landing,' he said, 'it was a case of "go east, lad", followed by fitness, firing and first aid.'

'Our Clansman radios were superb, and at no time – thanks to them – did the battle ever lack the means of command and control,' the Colonel stressed. 'But our Satellite Communications (SATCOM) – initially established ashore at San Carlos – were unbelievably good too: they opened up to us a world we didn't know existed before.' 'Major-General Jeremy Moore, who took over as the wartime Land Force Commander, describing SATCOM, called it "the only way home". It gave him the vital means of talking to Headquarters back in Northwood every day.'

The Signaller's task has widened since the end of the war. Not only has SATCOM been maintained, but other links, alternatives and trunk systems are required to Ascension, Britain and, of course, to South Georgia. Domestic military trunk links, mainly based on radio relay, had to be established, and are being further developed, to connect all the military deployments in East and West Falkland, and to join these, too, to SATCOM.

All ground-to-ground communications required by the Royal Air Force, either at Stanley Airfield or to remote detachment sites, are also provided by 30 Signal Regiment, as are the links to the Royal Navy.

In Stanley, as a result of the war, nearly all the civilian telephone lines drooped from their poles like so many exhausted cat's cradles. The Royal Corps of Signals linesmen quickly set to in re-connecting, re-wiring and repairing the system. Soldiers up poles were a familiar sight, even in my time.

The Military Headquarters have recently opened a permanent station on the local Civilian Settlements' radio net which operates throughout East and West Falkland. It works rather like a 'CB' network and is the principal means of inter-settlement chat, messages or of raising a medical or other alarm or emergency. Participation in it introduces yet another dimension of partnership between the military and civilian communities. Obviously there is an important 'eyes and ears' security aspect, but it is also an additional means by which the military can quickly hear of possible requests for their assistance.

The Royal Signals 'COMCEN' or message centre here operates twenty-four hours a day, dealing with 1,500 signals to and from Britain daily. 'We've never seen anything like it ever before,' the operators told me, their telex positions flanked by rack upon rack of miles of punched tapes. The volume of traffic is three times that at the height of the Borneo Campaign, which then had four brigades deployed and two airfields in direct support. Even today, two and half months after the end of the war, there are still some forty-odd signallers here who landed with the initial waves at San Carlos, and who will not be returning home until November or December. 'With mud all over their ankles, yet they volunteer to go out and man remote equipments up in the freezing mountains,' Colonel Thompson told me. 'Normally in detachments of a Lance-Corporal and five men – entirely on their own. They welcome being stretched by the challenge and the responsibilities thrust upon them. They give a marvellous response, without which we could not possibly operate at the pitch we do. And,' he added, 'we simply don't get disciplinary problems.'

29 | MINE DETECTION: WEAPONS

All of Stanley Town has now been 'cleared' by the Royal Engineer Explosive Ordnance Disposal (EOD) teams. Colonel Derek Brownson's next priority – he is Commander, Royal Engineers – is now Stanley Common which is where the local population will want to stroll in the forthcoming Falkland spring, and where their nearest peat banks are. Once the EOD teams have cleared it, the RE minefields teams will put up marker fences delineating just how far it is safe to stray from town before encountering mines.

Captain Tony Harkin RE of 69 Gurkha Field Squadron took over the mines responsibility from Lieutenant John Mullin of 9 Parachute Squadron, Royal Engineers, a month ago, and Major John Quinn is the new Commander of 49 EOD Squadron.

Corporal 'Sandy' Sanderson RE, from Portland, leads the self-christened 'Black Aces' Search Team which I had not been to see in action for several weeks. I caught up with him just beyond the quarry, seven miles out along the Darwin road. His task is to check and clear the road for hostile objects, and up to five metres each side of it. After personally going ahead to check for trip wires and booby traps, examine culverts and spot anything else that looks potentially dangerous, he marks out the five-metre limits with pegs and wire as guides for his teams to follow. They, helped by some Queen's Own Highlanders, are using the German 4021 Forster Locator which detects density variations underground. I found it good and very sensitive, and its headphones need not be worn all the time.

A few days ago it detected two roadside-buried dead Argentinians by reacting to their webbing equipment. We blew up Corporal Sanderson's latest visual finds – two half-buried mortar bombs which were too dangerous to move, a rifle grenade and an Argentine 'Beehive' explosive charge.

Updating myself on the state of the minefield clearance problem, I learnt that a complete folder of the Argentine engineer battalion's detailed minefield records dating back to early April had just been anonymously handed in to the EOD office. For anyone looking through it, as I did, it was perfectly obvious what it was. But, tragically, without a copy of the related Argentine Engineers' gridded map, it cannot be properly related to the ground.

Two almost incredible things emerge. First, knowing the universal hazard of mines to civilians and military alike, that the folder's possessor only saw fit to hand it in two and a half months after the end of the war. Second, there

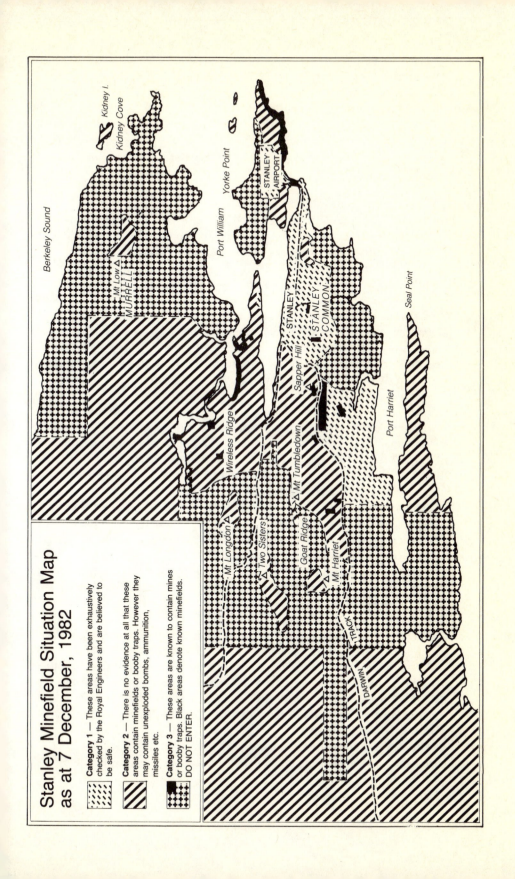

Stanley Minefield Situation Map as at 7 December, 1982

Category 1 — These areas have been exhaustively checked by the Royal Engineers and are believed to be safe.

Category 2 — There is no evidence at all that these areas contain minefields or booby traps. However they may contain unexploded bombs, ammunition, missiles etc.

Category 3 — These areas are known to contain mines or booby traps. Black areas denote known minefields. DO NOT ENTER.

Berkeley Sound

Kidney I.

Kidney Cove

Port William

Yorke Point

STANLEY AIRPORT

Seal Point

Mt Low △
MURRELL

STANLEY

Sapper Hill

STANLEY COMMON

Port Harriet

Wireless Ridge

Mt Longdon △

Two Sisters △

△ Mt Tumbledown

Goat Ridge

△ Mt Harriet

DARWIN TRACK

must have been a copy or copies of the Argentine Engineers' maps of the area available in Stanley at the time of the surrender. Where are these now, one wonders. No one knows. So, if you know of one being kept as a souvenir, either back home in Britain or elsewhere, persuade the owner to contact the Defence Ministry in London or HQ Land Forces, Falkland Islands, British Forces Post Office 666 with his original, or at least let it be photo-copied. The map could well be the means of Royal Engineers saving the limbs and lives of innocent civilians as well as of Servicemen.

There is still no complete answer to the detection and clearance of the totally plastic mines laid here in such quantity by the Argentinians. The only sure method remains the dangerous combination of the human eyeball and prodding by hand with a long metal skewer.

The initial tests of the bulldozer 'flail' have not been as successful as had been hoped, and modifications, such as lengthening the chains, are now being carried out. But, for the Falklands requirements of civilian safety, its flailed path would still of course have to be checked over by hand afterwards for any small detonators which the chains might have missed, and it is not really suitable for dealing with some types of mines. In the uneven terrain of the Falklands, with its many rocks set in among the peat and strongly tufted grass, the 'flail' can only ever be one of several methods of clearance available.

The Gazelle helicopter-mounted infra-red linescan detection equipment is still very much at the experimental stage, but better results may come when the grass-growing season gets properly under way and dug patches of ground show up better. There are significant changes in the earth's magnetic field in the Falklands, and this is a cause of some apparent unreliability in operating certain types of mine detector.

I had a go with the latest means of detection being tried out. First with the American 'Cubic' 156 PMD detector, which operates on the dialectic discontinuity principle of comparing the densities and moisture contents of adjacent pieces of ground. Although clever, I thought it far too complicated for practical operational purposes, especially in the uneven ground of the Falkland minefields. I am sure, though, it might work well on a bowling green.

In a different class was the British Irrado type 240 detector which I found easy to use, extremely sensitive, but, not being designed for military use, not robustly 'soldier proof'. As a civilian treasure-hunter, it is only really designed to detect ferrous and non-ferrous metals. Using it, however, I found I could easily detect the tiny piece of silver paper in the detonator slot of a Spanish P4B plastic anti-personnel mine from a good distance away, but I could get no reaction to an Argentine FMK 1 all-plastic anti-personnel mine.

The mine dogs are due out here soon, and I hope they will do well. One great advantage is that the rough terrain will not hinder them. But there are other difficulties – dogs cannot be worked for too long at a time; they can get bored if they fail to find enough objects; and the local peat has a strong pungent smell which may overpower that of the explosives. But they are yet another potentially valuable weapon well worth employing in the continuing mine battle. [In the event, the mine dogs were never deployed to the Falklands.]

But, despite all the aids and trials of equipment to date, the real position remains that the complete answer to clearance of small totally-plastic undetectable anti-personnel mines here in the Falklands, as indeed elsewhere, has yet to be found.

War souvenirs of Argentine weapons and ammunition are proving to be a very worrying Aftermath problem. Much of the still-scattered ordnance poses a grave risk of injury or death to less than knowledgeable souvenir seekers. This applies especially to those from Royal or Merchant Navy ships' crews who have at last been allowed a 'run ashore' to this war souvenirs' paradise. Some just 'pick' for themselves, but others, knowing very well the high prices which they can get for them elsewhere, particularly from the less adventurous on board ship, quickly grab up the most valuable pickings they can find.

Some of the uniformed Garrison, however, feel that civilians, some of whom are openly displaying their lethal treasures, are 'getting away with it', whilst the military authorities are applying increasingly strict disciplinary measures against Servicemen found 'in possession'. Certainly the problem of getting the highly independent civilians to surrender their proliferation of weaponry is a difficult one.

Mr Rex Hunt announced over the Islands' radio that those who possess Argentine weapons and ammunition are breaking the law. In the circumstances, however, he was giving a thirty-day amnesty for everyone to hand in the items they had acquired without risk of prosecution. Thereafter the full weight of the law would apply. The risk to people's safety is obvious, especially to the Islands' children.

Not many items were handed in, so the period of the amnesty was extended. Even as late as its edition of 6 August *The Penguin News* carried a short notice that Chief Superintendent Bill Richards 'will still accept, without charging the owner, any weapons that collectors now wish to give up'.

Eventually the situation changed dramatically when, quite by chance, a Seventh Day Adventist Falkland Islander in Stanley was found to have an extraordinarily large arsenal in his back room. His hoard only came to light when some Queen's Own Highlanders were looking for some wood to burn. They knocked on a front door, but were told, 'This is my home – no souvenir hunters'. But, even from the doorway, they had noticed some belts of ammunition in the house. Taking their leave, they reported the incident to the Royal Military Police.

When the Civil Police called round a little later, accompanied by the RMP and an RAOC Ammunition Technical Officer, they found an enormous cache of arms hidden under some blankets. It comprised 12,000 rounds of 7.62 belted ball and 100 rounds of 9 mm ammunition, thirty-seven rifle grenades and cartridges, seven rifles and three General Purpose Machine Guns with two spare barrels, boxes of Argentinian respirators, and of carbolic soap!

When asked to account for his possession of this amazing quantity of arms, the man replied, 'Every Falkland Islander has the right to defend himself.' He was subsequently charged in court.

30 | COMMANDER BRITISH FORCES FALKLANDS ISLANDS

The arrival in the Falklands of Major-General David Thorne on 17 July as Military Commissioner and Commander British Forces Falkland Islands provided the Aftermath with a much-needed tonic. His boundless energy transmitted itself throughout the Force, and his fresh enthusiasm came as an inspiration to all concerned.

After all, those who had fought the campaign had done their bit; many of them were understandably very, very tired and needed to return home. The future of the Falklands, rightly, was for others to shape.

As one Senior Officer put it to me, 'With General Thorne's arrival, things changed dramatically for the better; he was exactly what was needed to fill an increasing leadership vacuum.' With their eternal flair for aptness, the soldiers all knew the General as either 'Jumping Bean' or 'Action Man'.

In late August, sitting together for an hour in his office in front of a huge map, he reviewed the Falklands situation for me.

28 August, 1982

'Our task here is to defend the Falkland Islands, and for this anything short of a highly tuned, aggressive defence capability is unacceptable,' General Thorne told me.

'To create this effectively, we have forces from all three Services which, together with men from the Royal Fleet Auxiliaries and the Merchant Navy, make up one total team. It is a great challenge, and we have a huge area of ground to cover in both East and West Falkland. We therefore must have a very rapid and effective military response instantly available to draw the roots very quickly of anything hostile which could be mounted against us. I am sure that this message will already have reached the Argentine. Of course, for strategic reasons, development of the airfield had to be our first and over-riding priority.

'Yes, there is still a risk of Argentine action. Only 400 miles of sea separate us from them. They have a burning resentment at losing the war, and a deep-seated national understanding that what they call 'Las Malvinas' are theirs, and they have already demonstrated courage, ingenuity and initiative.

'We must therefore sustain our high state of training to ensure that our minimum forces are at maximum efficiency at all times, ready to carry out their operational tasks. You already know the tremendous motivation that everyone has here, so clearly demonstrated, for example, by the new AM2 matting surface-laying operation being completed in four days less than had been expected. The Royal Engineers, the Gurkhas, assisted by The Queen's Own Highlanders, worked in shifts around the clock in appalling weather conditions to do it, even running a competition for the fastest laying time. They were marvellous.

'Soldiers can work up a natural momentum which, once under way, is almost unstoppable and leads to great achievements. The problem is not starting them off, but often in stopping them once launched.

'Our other immediate and very important task,' The General continued, 'is learning to live with the Islands and to woo the Falkland Islanders. After all, some 4,000 Servicemen added to the local population of only 1,800 is bound to exert a number of strong influences, especially socially and particularly in the context of future accommodation for the garrison, and of course we want to avoid any tensions.

'We are a highly talented and capable organization,' he pointed out. 'Gaining the support and confidence of the Falkland Islanders, and showing them we are trustworthy, is a very important priority indeed. We must have respect for each other. The future is a partnership between us – the military – and the Islanders. For instance, we must show in practical terms in our selection and use of training areas that we are sensitive to farming interests, and also to the conservation of the Islands' marvellous and unique wildlife. In co-operation with the Settlement landowners – for example, Robin Lee of Port Howard – we are now drawing up a mutually acceptable "code of conduct" for troops under training. This is an example of what I mean.

'We must not arrogantly presume, but be prepared to be humble and quietly listen to what those in the Settlements have to say, try to understand their problems and gain their confidence. Patience is essential, as is dialogue. It has taken a little time, but I have now talked with those who live in all the main Settlements, and in due course hope to visit all the remainder. I am sure that by leaving everyone's natural human qualities to develop, by early March next year relationships will have settled down, and the Falkland Islanders will continue to welcome Servicemen here.

'I am sure that with this partnership approach, in training areas, in siting our permanent camps, in clearing up the aftermath of war, but above all in achieving the defensive task for which we are here, we will make the joint progress which is so essential. I consider the six-month tour "door-to-door" to be right, during which men may be called upon to work seven days a week, as indeed they are now. Certainly all our units will leave the Falklands at the end of their tours peak trained, and far fitter than when they arrived.'

[*General Thorne handed over as Military Commissioner and Commander British Forces Falkland Islands to Major-General Keith Spacie on 16 April, 1983, and was appointed a KBE in the 1983 Birthday Honours.*]

31 | 'GOING NORTH' – AND HOME

It took twenty-eight hours to fly in an RAF Hercules from Stanley to Lyneham in Wiltshire, with only a brief stop at Ascension, with a cheerfully efficient and friendly aircrew who until March of this year had spent their flying time 'flogging the route' to Norway, Cyprus, the United States and Hong Kong. In the immediate Aftermath they had become a vital link in the Falklands 'air bridge' between Stanley and Ascension.

During the time Stanley airfield had been closed for the runway extension work, the Hercules' norm had been to fly the fourteen hours from Ascension overhead Stanley with two nerve-racking mid-air refuellings, and then carry out several air-drop circuits followed by a couple of pick-up runs 'snatching' mailbags, using the trailing hook technique, before heading back, hopefully with a good following wind, the thirteen hours to Ascension.

After order and counter-order from the RAF element of the Commander-in-Chief Fleet's Headquarters at Northwood in Britain, I eventually flew out in the first passenger-carrying aircraft to take off from the newly opened Stanley runway. The problem was that the new AM2 matting surface on Stanley airfield had not yet been officially trialled to see whether it was safe for take-off by passenger-carrying Hercules. The AM2 matting, needless to say, held firm as a rock and defeated the earlier possible fears of any risk which, as I was pointedly told by the Movements Staff, I was anyway 'old and ugly enough' to take! Nearly all my companions were men who had been through the campaign, but whose various specialist skills were in such short supply that they had had to be retained these additional months before reliefs for them could be found and they could go home.

I left behind a very competent military organization of all three Services, well capable of defending the Falkland Islands. It was actively taking the lead in, and making a very positive contribution to, the rehabilitation and future of the Falkland Islanders themselves. One is just concerned whether, since the months have passed and no senior representative of Government has yet visited the South Atlantic, that in the initial aftermath of victory the Government will be as supportive and understanding of the military's many problems, and as keen in making decisions and in solving them as it should.

However, it is understood there is now a likelihood that someone may visit the Falklands this autumn. [It was later announced in mid-September that Mr John Nott, Secretary of State for Defence, and Mr Cranley Onslow, Minister of State at the Foreign Office, were to visit the Falkland Islands in October.] One would like to think that he, too, whoever it is, will 'hack it' to and from the Falklands by normal and not VIP-fitted Hercules. If your retired Army, ageing Defence Correspondent can do it – and so get the real flavour – so, one would like to think, can he.

One still has to sit close-packed, side by side, on nylon-covered bench seats with knees touching those in the opposite row, and having to wear cotton wool in the ears to deaden the roar of the engines. The light is not good enough for reading, there are no washing facilities whatsoever and only a screened off 'Elsan' by the aircraft's tail. You work out for yourself when during the journey you will eat the contents of your two issued cardboard food boxes.

The bars and struts of the Hercules' interior are like some strange airborne gymnasium from which the Air Loadmaster swings when briefing you. For most of the journey the passengers slump in snatched dozes, leaning on each other's shoulders like falling dominoes. Perhaps the one passenger who should try it the hard way is the civil servant in the Ministry of Defence's General Finance Department who assessed the repayment cost of a single flight for 'non-entitled' passengers as being £1,000. [On 1 November, 1984, the MOD's 'assessed fare' was £3,000 return!] Even the first Command Secretary (Civil Servant Financial Adviser) to be appointed to General Thorne's staff, after his own flight 'down South', told me he reckoned he should have been paid extra to do the journey at all – the Hercules way!

We reached Ascension to find that there was no connecting VC10 flight on to Britain, so on by Hercules it was to be. But, during our brief stopover to re-fuel, there was time for a quick re-visit to the incongruous Green Mountain with its Devonshire-like lane and flowers, and I was delighted, as we came down the steep road, to pass my South Georgia host Captain Jim Weatherall of HMS *Andromeda* on his way up.

Later, looking out from the small quay at Georgetown, I was able to see that the trio of frigates – *Andromeda*, *Penelope* and *Avenger* – had all reached Ascension together and were about to depart on the last leg of their prolonged voyage back to their home ports.

We were all on our respective ways north, our vivid and varying experiences now over. For them, it had been a short but hard battle campaign; for me – I was coming back with many of the elusive answers, the search for which had been the personal imperative which had driven me down to the South Atlantic some six weeks earlier.

We filed out from Wideawake airfield's soulless canvas shelter across the apron to the low-bellied Hercules, and clambered on in the accepted silence of very tired travellers. The muffled roar of the four engines easily penetrated the wisps of cotton wool in our ears and, lap-strapped into our inward-facing flimsy 'para' seats, our bodies tilted automatically towards the tail as the huge loaded hulk accelerated down the runway, lifted laboriously into the air and headed north.

In compensation for the extra-long journey, I was lucky enough to be invited up to the Flight Deck to take over in the Hercules' second pilot's right-hand seat, and for a while urge the great aircraft along its successive bearing headings towards home. After flying an Army Air Corps Beaver some years earlier, it was like driving a London bus.

EPILOGUE

The Falkland Islands have experienced many changes since the late summer of 1982, but the most significant constant to date is that Argentina has yet, at the time of writing, to declare a cessation of hostilities against Britain in the South Atlantic. The first other constant is the British Government's policy that the sovereignty of the Falkland Islands is not negotiable. The second is that Britain still maintains the integrity of a 150-mile radius Protection Zone around the Falkland Islands (the FIPZ) from which the Argentinians are excluded; but against which by sea and air the Argentinians provocatively initiate potentially intrusive action with the aim of expensively tying down, keeping on the alert, and otherwise testing the operational reaction time of a significant level of Britain's already stretched defence forces in the South Atlantic. The third constant is the continuing presence in the Falkland Islands for the forseeable future of so many Argentinian mines, albeit mainly fenced off.

In theory, at least, the campaign in which so many fought and so many died is thus still extant. This means that the Argentinian threat against the Falkland Islands and the Dependencies must still be continuously assessed, and in turn dictates – consistent with the Armed Forces' resources available and any other Falklands-related developments – the force levels which Britain has to maintain in the South Atlantic for the defence of the Falkland Islands, South Georgia and the other Dependent Territories; and for the continued operation of the FIPZ. Argentina has considerably re-armed herself following her Falklands losses.

The South Atlantic Fund was constituted on 15 July, 1982, to aid the victims of the Campaign and their families. By the autumn of the year the public's tremendous support had contributed the astonishing sum of £11 million. (Initially it was envisaged that the Fund would remain extant for the five years up to July, 1987, before being wound up. A recent decision of the Trustees, however, has extended this period up until July, 1988, but with a review of the position to be undertaken in December, 1987.)

On 4 November, 1982, Falklands War Artist Linda Kitson's work went on show at the Imperial War Museum, whose Artistic Records Committee had appointed her. The ninety-four drawings covered her experience from 12 May – sailing south on the *QE2*, arriving on the *Canberra* at San Carlos Bay, and then following 5 Infantry Brigade to Stanley. The Exhibition subsequently went on tour throughout Britain.

The sage Bob Hutchinson of the Press Association and the ebullient Paul Maurice of Independent Radio News together decided that members of the media who had so valiantly fought the difficult Whitehall campaign should be rewarded with a decoration. It was not a medal, though, but an exclusive tie Paul designed with a dark blue-water background carrying three motifs: a Royal Navy anchor to represent the Task Force – a penguin for the Falklands – and a red question mark to commemorate the fact that for most of the time the media 'were not told what the hell was going on!'

It had indeed been a traumatic campaign, devoid of 'gung-ho' for the participants, and the overwhelming attitude of the troops who had fought in the South Atlantic was 'Well, that's now behind us – let's get on with the next job.' In February of 1983, while visiting 3 Commando Brigade's annual Winter Warfare training deployment in Norway, Captain Rod Bell put it to me like this: 'The most important thing now is to look forward – away from the success of the Falklands and towards keeping tuned up to the Brigade's operational priority tasks here in Northern Norway. The Campaign confirmed for us only too well the training techniques and standards which the Brigade has evolved out here over the years.'

Later in the deployment, near Harstadt, Royal Marine Lance-Corporal Barry Gilbert from No 1 Raiding Squadron was ferrying me across a fjord from one snow-covered shore to the other in a Rigid Raider craft. I happened to know that he had been awarded a Mention-in-Despatches for some special tasks carried out in Stanley during the Campaign. His comment on the whole affair was typically pertinent, low-key and humorous. 'I much enjoy it up here,' he said, 'but I really feel I've been continuously cold now for a whole year on end.'

In Belize the following month I was talking to Corporal Mick Leather of 9 PARA who, as a Minefield Recce Party NCO, had 'tabbed' his way across East Falkland with 3 PARA. 'You know,' he said, 'I've really forgotten what happened down there, I'm far too busy with the work I've got on here in Belize.'

In late 1982, the only piece of metalled road in the Falkland Islands ran between Stanley and its airfield; as a result of the war, even this suffered badly. Constructed between 1974 and 1976, only 1,250 metres long and forty-five metres wide before being lengthened and reinforced by Royal Engineers in July/August 1982, the airfield itself still had severe limitations which, together with its distance from Ascension, precluded other than certain Royal Air Force aircraft flying to it from Britain. Stanley's only small timbered quay was both inadequate and damaged.

The British Garrison lived in civilian billets, in tents, on board ships, in public buildings and in sheep-shearers' bunk houses. Communications with the Settlements out 'in the Camp' were primitive to say the least, that is if you could not hitch-hike on a helicopter. The alternatives were to ride, steer your own Land-Rover or tractor across the peat making your own new track, or hitch a ride round by boat when and where you could – courtesy of the Royal Navy.

This book on the early Aftermath of the British-Argentinian campaign is not the place to chart all the many civil and military, political and social developments or the successes and failures which have taken place between 'then and now'; that is something to be covered by others in due time. Nevertheless there have been a number of significant changes and developments, particularly in 1983, which must be mentioned in any post-1982 Falklands volume.

The most outstanding development, without doubt, was the opening of the new international airfield at Mount Pleasant on 12 May, 1985, by HRH Prince Andrew, in the presence of Mr Michael Heseltine (Minister of Defence) and others. By thus enabling wide-bodied passenger transport aircraft to fly in and out from Britain, calling in at Ascension to refuel, a completely new form of direct military reinforcement and civilian outlet linkage was established between Stanley and London. It was a very expensive development – some £350 million plus – whose potential has yet to be either fully ascertained or exploited.

One consequence of the opening of the new airfield is that the American AM2 matting, with which the old Stanley airfield was lengthened and developed to the appropriate operational standard in August, 1982, with so much 'sweat and blood', has now all been picked up and shipped back into store in Britain. Ready for some future occasion, one wonders. Starting in November, 1986, the task was done by 25 Engineer Regiment from the British Army of the Rhine, assisted by a Company of the Royal Pioneer Corps. The Sappers also dismantled the twenty Rubb Shelters which had been housing the RAF Phantoms and their supporting 'back up' and cleared the Class 60 aluminium trackway roads, the Rapier sites and all the protective field defences which had been earlier erected around the airfield. Much of the salvaged timber and scrap metal was sold to local Falkland Islanders at the 'tip' established at Mary Hill Quarry.

The development and opening of the Mount Pleasant project moved the centre of gravity of the British Forces' presence 'off the backs' of, and away from, the civilian population's natural focus of its own capital of Stanley. The execution of this immensely complicated engineering project, 8,000 miles from Britain, was an outstanding feat. A brief account of it is given in Annex D.

This shift from Stanley to the new complex in May, 1985, was reflected in a significant change in the military command arrangements for the Falklands. During 1984 the Ministry of Defence had felt that once the Mount Pleasant airfield was opened, there could be a shift of emphasis 'down South' to an airfield-based reinforcement defence strategy, and it was thus for consideration whether thenceforth to alternate the top post of Commander British Forces Falkland Islands between the Army and the Royal Air Force. In the autumn of 1984, however, the Ministry eventually decided to make the appointment a fully Joint Service one to be rotated between all the three Services. Consequently, in December, 1984, the Ministry announced that a Royal Air Force officer, Air Commodore 'Kip' Kemball, then Commandant of the RAF Central Flying School, would succeed Major-General Peter de la Billière, on completion of his tour in July 1985, as CBFFI in the rank of Air Vice-Marshal. In 1986 AVM Kemball was succeeded by Rear-Admiral Kit Layman, who in turn is due to be succeeded by an Army Brigadier, Neil Carlier, promoted to Major-General: 'La ronde' will then be complete – first time round!

Leaving aside the difficult questions of costs within a strained defence budget (a planned £552 million in 1985/86 and £442 million in 1986/87) and Service overstretch of resources, there was and still is concern by many over the concentration of the Falklands' defence strength around a large static and precisely definable target – identifiable by a suitable rocket weapon fired from the Argentinian mainland – which, together with the continuing Stanley airfield, appears to increase the complexity of the overall defence task. Putting the new 'reinforcement' airfield out of action would obviously be any determined aggressor's earliest and top priority target.

Taken together with the task of patrolling and protecting the extensive remote areas of difficult terrain on both East and West Falkland, and the essential maintenance of a South Georgia deterrent presence, it creates grave doubts – despite the arguments of the 'rapid reinforcers', the 'trip wire' enthusiasts or the Falkland Garrison political detractors – by how much, if at all, the size of the South Atlantic Garrison can ever be safely reduced militarily prior to any satisfactorily agreed major political change, if such a thing ever comes to pass. Ultimately, of course, money 'shouts' extremely loudly in the context of domestic politics at home and could become the dominant factor.

Whereas Britain's Armed Services can always be relied upon to do their very best with the resources they are given, and do well under the most adverse conditions, nevertheless the fact that the Mount Pleasant site is some thirty miles from Stanley along a rather uncomfortable road, with currently no public transport service, has caused some concern on three counts. First, that this geographical separation of the centre of the military presence away from the centre of the civilian population will jeopardise the hitherto close partnership and co-operation between the two communities, at all levels, which has been, is and will continue to be so vital an element in assuring and developing a new future for the Falkland Islands.

Second, the physical separation of the Governor in Stanley from the Commander British Forces Falkland Islands in Mount Pleasant – the two key 'top' people who need to operate together as one in so many fields – runs counter to all the obvious and accepted proper teaching. In addition, the presence of CBFFI and his staff at the isolated airfield could be inhibiting to the local commander, but need not be if tactfully played.

Third, there is the all-important factor of morale. Many Servicemen and Servicewomen will now be virtually tied to an isolated 'big base' for their tour – one which is thirty miles and an expensive ride away from the only civilian 'city' outlet. Then there are Falkland Islanders for whom entertaining and 'having around' Servicemen and Servicewomen has become such a way of life that they are not best pleased at seeing them all disappear 'to the Camp'. The move just increases the leadership challenge for those responsible for both elements.

On the civilian side, Mrs Thatcher made an emotional visit to the Falklands in January, 1983. She flew the final 'leg' from Ascension to Stanley in a RAF Hercules which had been fitted out with a caravan lashed down to the floor of its large combined passenger and freight bay. She received a great welcome from the Islanders. The Prime Minister's journey home, however, was far less comfortable. Her Hercules had engine trouble on take-off and so the flight had to be aborted. Her time schedule for getting back to Britain was necessarily an extremely tight one. The RAF worked frantically against time with the result that virtually within an hour she and her party were transferred – but unfortunately without the caravan – to another 'normal' Hercules for the long flight back to Ascension. Mrs Thatcher, who, reports say, spent much of the journey up on the Hercules's flight deck, eventually arrived back just in time to appear in the Commons for Prime Minister's Question Time!

The Civil Commissioner, Rex Hunt, having been created a Knight in October, 1982, was extended in his tour.

The second most significant post-1982 development on the civilian side, after the new airfield, was the translation into reality of Lord Shackleton's recommendation to establish the Falkland Islands Development Corporation (FIDC). It was constituted on 14 June, 1984, on the coming into force of the Falkland Islands Development Corporation Ordinance 1983 (Appendix 1).

The FIDC is funded by grant-in-aid from the Overseas Development Administration, and in certain circumstances it is empowered to borrow on its own account.

The inaugural meeting of the FIDC took place on 14 July, 1984, presided over by its first Chairman, Sir Rex Hunt. Its members are nominated in accordance with its founding Ordinance. The General Manager, Simon Armstrong, arrived on 22 July, and on 4 September he made his recommendations to the Corporation regarding its priorities and future strategy.

The Corporation's initial goals were:

1. To increase the range of employment opportunities, particularly by encouraging diversification of the economy.
2. To increase population levels through selective immigration.
3. To increase the long-term capacity of the Falkland Islands to develop, with the eventual aim of self-sufficiency.
4. To improve community facilities.

In adopting a broadly-based strategy in order to fulfil its stated goals, the FIDC set out to build upon the Islands' traditional agricultural and natural resources bases, whilst at the same time seeking to encourage diversification of the economy into fisheries, tourism, industry and service sectors.

Since its inauguration, FIDC activity has been well spread, and it has helped to start up a number of businesses – for example The Stanley Dairy Ltd, Falkland Islands Seafood Ltd, The Falkland Mill and Falkland Islands Home Industries. It has encouraged tourism, as at Sea Lion Island, Pebble Island and Port Howard, and has initiated studies into fisheries, transport, wool, the abattoir, housing and a farmers' co-operative. Perhaps the most important of all, it has granted soft loans to farmers enabling them to buy their own farms, mainly subdivisions of larger absentee-landlord owned farms.

Moves to draft a new Constitution for the Falkland Islands started after the elections for the Legislative Council held in 1981, and a Select Committee of elected Councillors was set up for the purpose under the chairmanship of Councillor Tim Blake. The existing Constitution was considered clumsy, and in particular included a pedantic procedure for electing the six Members of the Legislative Council which was neither satisfactory nor foolproof.

The Select Committee's recommendations were adopted by the Legislative Council and put to the Foreign Office in August, 1983. There followed over two years of prolonged, and at times heated, negotiations between the two Governments, particularly over the status of the Falkland Islands Dependencies, and over the question of a one or a two Chamber form of Government, the British favouring the abolition of the Executive Council. In December, 1984, the British Government produced its draft version of an appropriate Constitution.

After even further discussion, a new Constitution eventually came into force by Order in Council on 3 October, 1985. It is interesting to record that the finally agreed and vitally important clause in the Constitution allowing the right to self-determination – so much welcomed by the Falkland Islanders and only inserted at the last moment – was actually proposed by Legislative Councillor Tony Blake. The British Government's view had been that the principle of self-determination was enshrined in the United Nations Charter anyway.

Two other significant changes took place under the aegis of this Order in Council. After intense Falkland Islands lobbying, Sir Rex's title of Governor was restored in place of 'Civil Commissioner', and that of 'Military Commissioner', held since 1982 by the Commander British Forces Falkland Islands, was formally abolished. In fact the latter title was put into suspense, in anticipation of implementation of the new Constitution, when Air Vice-Marshal Kip Kemball took over as CBFFI from Major-General Peter de la Billière in late July, 1985.

On 15 October, 1985, Sir Rex Hunt was relieved as Governor by Mr

Gordon Jewkes and, after a remarkable six years of devoted service to the Islanders, returned to Britain on retirement from the Foreign Service.

One 'running sore' in Falkland Islander-British relations however, has been the British Government's refusal – largely because of the expense and of the practical difficulties in providing the resources necessary to police it – to declare a 200-mile Exclusive Economic Zone around the Falklands. The Islanders particularly wanted this in order to preserve the once extensive fish stocks which they and Lord Shackleton in his report rightly saw as one of their principal assets. They were understandably somewhat bitter as they watched 'their' stocks being fast depleted by trawler fleets from Japan, Poland, the Soviet Union and other Eastern Bloc countries, Spain and Taiwan, without a 'by your leave', thought for conservation, proper management or any satisfactory agreement.

In fact, the 150-mile radius Falkland Islands Protection Zone (FIPZ), declared in 1982 and still extant, has provided an unofficial 150-mile Fishery Protection Zone ever since for those shrewd enough to take advantage of it. The inevitable result has been that foreign fishing fleets in the South Atlantic have naturally concentrated their efforts within the FIPZ where, by default as it were, they have enjoyed the Royal Navy's secure protection – at no cost – against Argentine interference. Such fishing fleet deployment was especially advantageous in view of the fact that the Argentinians have arrested vessels, in one instance causing a death, which were fishing within 200 miles of the Falkland Islands but over 200 miles from the coast of Argentina. The situation was further complicated by Argentina having signed fishing agreements with the Soviet Union and Bulgaria relevant to the Argentinian Exclusive Economic Zone (EEZ) which, according to them, covers waters within 200 miles of the Falkland Islands.

The Falkland Islanders thus had to put up with the worst of both worlds in that, firstly, a 150-mile-radius de facto protected fishing zone belonging to them was being exploited by sundry foreigners: secondly, they were getting no compensation for such pillaging of stocks by way of licences, taxes or any charges whatsoever; and thirdly, with no conservation or control measures in operation, the Falkland Islands waters were fast being denuded of what fish stocks they contained.

It is a matter of record that the number of vessels fishing around the Falkland Islands, one of the world's largest unregulated fisheries, rose from some 200 to over 600 in the three years up to 1986. In April, 1985, the United Nations Food and Agriculture Organization's Committee on Fisheries (FAO) held a conference at which concern about conservation was strongly expressed. Following a British proposal, a FAO Study of the Falkland Islands Fishery was initiated in November, 1985, with a view to producing a completed report by June, 1986. Largely because of delays by the Soviet Union, Spain and Japan in producing required data on time, completion of the Study by June became impossible and the end of December, 1986, became the new target date for a first draft.

The threat of fishing fleets from the Far East mounting a massively increased effort targeted on the squid in the Falkland Islands Fishery prompted Britain to try and introduce Voluntary Restraint Arrangements (VRAs) as a means of preserving the integrity of the FAO Study. As soon as it became clear that there was no prospect of multilateral arrangements being negotiated in time for the 1987 fishing season, Britain sought to renew and extend the concept of VRAs to all the nations interested in the Falkland Islands Fishery.

With some nations being particularly tardy in responding to Britain's VRA approach, and with the need for national fishing fleets to set sail in December, 1986, in order to be in position to start catching fish when the season opened in February, 1987, time was running out fast for any agreement at all and the prospect was that once again the Falkland Islands Fishery would be a 'free for all'.

It was against this rather depressing background and need for firm action over the squid issue that Sir Geoffrey Howe, the Foreign Secretary, announced in the House of Commons on 29 October, 1986, that the British Government had decided to establish a Falkland Islands Interim Conservation and Management Zone (FICZ) from 1 February, 1987, extending for a radius of 150 miles around the Islands. It would be the responsibility of the Falkland Islands Government to run the FICZ and police it with two civilian fishery protection vessels and one civilian aircraft.

Sir Geoffrey stressed that the setting up of the FICZ was only an interim measure which would remain in force until permanent collaborative multilateral arrangements could be satisfactorily negotiated. The aim would be to promote conservation of fish stocks and, by granting of licences, help develop the Falkland Islands economy and its fishery, while at the same time benefiting the foreign fleets concerned.

The published limits of the FICZ showed it to be co-extensive with the existing 1982 FIPZ except for a minor segment in the south-west quadrant, nearest to Argentina and adjacent to the Falkland Islands – Argentina geographical median line. In this area, over 150 miles long, the FICZ perimeter is smaller than that of the FIPZ by up to a maximum of some thirty miles.

Falkland Islands fish thus have deep political and economic international connotations, and they continue to bedevil the development of Anglo-Argentinian relations. By comparison, animals are relatively simple After-math subjects over which the Islanders have fared much better: they received a virtual 'Noah's Ark' worth from Britain as replacements for those lost as a result of the Argentinian Occupation and the subsequent Campaign.

[It is very satisfactory to record that in 1987, since this chapter was drafted and at long, long last, the Falkland Islands Government's revenue from its new fishing licences has been substantial. Indeed, editorial comment in the *Falkland Islands Newsletter* of August 1987 reported 'The financial results of the first season's controlled fishing in the Falklands have borne out all our predictions. They have been dramatic, transforming the Falkland Islands economy. . . . The fishing is successful: now lets go for the oil! How long the income from fishing licences will continue, however, depends largely on whether the fish conservation measures now being taken, especially for squid, can preserve sufficient stocks for the future.]

Leaving aside the United Nations debates, the subsequent politically-motivated fuss over the *Belgrano*, and the continuing British and Argentinian political moves vis-à-vis the Islands, the Government and House of Commons Committees have produced various Reports and Reviews on the Falklands over the years, notably Lord Shackleton's updated Report of September, 1982, entitled 'Falkland Islands Economic Study 1982', the 'Falkland Islands Review' Report of a Committee of Privy Counsellors chaired by Lord Franks in January, 1983, and the Ministry of Defence's 'The Future Defence of the Falkland Islands' in October, 1983. Commons debates have been frequent on various aspects of the Islanders' future, the political 'way ahead' as regards Argentina, the Service force levels, the costs of the Garrison and the welfare of those who constitute its remote populations: throughout, the Falkland Islands Association's *Newsletter* has been forthright in consistently presenting the Islanders' problems to a wide audience.

The Aftermath 'war' against the mines, booby traps and abandoned and unstable ammunition and explosives has continued to be energetically pursued.

By 30 January, 1983, for instance, when they arrived back in Britain on completion of their tour, Major Peter Courtney-Green and his men who first manned the RAOC's Composite Ammunition Company, operating in conjunction with the Queen's Gurkha Engineers, had 'surface cleared' forty-seven battlefield sites. These included Wireless Ridge, Sapper Hill and Mounts William and Tumbledown from which eighty-seven tons of unexploded objects had been recovered. They had also completed removal of the improvised 'cocktail' dump of assorted ordnance just off the road leading to the old Royal Marine Barracks at Moody Brook, and of the gun and mortar ammunition dump by Murrell Bridge by the track leading to Estancia House.

Captain Nick Bell and Sergeant Jack Horner had been responsible for dealing with Goose Green and Fox Bay where they had to dispose of many 2.75-inch SNEB rockets and other items originally destined to be fired by Argentinian Pucara aircraft against British troops. Warrant Officer Class 1 Steve Harman spent three weeks in South Georgia 'surface clearing' the battle areas at Grytviken and Leith.

The RAOC Company had found, dug up and dealt with nearly 3,000 tons of Argentine ammunition – worth £8–9 million of which some 1,000 tons, comprising 4,750,000 items, passed inspection for further use elsewhere. A large quantity of other ammunition was found to be in good enough condition to be used for live firing training in the Falklands.

A further total of 41,000 Argentine crates and boxes and individual shells, rockets, mines and rifle grenades as well as gun, mortar and other ammunition were actually destroyed.

British ammunition recovered included 1,600 tons from Ajax Bay – the Red beach of the original landings – and from the superbly laid out dump at Teal Inlet established at the height of the campaign by the Ordnance Squadron of the Commando Logistic Regiment.

The EOD Battle Clearance work continues still. In the latter six months of 1986, for instance, the teams concentrated on the Goose Green and Wireless Ridge areas. The result was some 250 hectares of battlefield 'cleared', involving the 'disposal' of 15,000 items of ammunition of various kinds in varying states of safety. In addition a recently discovered crashed Argentine Pucara aircraft had to be divested of its unexploded rockets and canon shells.

Whereas the known Argentine minefields are now fenced off and marked with warning signs, the persistent menace of coming across unmarked stray mines still calls for constant vigilance, and the strict maintenance of the mine fences. There is the newly-encountered phenomenon, too, of 'floater' mines which add a further dimension of danger: these are mines, originally laid inside the now marked and fenced minefields, which 'float' in the peat and, over time, travel by themselves under the perimeter fences and out into the unmarked areas.

The latest device to be tried out, produced in a record four months by the Royal Armaments Research and Development Establishment at Chertsey, is the 'Remote Explosive Destroyer Falkland Islands Royal Engineers' – known as REDFIRE for short. It is a modified form of the Explosive Ordnance Disposal remotely-controlled-by-radio Mark 8 'Wheelbarrow' equipment. On visibly discovering a mine, the operator has the choice of using one of three of the machine's 'disposal options'. First, a Propane gas burner jet which melts the plastic mine covering and then burns away the explosive content: second, a 'placer' with which to deposit and then detonate an explosive charge on top of a mine: and, third, a mine recovery attachment which will grab and carry the mine away to be dealt with elsewhere. But of course both the operator and the machine are vulnerable to unexpected contact with a mine the operator does not see, as experience in the Falklands has shown. So far REDFIRE has dealt with nearly 100 plastic mines, including 'floaters'. Certainly it is a useful equipment, but not the ultimate 'clearer' of all mines visible and invisible of which all Sappers dream.

Reminders of the ever-present danger are the two Royal Engineer

Majors belonging to 33 Engineer Regiment EOD who both lost a leg in the more recent Aftermath. Major Steve Hambrook lost his at Fox Bay East on 15 January, 1983, when walking along a well-used path believed to be mine-free. Retired, he is now a Permanent Staff Administrative Officer with 591 (EOD) Squadron (Volunteer). Major Geoff Ward lost his leg inside the outer fence of the Stanley Common Minefield on 15 October, 1983, thanks to an Argentine anti-personnel mine 'floater' getting itself outside the inner minefield fence to where Major Ward was working. He is still serving – as a Staff Officer in Northern Ireland.

The reality is that there is, as yet, no 100 per cent certain means of detecting the many thousands of plastic mines still in the ground. The nature and varied content of the soil, ranging from soft to rocky and with a very uneven surface, adds to the difficulty of finding appropriate satisfactory techniques of safe clearance.

The Ministry of Defence has so far spent millions of pounds on research for a practical solution. There are some scientific techniques – reflected radar pulses, soil density variation detectors and so on – which have all held out possibilities, but the problem of translating the laboratory theories and tests into workable, 'soldier-proof', equipment at realistic cost remains as elusive as ever. The world, and particularly the British Army, still awaits that long-promised scientific breakthrough. When it comes, the technology may well have even more and lucrative civilian applications than military ones.

The subject of Falkland Islands mines is a sensitive one. With the Defence Vote under severe pressure, naturally the Ministry of Defence has to consider the relative priorities of spending further large sums on plastic mine detection research vis-à-vis its other requirements for the maintenance of Britain's four main pillars of NATO and Home Defence, and it could be argued that there is really no *military* imperative to remove the Falkland mines. The Foreign Office, on the other hand, would naturally be expected to resist any pressure on it to provide money to fund what it could claim was a purely military matter. The Falkland Islands Government could well argue that the enormous cost of mine clearance was certainly not its responsibility. The Argentine Surrender terms made no mention of reparations or mines.

Major-General Jeremy Rougier, the Army's Engineer-in-Chief, summed up the situation in 1987 by saying, 'We have not yet been able to find a cost-effective way of clearing the mines to the safety standards required in peacetime.' The result is the current British Government policy whereby Servicemen's lives will not be put at risk to clear the large areas of uncleared Argentine minefields. If and when a suitable technique is discovered, which could undertake the task safely and cheaply, then the whole matter would be re-considered.

An interesting view was recently expressed by a Falkland Islander. 'With the main areas of normal activity safely cleared of Argentine mines –

as they have been – the remaining mined areas should now be left uncleared as an ever-present reminder to the Governments involved in the conflict of what can go wrong, and of the continuing price which has to be paid for such adventures.

A map of the Stanley Minefield and Clearance Situation as at 7 December, 1982, is given on page 135.

Logistics have also been a continuous and extensive problem for the Garrison. For example, in April, 1983, twenty-five merchant ships on charter to the Ministry of Defence were required to keep it supplied from Britain with fuel, food, supplies and stores of every description. Royal Fleet Auxiliary vessels were similarly operating in support of the Royal Navy.

In addition some 1,000 Servicemen and Merchant Navy Seamen had to be ferried each way between Ascension and the Falklands every month, demanding a further two chartered vessels – the *Uganda* and the *Cunard Countess*. The latter was later replaced by the ex-British Sealink ferry *St Edmund*, subsequently bought by the Ministry of Defence, renamed the *Keren* and operated by Blue Star Ship Management Ltd.

Turning to accommodation, the seven strategically-sited camps for the troops deployed out of Stanley alongside the Settlements, designed to give the men 'a solid roof over their heads instead of tent covers', were a first priority. General Thorne laid down the target date of April, 1983, for these to be completed, just before the onset of the Antarctic winter – a date later amended to May. Fully equipped with water, power and sewerage, based on 'Portakabins' for accommodation and other types of prefabricated structure for other buildings, they were completed in early May.

The next major leap forward in troop accommodation for those based in the Stanley area was the introduction of 'Coastels'. These are fully self-contained floating accommodation vessels designed for use in inshore waters and having a 'walk on/walk off' link to the shore. In reality they are huge flat-topped barges carrying multi-storey accommodation of cabins for some 900 men, with ablutions and lavatories, recreation and dining rooms, and kitchens. Electric power, heating, fresh water, ventilation, sewerage and laundry facilities are all on board.

The first Coastel taken into use was the *Safe Dominia*, chartered from Sweden, moored in the Canache. The second, similarly chartered, was the *Safe Esperia*, which included four squash courts, two swimming pools, a gym, and a NAAFI. Both these vessels are operated by Swedish-based Consafe under a pooling arrangement with Bibby Line.

Pursuivant (5,500 tons), the third unit taken into use, was built by a consortium initiated by North Venture Shipping Agencies Ltd including firms from Hull, Lowestoft and Penryn in Cornwall. The first British-built floating five-level accommodation barge for nearly 900 Servicemen, it left for the Falklands in mid-July, 1983, and is managed by United Towing Ltd of Hull and crewed by Servicemen.

The long and very laborious operating of Stanley's port by lighterage came to an end with the opening on 26 April, 1984, of a £23 million floating port and warehouse complex – called 'Flexiport' – which provided a 'ship alongside offloading capability'. Officially known to the Ministry of Defence as the Falkland Intermediate Port and Storage System (FIPASS), and built by ITM (Offshore) Ltd and its subcontractors, it consists of six linked standard 800-ft-long North Sea oil rig support barges, each supporting a quay and securely moored to special piles called dolphins. Four of the barges carry warehouses; there is also refrigerated storage, accommodation, offices and messing facilities for 200 people. Sections of Flexiport were shipped out to Stanley from the Belfast shipyard of Harland and Wolff.

Positioned not far from the Services' 'Coastels', Flexiport's quay is connected to the shore via a linkspan (in reality a seventh barge) and a 623-ft-long causeway which takes two-way traffic of thirty ton vehicles. A new road to connect with the end of the causeway, using over 4,000 tons of local quartzite rock, was constructed by 37 Regiment, Royal Engineers. FIPASS accepts vessels of up to 1,000 ft long and is designed to withstand winds of 100 knots.

The complex, estimated to have saved up to £15,000 per day through release of chartered vessels retained for store-holding and refrigeration purposes, is operated by the Falklands Logistic Battalion.

The first members of the Women's Services to arrive in the Aftermath were fourteen officers and Servicewomen of the Queen Alexandra's Royal Army Nursing Corps led by their Matron, Major Margaret Nesbitt. Members of 2 Field Hospital, they had sailed from Britain on the *Rangatira* on 19 June and arrived on 11 July, 1982.

The Field Hospital's original tentage had been lost when the *Atlantic Conveyor* was sunk. Because the only alternative accommodation available to it would have been new tentage, the Falkland Islands Government invited the Field Hospital to share the facilities of the civilian King Edward Memorial Hospital in Stanley – 'old and cramped and inadequate', according to one civilian authority, as it was. The offer was gratefully accepted.

This was not only the only hospital in the Islands, but doubled up as the Islands' only Old People's Home. Appreciating the problem, the elderly residents volunteered to give up their single rooms to move in two, three and even four to a room in order to free space for military medical use. 'It was their way of showing how grateful they were to their liberators', I was told.

This dual occupancy of the Hospital gave rise to the affectionate name being bestowed on it of 'The QUAAKE' ('the Queen Alexandra and King Edward').

Set a little back from the Stanley waterfront, and adjoining the start of the Darwin track, the Hospital was a long 'T'-shaped bungalow-style building, white-roofed and clearly identifiable by its large 'Red Cross' marking. Old and cramped, and despite the broken windows, leaking radiators, and shortage of linen, it nevertheless possessed the vital assets of any hospital – beds, warmth, medical equipment and, above all, skilled doctors and nurses. The arrival of 2 Field Hospital, with its RAMC and especially its QARANC nursing staff, was an excellent tonic for morale.

The cases which passed though its doors varied very widely, from blast injuries involving amputations to severe cases of 'Galtieri's Revenge', later on turning to an increase in burns and fractures. The 'QAs' lived aboard the *Rangatira*, mastered the art of the rope ladders, and usually commuted to work by landing craft.

Sadly, part of 'The QUAAKE' was destroyed by fire in 1983, but now a new Hospital is being built to replace it. The Field Hospital has changed its number from '2' to '22', but the 'QA' strength has been maintained at around six officers and eight Servicewomen, including dental-trained girls, serving on a four-month tour.

Latterly, patients have included men and women from the Services, as well as Falkland Islanders, civilian contractors, even Russian and Chinese fishermen, and, to date, one genuine explorer!

The first 'Wren' to be posted to the Falkland Islands in the Aftermath was Second Officer Heather Robinson who arrived in the autumn of 1982 to fill a special post on the Commander British Forces's Staff. She was relieved in January, 1983, by Second Officer Marion Greenway who returned to Britain in May and was not replaced.

In January, 1984, 'Wren' Petty Officer Di Keeling, a writer/general, was posted as Personal Assistant to the Commander; she returned home in early May of the same year, having been relieved by a male Army Staff-Sergeant. These first trial appointments having been completed, there followed a long 'gap' with no member of the Women's Royal Naval Service in the Falkland Islands.

Following a new policy decision by the Royal Navy, however, a permanent WRNS presence in the South Atlantic was established in November, 1985, on the basis of regular four-month tours. Second Officer Sandy Pearce was posted out that month; six women ratings followed her in January, 1986, and a further four in March, 1986. The same level of WRNS representation at around eight to ten all ranks has been maintained ever since. The officers have been employed variously on operations and intelligence duties, as Secretary to the Senior Naval Officer Falkland Islands (SNOFI), and Second Officer Caroline Tapsell was ADC to the Commander; the ratings have come from the communications, radar and secretariat specialist trades.

Commanded by Captain Diana Foster, twenty Women's Royal Army Corps members, all volunteers, flew out in July, 1983, for a four-month experimental tour to undertake clerical, postal, supply and catering duties with units in the Stanley area. The idea proved successful, and in December a second team, commanded by Captain Lorna McGregor, replaced them. The WRAC presence has been maintained ever since.

Flight-Lieutenant Sandi Singleton and three members of the Women's Royal Air Force were posted to the Falkland Islands on 18 August, 1984. She worked at RAF Stanley, and the girls at HQ British Forces Falkland Islands where they were communications operators and 'P & A' clerks. The party returned to Britain in November after their four-month tour.

In September, 1985, a WRAF Flight was established at the new Mount Pleasant airfield which was soon built up to a strength of three to four Officers and twenty-four Other Ranks, plus a further three working at HQ BFFI. The spread of their specialist duties included Assistant Traffic Controllers, telecommunications operators, 'P & A' clerks, painters and finishers, medical assistants, suppliers, drivers, cooks and stewardesses. The WRAF's aim is to maintain a Flight strength 'down South' of some fifty all ranks. One nurse from the Princess Mary's Royal Air Force Nursing Service is permanently deployed for duty in the Medical Reception Station.

In December, 1983, the first NAAFI girls, six volunteers, flew out to the Falkland Islands on a five-month tour to run clubs and bars in the Garrison. They were the first women to be recruited into the NAAFI's operational unit – The Royal Army Ordnance Corps (Expeditionary Forces Institute) commanded by Major Bob Randerson – since 1949; and the first to wear military uniform since 1945. The experiment was an instant success and the number of EFI girls was consequently increased to around twenty-five, a level which has been maintained ever since.

An interesting reflection on the Falklands NAAFI duty is that some of the EFI girls have volunteered for a twelve-month tour, and some are now returning there for their third tour.

NAAFI runs shops on all three Coastels as well as other clubs and shops on the Islands proper, principally at Mount Pleasant and Fox Bay. Two EFI girls run the Rest and Recreation ('R & R') Centre at San Carlos Settlement. The NAAFI establishments at Port Howard, Goose Green and San Carlos have been closed. There has never been one in South Georgia where the small Garrison has instead run its own company club.

The RAF NAAFI club at Mount Pleasant, opened in April, 1986, soon proved to be insufficient on its own to cope with the enormous demand put upon it; its takings were more than £20,000 per week! A new Army club, opened there in December, 1986, should now ease the pressure. NAAFI have also opened a new Bulk Issue Store at Mount Pleasant, to which stores will now have to come from the Falklands Intermediate Port and Storage System (FIPASS) via Mare Harbour and thence by road. The opening of these latest NAAFI facilities has meant the closure of the clubs at Kelly's Garden and at Navy Point, and of the Kelper Store.

In March, 1983, civilians Midge Buckett and Crystal Mercer started up Stanley's first mobile fish-and-chip shop.

The Falkland Islands Broadcasting Service has been dramatically developed since 1982 in parallel with the Forces' radio broadcasting requirements. On 4 December, 1986, a new taped television service for the Falkland Islands Garrison was inaugurated. Run by the Services Sound and Vision Corporation from their new broadcasting complex at Mount Pleasant, it transmits a blend of taped current BBC and ITV programmes for four hours daily. There is even a nine-hole golf course by Stanley, twinned with the Salisbury and South Wilts Golf Club. Warrant Officer Class 2 T. Collins of the Royal Engineers recently wrote in *The Sapper* that 'The fairways are covered with craters – courtesy of the Task Force – which are in lieu of bunkers. Depending on the weather, you can have a fun day hacking your way through the tussock grass and bouncing off the rocks.' It must be the most southerly golf course in the world!

The first golf course at Stanley was laid out in 1922, according to a local authority. It was rebuilt into the current course in 1939 by a group of Anglo-Argentinian rugger players from the Tabarin night club in Buenos Aires: they had come to the Falkland Islands to help defend it against the Germans in the Second World War. Some of the holes had to be re-aligned in late 1982 to avoid the British shell craters and the Argentine ammunition dumps.

The vital importance of preserving the Island's very special wild life has been a prime concern of each Commander British Forces Falkland Islands.

In late 1983 a twenty-minute video film of South Atlantic wild life was produced, which has since been shown to all Servicemen before they leave Britain. Put together from the excellent material shot by the naturalist photographer Cindy Buxton – who with Annie Price survived in South Georgia throughout the Argentine occupation there – it clearly demonstrates the reasons for the troops to take particular care to avoid upsetting the Falkland Islands' unique wild life.

For instance it shows Great Skuas robbing temporarily unguarded penguins' nests of both eggs and young chicks. It also contains some delightful shots of Rock Hopper penguins comically sliding and somersaulting their way towards the sea and then, just like so many humans, dithering at the rock 'diving board' edge before taking a header into the breakers below.

The film puts over three golden rules which the Defence Ministry and Falkland wild life conservationists suggest should govern the troops' behaviour. First – do not chase anything: second – do not disturb anything:

and third – 'if you wish to photograph anything, sit down, stay quiet, and let the wild life come to you: it's so tame, it probably will'.

Communication networks, both civil and military, have been considerably improved over recent years. Cable and Wireless Ltd put in an Earth Satellite Station which for the first time allowed people in the Falklands to dial telephone numbers in Britain directly.

Introduction of The Falkland Islands Trunk System (FITS) revolutionized military communications throughout the territory. Its microwave radio container sub-system, made by Marconi Communications Ltd, interconnects remote military sites with the centre in Stanley from whence, if necessary, they could be routed via the Earth Satellite to the Ministry of Defence in London.

For many of the families and relatives of those who were killed in the campaign, the most significant and poignant Aftermath event was their pilgrimage to the Falklands in April, 1983.

Having flown from Britain to Uruguay on 6 April, the 545 mourners were taken from Montevideo to Stanley on board the *Cunard Countess* which had been diverted for the occasion from its normal MOD Ascension–Falklands run.

On 10 April, 1983, they took part in a moving Service at the new War Memorial and War Cemetery at San Carlos, the latter having been relocated from its original site at Ajax Bay. The Civil Commissioner represented the Queen and the British Government; Field-Marshal Sir Edwin Bramall, then Chief of the Defence Staff, represented the British Armed Forces; and the address was given by the Right Reverend Stuart Snell, Bishop to the Forces.

The following day a Service was held in Falkland Sound in memory of those who died at sea. Later the relations visited Goose Green, Fitzroy and the other battlefields overlooking Stanley, whichever was personally special to them. The visit, as is only to be expected, was an extremely emotional one for all concerned. Before they sailed out of Stanley on 13 April, the visitors had met Sir Rex Hunt and many of the Falkland Islanders, and had seen for themselves the remote Islands for whose Britishness their loved ones had died.

Before the *Cunard Countess* had reached Montevideo on its return voyage, the feelings and closeness of those who had travelled on this Government-sponsored trip gave rise to the formation of the Falklands Families Association. A second pilgrimage took place in April, 1986, but this time the relatives were able to fly direct to the Falkland Islands in an RAF Tristar aircraft. A further visit is being planned for late in 1989. Currently the Chairman of the Falklands Families Association is Mr Des Keoghan, and his Vice-Chairman is Mrs Sara Jones, widow of Lieutenant-Colonel 'H' Jones, VC. A separate organization, the Association of Parents of Unmarried Sons killed in the Falklands, whose Chairman and Secretary are Mr Stockwell and Mrs J. Steward respectively, was also started on the *Cunard Countess* original return journey to Montevideo; some relatives belong to both Associations.

The Supplement to the *London Gazette* of 8 October, 1982, dated 11 October, published the Honours and Awards approved by the Queen for Service in the South Atlantic. The next day, 12 October, 1982, the City of London's 'Salute to the Task Force' took the form of a Parade March through the City from Armoury House to the Guildhall by representatives of all units of the Services which had participated, and from the Merchant Navy, with the Lord Mayor taking the Salute at the Mansion House. There were two Fly Pasts – the first by helicopters and the second by fixed wing aircraft of the types used in the Campaign. There followed luncheon in the Guildhall.

The Supplement to the *London Gazette* of 13 December, 1982, published on the 14th, contained the 'Despatch of Admiral Sir John Fieldhouse, Commander of the Task Force Operations in the South Atlantic April to June, 1982'.

In the House of Commons on 25 October, 1983, Mr Michael Heseltine, Secretary of State for Defence, announced the Queen's approval of the award of particular Battle Honours to ships and units of the three Services and the Merchant Navy; and on 30 July, 1984, he similarly announced the award of Theatre and Battle Honours to Regiments of the British Army.

Lastly, on Friday 14 June, 1985, the third anniversary of the Argentinian surrender in Stanley, the Queen unveiled the South Atlantic Campaign Memorial in the Crypt of St Paul's Cathedral. The Service in the Cathedral, of which the unveiling formed part, was attended by members of the Royal Family; the Prime Minister, Ministers and other political leaders; representatives of all the Services and the Merchant Navy, and of units and ships which had taken part in the Campaign; by 777 wives, children, parents and other relatives of those who died; and by representatives of the many welfare and other organizations which had supported the Task Force, a congregation of some 2,200 people.

The inscription on the striking Memorial of green Cumbrian slate, sculpted by Mr David Kindersley and dedicated by the Archbishop of Canterbury, is simply and fittingly headed:

IN HONOUR OF THE SOUTH ATLANTIC TASK FORCE
AND TO THE ABIDING MEMORY
OF ALL THOSE WHO GAVE THEIR LIVES

Underneath are listed alphabetically by Service – Royal Navy, Royal Marines, Royal Fleet Auxiliary, Army, Royal Air Force and Merchant Navy – the names of the 255 people who lost their lives. At the bottom, and separated by an outline map of the Falkland Islands, are inscribed in words the dates of the Campaign:

APRIL–JUNE

NINETEEN EIGHTY TWO

SOUTH GEORGIA

A small Garrison, found primarily by the British Army's Infantry Battalion on duty in the Falkland Islands, has been continuously stationed at the British Antarctic Survey's base at Grytviken ever since the Argentinian surrender of South Georgia by Captain Alfredo Astiz on 24 April, 1982.

Responsible for the defence of South Georgia, the Garrison sends out patrols to the other abandoned whaling stations of Leith, Stromness and Husvik.

Although there is a small quay at Grytviken, owing to the extremely steep and mountainous nature of its terrain South Georgia has never had an airfield of any kind. Looking to the unpredictable future of Antarctica, and indeed of the Falkland Islands, there is considerable attraction in South Georgia having some kind of airfield for both civilian and military use even if on account of the appalling weather it could not be open all the year round. To build and maintain one, however, would be extremely expensive and difficult, in political and economic terms, to justify.

Nevertheless, in 1983 an airfield reconnaissance was mounted.

24 August, 1983

A Joint Service Reconnaissance Team has recently investigated the possibility of constructing an airfield and an adjacent new military port and base in South Georgia. Some 700 miles east of the Falklands it is an island over which the Argentinians have never had even the basis of any sovereignty claim whatsoever. It has no indigenous human population.

The strategic concept of building an airfield on South Georgia was strongly advocated last summer in the immediate wake of Britain's South Atlantic victory. Some preliminary study was carried out, with British Antarctic Survey advice, and a candidate site was suggested west of Grytviken on one of the island's few stretches of narrow coastal plain which occur on its northern side.

Building any airfield on South Georgia would be difficult and very expensive, given the harshness of its steep terrain, the strong katabatic wind patterns and the sudden unpredictable changes of the weather from clear to instant 'white out' conditions. In winter, as I found out last year, one has to wear snow shoes to traverse the not-unusual 15 ft depth of snow.

The visit of this year's joint Navy/Army/Air Force Team – well briefed by the Royal Navy 1981/82 Expedition's leader and fully prepared for the hostile Antarctic conditions there – was preceded by intensive study of maps, air photographs and detailed analysis of all the available data. Some of the Team's members had previously worked on the reconnaissance of the Falkland Island's new airfield. The Army element was found by 62 (Commander Royal Engineers) Construction from Barton Stacey, Hants.

After flying to Stanley, the team embarked on HMS *Hecla* (1,915 tons) for the four-day voyage to South Georgia. On arrival the ship's 'Wasp' helicopter – christened Hector – was used exhaustively to make site reconnaissances at various points along the coast. Having finally selected one promising site, the Team was put ashore, its Land-Rover and Smalley excavator having been gingerly off-loaded from the ship on to a raft.

For seventeen days the Team worked ashore at a site on which probably no one had ever set foot before. It was kept under constant close surveillance throughout by King Penguins, Elephant and other types of seal. In the end a runway alignment was selected and the Team carried out a tacheometric and grid survey of the runway and of the proposed aircraft apron and permanent camp site areas. Vital soil samples were collected for laboratory analysis back in Britain.

In the meanwhile HMS *Hecla* carried out the necessary hydrographic work, and prepared a study of the sea approaches, anchorages, shore landing sites and the other essentials related to the naval side of creating a small airfield complex ashore.

Severe Antarctic blizzards, and the usual South Georgia winds, gusting up to over forty knots, made the Team's work very challenging. But, with the runway alignment finally set out, a Royal Air Force Hercules aircraft was guided in to make low passes to 'prove' the selected airfield's approaches feasible. The aircraft reciprocated by air-dropping welcome and urgent spares.

In appalling weather conditions, the Team and all the equipment were eventually safely re-embarked, and the detailed work on the possibilities which were reconnoitred is now continuing back in Britain.

No further action regarding an airfield on South Georgia has been taken since the Joint Service Reconnaissance Team's visit. However, in the late autumn of 1986 a detachment of Sappers from 25 Engineer Regiment started rebuilding the jetty at Grytviken – a task codenamed Operation JURAL.

The story of Sir Ernest Shackleton's escape with his Expedition in 1916 from the Weddell Sea pack ice to Elephant Island, and of his own incredible journey to and across South Georgia in order to seek rescue for his team left behind on Elephant Island, is one of the world's legendary feats of heroism.

The idea of re-tracing Shackleton's steps from King Haakon Bay to Stromness first came to Captain Roger Morgan-Grenville of 1st Battalion The Royal Green Jackets South Georgia Garrison (commanded by Major Christopher Mieville) after reading Shackleton's book *South*. It was crystallized into reality by a challenge from Major-General de la Billière, Commander British Forces Falkland Islands.

With the help of a plan of the route taken by Commander Malcolm Burley's Combined Services Expedition of 1964, the Garrison's experienced Royal Marine Arctic Warfare Instructor, Sergeant Derek Wilson, and a combined contingency 'back-up' of radios, a homing beacon, the frigate HMS *Berwick*, the RFA *Tidespring* and support helicopters, a patrol of eleven Green Jackets, Sergeant Wilson and RAMC doctor, Captain Peter Gilbert, set off from King Haakon Bay on 31 January, 1985, on what had now become Exercise GREEN SKUA.

In unexpectedly soft snow at the base of the Murray Snowfield, using their Hjelper Sledges was 'like towing a Morris Minor through porridge' so these were quickly put away. The patrol crossed the Trident Ridge, and on moving forward towards the Fortuna Glacier they soon found that they were not just crossing 'a huge frozen lake' as it had looked from afar, but an area where 'three glaciers converge on each other . . . crevassing is not restricted to one line, rather it appears to be a million giant broken lavatories moving slowly seaward.'

On the western final approach to the Fortuna, the patrol gained temporary shelter for a 'brew up' in the remains of a Wessex helicopter of C Flight 845 Naval Air Squadron still lying where it crashed during the exceptionally brave rescue attempt of a patrol from D Squadron SAS during the Falklands Campaign.

The patrol eventually entered Stromness thirty-one hours, forty minutes after leaving King Haakon Bay, an excellent feat. Sir Ernest Shackleton had taken thirty-six hours but, as Roger Morgan-Grenville pointed out, in 1916 the journey had never been done before; the only charts available to him were 'hideously inadequate' for land navigation; prolonged hardship had taken its physical toll; there was no back-up and there could be no second attempt.

Captain Morgan-Grenville's account of his patrol in The Royal Green Jackets *Regimental Chronicle* ends with the delightfully underwritten conclusion:

'It is now a mini-expedition well within the capabilities of the resident military detachment based at Grytviken – a couple of day's entertainment in some three-dimensional and very attractive countryside. It was not ever so: the last party but one to walk from King Haakon Bay to Stromness could have testified to that.'

ASCENSION

In Ascension, the vital staging base en route to the Falkland Islands in constant use since the Spring of 1982, a new Services' accommodation complex was completed in early 1984 at Travellers' Hill, near Georgetown. It replaced a variety of improvised accommodation, including the well-known 'Concertina City' of prefabricated quarters, made of a type of corrugated material which telescopes almost flat for freighting.

At Wideawake airfield, a major project was also undertaken to enlarge the apron and extend the taxiways. These improvements were necessary in order to ease the problem of handling the wide-bodied transport aircraft due to stage through Ascension en route to the Falklands once the Mount Pleasant airfield opened. The cost of the Ministry of Defence's capital improvements to the Garrison's facilities over three years was estimated at £70 million.

Twenty members of the Women's Royal Air Force, under the command of Flight Lieutenant Jane Ward, were deployed to Ascension in April, 1984 – a new 'first' in overseas postings for them. Their tasks included air traffic control, telecommunications, supply, driving, clerical and stewardess duties. A Princess Mary's Royal Air Force Nursing Service nurse was similarly deployed for duty in the Medical Reception Station. No members of either the Women's Royal Navy Service or the Women's Royal Army Corps have yet been stationed in Ascension.

In April, 1984, there was a brief but unusual threat to the Falklands supply 'air bridge' operating between Ascension and Stanley. It came not from the Argentinians but from huge numbers of migratory locusts, and Dr Nick Burgess, the Ministry of Defence's Senior Entomologist, was flown out to deal with it.

Normally solitary insects, the locusts, due to unusually heavy rains, had suddenly showed signs of swarming, a process that could result in a density of fifty million to the square mile. If this were to include Wideawake airfield, it could quickly clog up aircraft air intakes, engines, turbines and external controls – effectively grounding the entire RAF fleet and thus cutting the Falkland Islands Garrison's umbilical cord.

This locust phenomenon hits Ascension on a roughly twenty-five year cycle, the last recorded instances being in 1934 and 1958. On this occasion, however, the potential threat had been spotted in time, special equipment was positioned at Ascension, orders given for what to do and the threat safely contained.

The Royal Air Force are also concerned with one other unusual responsibility. It is taking great care to minimize the effect of Garrison development on the large numbers of Brazilian Green Turtles which come ashore on the Island's Long Beach each year to lay and bury their eggs in the sand.

Annex A

Mines used by the Argentine forces in the Falkland Islands Campaign

1   *Argentine FMK1 anti-personnel mine.* Made of plastic, this mine contains 152 grams of explosive and has a removable detecting ring. It may be used with trip wires to operate as a booby trap. Its diameter is eighty-two mm, and its detonating pressure is approximately fifty kilograms.

2   *Argentine FMK3 anti-tank mine.* Made of plastic, and with a diameter of 240 mm, this mine contains 6.1 kilograms of explosives. It is initiated by an inserted FMK1 anti-personnel mine specially set to detonate at approximately 150–280 kilograms.

3   *Spanish P4B anti-personnel mine.* This is a plastic mine containing 100 grams of explosive. It has a diameter of seventy-seven mm, and a detonating pressure of approximately ten to fourteen kilograms.

4   *Spanish C3B anti-tank mine.* Sometimes found linked to large buried bombs, this plastic mine contains five kilograms of explosive. Its diameter is 270 mm and its detonating pressure is approximately ninety-one kilograms.

5   *Italian SB33 anti-personnel mine.* This plastic mine is dispensable by helicopter and, as a special aid to camouflage, its absorbent surface attracts fine dust particles from its surroundings. It has a diameter of ninety mm, an explosive content of thirty-five grams and is activated by a pressure of approximately eight kilograms.

6   *Italian SB81 anti-tank mine.* Well waterproofed and dispensable by helicopter, this plastic mine detonates under pressure of approximately 150–350 kilograms. It has a diameter of 240 mm and contains two kilograms of explosive. A good 'floater' for the tide to shift along the shore.

7   *Israeli No 4 anti-personnel mine.* This is a box-type mine, very similar to an American design. It is normally used as a booby trap using push or pull switches, or trip wire. It is detectable, 145 mm long, and has an explosive content of 155 grams. The detonating pressure is approximately eight kilograms.

8   *Israeli No 6 anti-tank mine.* This detectable metallic mine is almost identical to the Soviet TM 46. Its diameter is 300 mm, the explosive content six kilograms and it is activated by a pressure of approximately 260 kilograms.

9   *United States M1 anti-tank mine*. This is a detectable metallic mine from the Second World War of 1944 vintage. Its diameter is 203 mm, the explosive content 2.72 kilograms and the detonating pressure is approximately 113–226 kilograms.

The detonating pressures given are only approximate because a number of different factors can affect the actual pressure required to set off any particular mine in varying circumstances.

Annex B

Standard Argentine minelaying procedure

The standard Argentine drill was to lay eight or sixteen mines (*minas*) in a row, with one mine buried or laid directly under each of the eight small circular spacing rings which were unequally spread out and rigidly fixed (up to four metres apart) along a special minelaying line.

Three rows of mines constituted a normal Mine Panel (*Trecho de Faja*), which covered an area approximately thirty-two metres long by twenty-five metres deep, but sometimes there were six rows. The mine rows in the Panel were staggered, with the aim of increasing the likelihood of a person or vehicle setting off a mine when crossing the minefield.

At each end of a minelaying line were three separate metal D-rings. The staggering was achieved by starting the successive mine rows from different D-rings.

From two to six Mine Panels, laid in a straight or dog-legged line, constituted a Minefield (*Campo Minado*). Being only one Mine Panel deep, however, the minefields were much 'thinner' than British ones. Normal markings varied from low pickets or a single low strand of barbed wire, on the home side only, up to a proper two-strand wire fence.

For recording purposes, Mine Panel Points of Origin were linked by magnetic bearings and distance to Intermediate Points, which in turn were similarly linked to Base or Reference Points (*Punto Base*). Infantry 'safe lanes' through the minefield were made two metres wide and vehicle lanes four to eight metres wide.

ANNEX C

Argentine equipment collected in as at 26 July, 1982

1 *Guns*
   a Five Oerlikon 35 mm twin-barrelled air defence guns.
   b Three Rheinmetall 20 mm air defence guns.
   c Ten 105 mm pack howitzers.
   d Four 155 mm howitzers.
2 *Missiles and Launchers*
   a One Roland missile launcher (plus missiles).
   b Four Tigercat missile launchers (plus missiles).
   c One Exocet land-based launcher (with four missiles).
   d SAM 7 launchers (with missiles).
   e Fifteen 120 mm RCL (plus missiles).
3 *Radars*
   a One Super Fledermaus radar.
   b Three Skyguard radars.
   c Two ELTA and RASIT radars.
   d Two Radar Cabins.
4 *Aircraft*
   a Seven Pucara aircraft.
   b Two Augusta 109 helicopters.
   c Five Iroquois helicopters.
   d One Puma helicopter.
   e Two Chinook helicopters.
5 *Armoured Cars*
   Twelve Panhard ERV 90.
6 *Soft-skin Vehicles*
   A minimum of fifty Mercedes $\frac{1}{2}$ and $\frac{3}{4}$ ton trucks: ten Volkswagens: 45 assorted trucks and pick-ups.
7 *Small Arms* (Up to .5 inch Browning machine gun and including small mortars) 7,900 items.
8 *Communications and Electronic Warfare Equipment* Various.
9 *Surveillance Equipment*
   Night vision goggles, thermal imagers and portable surveillance radars.

This list does not include large quantities yet to be brought in from a number of known gun positions near Stanley, from outlying areas of East Falkland, from West Falkland, the battle areas or the uncleared minefield areas.

[In December, 1984, the Royal Air Force announced that a new Royal Auxiliary Air Force Regiment Squadron was being specially raised and equipped with anti-aircraft guns. It would form at R A F Waddington, Lincolnshire on 1 April, 1985, and be equipped with Twin 35 mm Oerlikon guns, and their associated Skyguard fire control system, captured from the Argentinians in the Falklands and refurbished to the latest operational standards. The acceptance of guns back into the R A F's current all-missile ground-based anti-aircraft weaponry was a change of policy largely influenced by lessons learnt in the Falklands campaign. The Squadron was duly formed.]

Annex D

The Falkland Islands airfield project at Mount Pleasant

The story of the Falklands airfield, conceived in June, 1982, and termed the largest and most unusual project ever undertaken by the British construction industry, is one of persistent challenge and endeavour. I well remember the following month helicoptering low over one of the very few alternative sites which had been selected by the 'recce team' of Colonel Robin Jukes-Hughes, Royal Engineers, and Mr Maurice Chammings of the Property Services Agency. It was a slightly depressed but noticeably a flatter run of peat than any others en route to Goose Green – a wild empty area. On 12 May, 1985, on that same site and less than three years later – whilst serving in Falkland waters as the Lynx helicopter pilot of the Type 22 frigate HMS *Brazen* – HRH Prince Andrew officially opened the Mount Pleasant airfield.

Six successive 'pictures' of the project's development are reflected in the following 'pieces'.

3 August, 1983

The first major shipment of men, engineer plant and materials for the new £215 million strategic airfield for the Falklands is due to leave Britain in two ships in early September, the end of the South Atlantic winter.

An advance party of geologists and surveyors is flying down there this month to undertake the preliminary site work.

The Joint Venture Consortium of Laing – Mowlem – Amey Roadstone Construction was awarded the contract for the construction of a main and a secondary runway, taxiways and aircraft hardstandings. Also included is the necessary infrastructure of bulk fuel installations, hangars, technical repair and storage facilities, together with accommodation, messing and recreational facilities for the Royal Air Force at the Mount Pleasant site.

One of the first tasks for the workforce on its arrival is to provide access to the airfield construction site. This will be done by building a rock-filled causeway stretching out from the shore which will then be connected by a Bailey Bridge to a jetty head formed by an anchored vessel. Eight kilometres of road will then have to be built to connect the causeway to the airfield site itself.

The construction team, which will average 1,000 men, with a peak of 1,400, will live initially in a field camp of prefabricated units, with its own water supply plant, until more permanent housing arrangements arrive at the end of the year. Due to the remoteness of the site, the construction team will have to be both self-supporting and self-sufficient right from the start.

To date the Joint Venture Headquarters at Surbiton has received more than 6,000 applications from people keen to work on the project. Rates of pay will undoubtedly be high, but what these actually are the Consortium regard as 'confidential'.

11 August, 1983

A large fixed-price contract to design, manage and co-ordinate the supply and installation of all the Government-provided electronics and communication equipment for the new Falklands airfield at Mount Pleasant has just been awarded to Plessey Airports Ltd. A team of the Company's experts will shortly be leaving for the Falklands in order to survey the site and to establish the exact locations for the airfield's navigational aids and other communications systems.

In view of the special strategic considerations which apply to the South Atlantic Garrison's role, the Royal Navy, the Army and the Royal Air Force will all be involved in the specifications for the operational requirement for the subsequent complete design and, eventually, the continued operation and maintenance of the various installations. It is understood that this is the first time the Defence Ministry has awarded a contract for the technical co-ordination of work at a military airfield.

The Company will be responsible for the overall systems and installation design, and also such quality assurance as is necessary to establish Mount Pleasant as a fully operational airfield. The design programme will last for forty-four weeks, during which time Plessey Airports Ltd will be working very closely with the Government's Property Services Agency, and with the consortium of Laing–Mowlem–Amey Roadstone Construction.

12 August, 1984

The 'taking shape' of the new airfield at Mount Pleasant and the construction of a jetty by Port Stanley are two of the dramatic changes which have taken place in the Falklands over the past months.

All the basic foundations for the main airfield runway, which now stands out well from the air, have been completed, and considerable progress has been made with the associated accommodation. Part of the indoor recreational area is now functioning, and a visiting Combined Services Entertainment party was recently able to perform there under cover.

The 'alongside' jetty at Mare Harbour, to the south of the Airfield, is performing well and the 'haul road' connecting the two is now well established. Both the Property Services Agency and the Laing-Mowlem-Amey Roadstone Construction consortium are said to be very confident that an airfield 'with an initial operating capability' will open on target in April, 1985. This means that wide-bodied aircraft from Ascension can land, refuel and be 'turned round' for the flight back. Development to a fully operational airfield, with all its attendant operational facilities, will follow later.

27 February, 1985

A new era in the South Atlantic will open when, late this spring, the first wide-bodied RAF 'Tristar' aircraft lands on the Falkland Islands' new permanent airfield at Mount Pleasant.

Political and strategic considerations apart, the construction task alone has been a historic one of the greatest magnitude. Whereas the technical design aspects of the project were not difficult – so far it has involved 22,500 separate drawings with some 300 more to come – it was in overcoming the gigantic logistic problems associated with the sheer remoteness of the site where the secret of success has lain. One very important aim throughout, by both planners and constructors, has been to minimize wherever possible the damage done to the environment and to the Falkland Islands' exceptional wild life.

Mr John Parr-Burman, a director of Mowlem International and the Project Director for the Laing-Mowlem-ARC Joint Venture Company which won the contract, recently highlighted the scale of the project and the speed at which it has developed.

The Government's decision to build a new Falklands airfield was taken in July, 1982, and, after the initial joint military/Property Services Agency (PSA) ground reconnaissance had found a suitable site, the PSA started planning work on the project in September. In February, 1983, interested contractors were brought in, priced documents were due in by early May, and at the end of June the Government accepted the Joint Venture's tender for a contract initially worth about £200 million.

There are six key elements of the new airfield complex. First, an 8,500-foot flexible-construction main runway with hardened ends. Second, a 5,000 foot cross runway, also with hardened ends. Third, a circulating road system. Fourth, the support buildings which include two power stations, the air traffic control tower and fuel installations, a major sewerage plant and a double-storey RAF camp and a single storey Army camp, all with full accommodation and recreational facilities.

Fifth, a thirty-mile all-weather road connecting the new airfield, which is situated half-way between Stanley and Goose Green, with Stanley. Sixth, a six-mile permanent road connecting the airfield with, in the long term, a new port handling facility at East Cove/Mare Harbour which is being built by another contracting Joint Venture Company.

The total thirty-month-long project of two runways and 100,000 square metres of buildings are to be handed over to the PSA in two phases. Phase One, due for handing over on 15 April this year, comprises an operating airfield with a main runway, together with the power station, air traffic control tower, main hangar and light, half the aircraft apron area and a usable road into Stanley. A temporary jetty at East Cove, together with a temporary road connecting it to the site, are both already completed – they had to be built early on in order for construction of the airfield to start and subsequently develop.

Phase Two, comprising the remainder of the work, is due to be handed over to the PSA early in 1986.

Mr Parr-Burman stressed that the Mount Pleasant task was different in that, as far as he knew, it was the first fully operational airport constructed overseas by a totally UK-based work force, on a totally virgin site, where everything had had to be set up from scratch. Everyone working on it had had to be brought the 8,000 miles from Britain. Similarly, all the engineer plant (£25 millions worth of it), the equipment and the materials had had to be brought in with the exception of water and rock both of which were available aplenty in the Falklands. To date, over one and a quarter million tons of rock has been quarried locally and used on site.

It had also been a condition of the contract that the Joint Venture Company had had to establish its own lines of communications to the site, without using or even impinging on the existing Service communication links between Britain and the Falklands.

The first requirement of the construction task had been to build a jetty for unloading the shipping carrying all the early stores and engineer plant. This problem was solved by buying the 13,000-ton vessel *Artico* in Cadiz, altering her structurally and re-registering her as a British ship, the *Merchant Providence*, securing her to the mainland at East Cove in the Falklands, and connecting her up with a Bailey Bridge over which everything could be unloaded. A temporary base camp had then to be built for the men, and a working road carved out leading up to the airfield site.

The jetty was fully operational by 7 December, 1983, and, with the road done, full work started at Mount Pleasant on 1 January, 1984, only six months after the contract had been awarded.

The workforce, which has peaked to about 2,000 on site, with a monthly movement to and fro to Britain of some 300, sign on for a fourteen-month 'package', are on individual staff contracts and are paid in Britain. They fly out to South Africa, and from thence sail in the Joint Venture's chartered Cunard vessel, the ex-Danish ferry MV *England*, on the ten-day voyage to the jetty. To date, of those who have completed their contract, some fifty per cent have renewed them. 'There has never been any shortage of volunteers,' Mr Parr-Burman said.

The stores and freight, some 30,000 tons worth per month, are first carefully packaged at Dudley, Worcestershire. They are then sent by road for loading at Avonmouth into the Joint Venture's four 25,000 ton vessels on charter from Cenargo Ltd for the three-week voyage down to East Cove.

11 February, 1985

The decision taken in June, 1982, to build a new Falklands airfield 'was bold and courageous', said Mr Kenneth Baker MP, the Environment Secretary, introducing the London premiere of the excellent thirty-five minute film *80 Weeks to Touchdown* which tells the story of the remarkable achievement of turning a peat-ridden virgin site half a world away into a modern airfield.

The audience included representatives of all those who had been involved in creating the Mount Pleasant airfield – the Property Services Agency, the Defence Ministry, the Foreign Office and the Laing-Mowlem-ARC Joint Venture consortium who actually built it, together with their many supporting British contractors in engineering, transport and heavy plant, shipping and supply.

After a year's design work run by the PSA, the consortium's first ship arrived after an 8,000-mile voyage to unload the first bulldozer across an unprepared beach on 25 October, 1983. Using a peak UK labour force of 2,000, some 513,000 tons of materials, plant and equipment all of which had to be ferried out and 1.5 million tons of locally quarried stone, the airfield was opened to wide-bodied aircraft by HRH Prince Andrew on 12 May, 1985.

Mr Baker passed on to all concerned 'the personal congratulations' of Mrs Thatcher, as well as his own. This all-British project which was 'the largest and most unusual project ever undertaken by the British construction industry,' he said, 'reflected great credit on all involved. The key to building the airfield was its logistics; everything, down to the last screw, had had to be ordered months ahead.'

Mr Wynn Kenrick took over as Project Manager (UK) in the Spring of 1985 on return from his tour on site in the Falklands. In the event, largely because of the MOD's increased requirements, the amount of work to be carried out in Phase Two of the Mount Pleasant airfield complex was much greater than had been originally envisaged. In May, 1986, however, the secondary runway, the further taxiways and dispersal areas, the accommodation and a host of other buildings were handed over to the Property Services Agency by the Joint Venture Consortium.

Since May, 1986, further buildings have been handed over, one by one, as and when they were completed.

Speaking to me on 28 August, 1986, Mr Kenrick said that the whole Joint Venture operation was well into its 'demobilization' phase, and only four of the total of 120 buildings remained to be handed over. The site work force had been sharply reduced to only 250 men, whose time was occupied more by taking down temporary buildings than by handing over new ones.

The M V *England* ceased its trips ferrying the work force to and from South Africa in June, 1985. Its last one was something of a 'macro' trip to re-adjust the reducing numbers, so that the remaining changes and returns home could be fitted in to available capacity on the new wide-bodied aircraft flying into Mount Pleasant.

The Cenargo vessels on charter were released in June, 1986, having completed a total of thirty-four trips delivering 750,000 tons of freight.

The remaining stores still required at the site were routed 'down South' via the Government Freight Agency.

On 22 August the *Merchant Providence*, the original vessel which had taken the first load of stores down to the Falkland Islands and which had been converted itself into the unloading jetty for the whole project, sailed away from the Falklands for home.

There then remained only two tasks for the Joint Venture to complete. First, a contract to refurbish the contractor's accommodation to the uprated standards required by the MOD for Service use. Second, to complete the contract maintenance on all the buildings and installations handed over – basically six months on buildings, and twelve months on mechanical and electrical installations. By the end of October, 1986, the strength of the Joint Venture work force left on site for these tasks would number less than one hundred.

Philosophizing about the Mount Pleasant Airfield Project, Mr Kenrick stressed four key aspects which had made it such an unusual and challenging task.

First, Mount Pleasant was 'a green field site' job 8,000 miles away. It all depended on the logistics – 'everything from a bottle of washing-up liquid to a D8 bulldozer had to be brought in from the UK' – and the concept of using a vessel as the unloading jetty was an outstanding success.

Second, major defence 'works' normally take many years to build. Designs are well honed and tested, much is done consequentially, and there are long lead times for almost everything. In the event, there is time and opportunity to change or modify things if needs be. By contrast, because of the Falklands Campaign and its Aftermath, everything for the airfield project had had to be done in an exceptionally short space of time. The varied design work had to be completed very rapidly, as had all the normal 'pre-monitoring' that goes into such an enormous project. All the various aspects had to be 'concertina-ed' and undertaken virtually concurrently, with some inevitable overlap.

Third, timings were so tight that, once decisions had been made and were being implemented, there was no time or opportunity to change them. 'It was a question of having to get it right first time, or not at all.'

Fourth, the Ministry of Defence, the Property Services Agency, the Joint

Venture consortium's management, designers and procurers of equipment had to work together throughout under very exceptional circumstances.

Another important point Mr Kenrick made, not readily appreciated and not easy to make publicly, is that all the publicity and show of the official opening of the Mount Pleasant airfield on 14 May, 1985, was followed by a remarkable 'construction explosion' in the year to May, 1986. Far more permanent building work was carried out in this succeeding time than was ever done beforehand. This achievement was due to the fact that whereas earlier so much effort had had to be put into developing a virgin site into a working one, now the work force was at last able to operate from an established base, and 100 per cent manpower could be diverted into actual construction work.

Annex E

The Royal Navy

I – *Royal Navy, Royal Fleet Auxiliary, Royal Maritime Auxiliary Service and Merchant Navy Vessels on South Atlantic Deployment 14 June to 1 September 1982*

Ship		Dates	Captain/Master
HMS	*ACTIVE*	dep 24 July	Commander P. C. B. Canter RN
HMS	*ALACRITY*	dep 15 June	Commander C. J. S. Craig DSC RN
HMS	*AMAZON*	arr 16 August	Commander I. D. G. Garnett RN
HMS	*AMBUSCADE*	dep 15 July	Commander P. J. Mosse RN
HMS	*ANDROMEDA*	dep 28 August	Captain J. L. Weatherall RN
HMS	*ANTRIM*	dep 9 July	Captain B. G. Young DSO RN
HMS	*APOLLO*	arr 29 June	Commander C. M. Sloane RN
HMS	*ARGONAUT*	dep 16 June	Captain C. H. Layman DSO MVO RN
HMS	*ARROW*	dep 26 June	Commander P. J. Bootherstone DSC RN
HMS	*AVENGER*	dep 28 August	Captain H. M. White RN
HMS	*BACCHANTE*	arr 29 June dep 20 August	Commander A. C. Lyddon RN
HMS	*BATTLEAXE*	arr 21 August	Captain D. B. Nolan RN
HMS	*BIRMINGHAM*	arr 29 June	Commander J. E. Culley RN

Ship		Dates	Captain/Master
HMS	BRECON	arr 26 June	Commander P. A. Fish RN
HMS	BRILLIANT	dep 29 June	Captain J. F. Coward DSO RN
HMS	BRISTOL	throughout	Captain A. Grose RN
HMS	BROADSWORD	dep 8 July	Captain W. R. Canning DSO ADC RN
HMS	CARDIFF	dep 16 July	Captain M. G. T. Harris RN
HMS	CONQUEROR	dep 25 June	Commander C. L. Wreford-Brown DSO RN
HMS	CORDELLA	dep 20 July	Lieutenant-Commander M. C. G. Holloway RN
HMS	COURAGEOUS	dep in July	Commander R. T. N. Best RN
HMS	DANAE	arr 6 July	Commander G. L. D. W. Gough RN
HMS	DIOMEDE	arr 6 July	Commander W. L. T. Peppe RN
HMS	DUMBARTON CASTLE	dep 5 August	Lieutenant-Commander N. D. Wood RN
HMS	ENDURANCE	dep 4 August	Captain N. J. Barker CBE RN
HMS	EXETER	dep 16 July	Captain H. M. Balfour MVO RN
HMS	FARNELLA	dep 20 July	Lieutenant R. J. Bishop RN
HMS	FEARLESS	dep 4 July	Captain E. J. S. Larken DSO RN
HMS	GLAMORGAN	dep 29 June	Captain M. E. Barrow DSC ADC RN
HMS	HECLA	dep 11 July	Captain G. L. Hope RN
HMS	HERALD	dep 5 July	Captain R. L. C. Halliday RN
HMS	HERMES	dep 11 July	Captain L. E. Middleton DSO RN

Ship		Dates	Captain/Master
HMS	*HYDRA*	throughout	Commander R. J. Campbell RN
HMS	*ILLUSTRIOUS*	arr 21 August	Captain J. C. K. Slater LVO RN
HMS	*INTREPID*	dep 6 July	Captain P. G. V. Dingemans DSO RN
HMS	*INVINCIBLE*	dep 28 August	Captain J. J. Black DSO MBE RN
HMS	*JUNELLA*	dep 20 July	Lieutenant M. Rowledge RN
HMS	*LEDBURY*	arr 26 June	Lieutenant-Commander A. Rose RN
HMS	*LEEDS CASTLE*	dep 5 August	Lieutenant-Commander C. F. B. Hamilton RN
HMS	*MINERVA*	dep 23 July	Commander S. H. G. Johnson RN
HMS	*NORTHELLA*	dep 20 July	Lieutenant J. P. S. Greenop RN
HMS	*ONYX*	dep in July	Lieutenant-Commander A. P. Johnson RN
HMS	*PENELOPE*	dep 31 August	Commander P. V. Rickard RN
HMS	*PICT*	dep 20 July	Lieutenant-Commander D. G. Garwood RN
HMS	*PLYMOUTH*	dep 29 June	Captain D. Penteath DSO RN
HMS	*SOUTHAMPTON*	arr 29 June	Captain H. G. de Courcy-Ireland RN
HMS	*VALIANT*	dep in July	Commander T. M. Le Marchand RN
HMS	*WARSPITE*	arr in July	Commander J. G. F. Cooke RN
HMS	*YARMOUTH*	dep 16 July	Commander A. Morton DSC RN
RFA	*APPLELEAF*	throughout	Captain G. P. A. MacDougall RFA

Ship		Dates	Captain/Master
RFA	*BAYLEAF*	throughout	Captain A. E. T. Hunter RFA
RFA	*BLUE ROVER*	dep 9 July	Captain J. D. Roddis RFA
RFA	*BRAMBLELEAF*	arr 16 August	Captain J. H. Armstrong RFA
HMS	*ENGADINE*	dep 16 July	Captain D. F. Freeman RFA
RFA	*FORT AUSTIN*	dep 20 June	Commodore S. C. Dunlop CBE DSO RFA
RFA	*FORT GRANGE*	throughout	Captain D. G. M. Averill CBE RFA
RFA	*OLMEDA*	dep 1 July	Captain A. P. Overbury OBE RFA
RFA	*OLNA*	throughout	Captain J. A. Bailey RFA
RFA	*OLWEN*	arr 28 June	Captain J. H. McLoughlin RFA
RFA	*PEARLEAF*	dep 3 July	Captain J. McCulloch RFA
RFA	*PLUMLEAF*	dep 20 June	Captain R. W. M. Wallace RFA
RFA	*REGENT*	throughout	Captain J. Logan RFA
RFA	*RESOURCE*	dep 9 July	Captain B. A. Seymour RFA
RFA	*SIR BEDIVERE*	throughout	Captain P. J. McCarthy OBE RFA
RFA	*SIR GERAINT*	dep 9 July	Captain D. E. Lawrence DSC RFA
RFA	*SIR LANCELOT*	throughout	Captain C. A. Purtcher-Wydenbruck OBE RFA
RFA	*SIR PERCIVAL*	dep 8 July	Captain A. F. Pitt DSC RFA
RFA	*SIR TRISTRAM*	throughout	No Captain. Severely damaged and initially used only for some

Ship		Dates	Captain/Master
			accommodation, the *Sir Tristram* was shipped back to Britain in mid-1983 in the Heavy Lift Vessel *Dan Lifter*
RFA	*STROMNESS*	dep 8 July	Captain J. B. Dickinson OBE RFA
RFA	*TIDEPOOL*	dep 30 July	Captain J. W. Gaffrey RFA
RFA	*TIDESPRING*	dep 10 July	Captain S. Redmond RFA
RMAS	*GOSSANDER*	throughout	Captain A. MacGregor
RMAS	*TYPHOON*	throughout	Captain J. N. Morris
MV	*ANCO CHARGER*	dep 3 August	Captain B. Hatton
MV	*ASTRONOMER*	arr 16 June	Captain H. S. Braden
SS	*ATLANTIC CAUSEWAY*	dep 20 July	Captain M. H. C. Twomey
MV	*AVELONA STAR*	arr 21 June	Captain H. Dyer
MV	*BALDER LONDON*	arr 14 June	Captain K. J. Wallace
MV	*BALTIC FERRY*	throughout	Captain E. Harrison
MV	*BRITISH AVON*	arr 25 June	Captain J. W. M. Guy
MV	*BRITISH DART*	dep 18 June	Captain J. A. N. Taylor
MV	*BRITISH ENTERPRISE III*	dep 13 August	Captain D. Grant
MV	*BRITISH ESK*	arr 27 June	Captain G. Barber
MV	*BRITISH TAMAR*	throughout	Captain W. H. Hare
MV	*BRITISH TAY*	arr 5 July	Captain P. T. Morris
MV	*BRITISH TEST*	dep 20 June	Captain T. A. Oliphant
MV	*BRITISH TRENT*	dep 23 June arr 23 July	Captain P. R. Walker
MV	*BRITISH WYE*	dep 29 June	Captain D. M. Rundell OBE
SS	*CANBERRA*	dep 3 July	Captain W. Scott-Masson CBE
MV	*CEDAR BANK*	arr 3 July	Captain R. F. Whitehead

Ship		Dates	Captain/Master
MV	*CONTENDER BEZANT*	dep 13 July	Captain A. MacKinnon
MV	*EBURNA*	dep 19 July	Captain J. C. Beaumont
MV	*ELK*	dep 4 July	Captain J. P. Morton CBE
MV	*EUROPIC FERRY*	dep 6 July	Captain C. J. C. Clark OBE
MV	*FORT TORONTO*	throughout	Captain R. I. Kinnier
MV	*G. A. WALKER*	arr 22 June	Captain E. C. Metham
MV	*GEESTPORT*	dep 11 August	Captain G. F. Foster
CS	*IRIS*	throughout	Captain G. Fulton
MT	*IRISHMAN*	throughout	Captain W. Allen
MV	*LAERTES*	arr 17 June dep 12 August	Captain H. T. Reid
MV	*LYCAON*	throughout	Captain H. R. Lawton
MV	*MONSUNEN*	throughout	Captain G. Betts – but see special note about this vessel at the end of this schedule
MV	*MYRMIDON*	arr 15 July	Captain D. T. MacLachlan
MV	*NORDIC FERRY*	throughout	Captain R. Jenkins
MV	*NORLAND*	dep 4 July	Captain M. Ellerby CBE
TEV	*RANGATIRA*	arr 30 June	Captain D. Liddell
MV	*ST EDMUND*	throughout	Captain M. J. Stockman
RMS	*ST HELENA*	arr 26 June dep 29 August	Captain L. M. Smith
MT	*SALVAGEMAN*	throughout	Captain A. J. Stockwell
MV	*SAXONIA*	dep 20 June	Captain H. Evans
MV	*SCOTTISH EAGLE*	throughout	Captain A. Terras
MV	*STENA INSPECTOR*	arr 20 June	Captain D. Ede
MV	*STENA SEASPREAD*	dep 1 August	Captain N. Williams
MV	*STRATHEWE*	arr mid July dep 8 August	Captain S. T. S. Household
MV	*TOR CALEDONIA*	dep 9 August	Captain A. Scott
SS	*UGANDA*	dep 28 July	Captain J. G. Clark

Ship		Dates	Captain/Master
MV	*WIMPEY SEA HORSE*	throughout	Captain M. Slack OBE
MT	*YORKSHIREMAN*	throughout	Captain P. Rimmer

Some ships' published arrival/departure dates vary slightly, depending upon which set of records are consulted. The Captains are shown with their Falklands Honours and Awards.

MV Monsunen

The MV *Monsunen* (315 tons) was a coaster employed by the Falkland Islands Company prior to the Argentine invasion as a shifter of general cargo between and around the Islands. Captured and used by the Argentinians, she was on a run from Darwin to Stanley on 25 May when she was intercepted by HMS *Brilliant's* Lynx helicopter in Choiseul Sound. With the aid of the frigate HMS *Yarmouth*, she was forced aground in Lively Sound, and was subsequently taken to Darwin by the Argentinians.

Recaptured by the British in early June, following the capture of Darwin, she was requisitioned by the Royal Navy and, after emergency repairs, operated by a combined RN/Civilian crew. Later surveyed by the Task Force's MV *Stena Seaspread*, the MV *Monsunen* was handed back to her original civilian Master (Captain George Betts) and his crew on 11 July, and returned to general cargo duties in the area. The vessel had to go into dry dock in Montevideo in 1986, but has recently resumed her duties in the Falkland Islands.

II – Royal Naval Air Squadrons serving in the South Atlantic in the period 14 June–1 September, 1982.

Squadron	Aircraft	Commanding Officer	Notes
737	Wessex	Lieutenant-Commander M. S. Tennant RN	Various Ship's Flights
800	Sea Harrier	Lieutenant-Commander A. D. Auld	HMS *Hermes*
801	Sea Harrier	Lieutenant-Commander N. D. Ward/A. R. W. Ogilvy RN	HMS *Invincible*

Squadron	Aircraft	Commanding Officer	Notes
809	Sea Harrier	Lieutenant-Commander T. J. H. Gedge RN	HMS *Illustrious*
814	Sea King	Lieutenant-Commander R. M. Turner RN	HMS *Illustrious*
815	Lynx	Lieutenant-Commander R. I. Money RN	Various Ship's Flights
820	Sea King	Lieutenant-Commander R. J. S. Wykes-Sneyd RN	HMS *Invincible*
824 (A, C, D Flights)	Sea King	Lieutenant-Commander I. Thorpe/D. J. Ackland RN	Special Falkland Islands Detachment: HMS *Invincible*, RFA's *Regent* and *Fort Grange*
825	Sea King	Lieutenant-Commander H. S. Clark RN	San Carlos FOB etc.
826	Sea King	Lieutenant-Commander D. J. S. Squier RN	HMS *Hermes*
829	Wasp	Lieutenant-Commander M. J. Mullane RN	Various Ship's Flights
845	Wessex	Lieutenant-Commander R. J. Warden RN	Various Ship's Flights
846	Sea King	Lieutenant-Commander S. C. Thornewill RN	HMS *Hermes*/Navy Point
847	Wessex	Lieutenant-Commander M. D. Booth RN	Various operations ashore
848	Wessex	Lieutenant-Commander D. E. P. Baston RN	RFA's *Regent*, *Olna*, *Olwen*
899	Sea Harrier	Lieutenant-Commander J. Gunning RN	Back up for 800, 801 and 809 Squadrons

It is quite impossible in one simple table to portray the very complex permutations and combinations of attachments and detachments of Flights, let alone of individual aircraft – not only from Britain but also between Squadrons afloat and ashore in the South Atlantic – which characterized the deployment of R N Air Squadrons in the early Aftermath period: and later complicated the pattern of their return to Britain on board so many different ships. The above table is therefore only a rough guide towards the reality of locations and deployments; dates have been omitted as being far too complex for simple presentation. For those interested in the actual detail of every Royal Navy (and indeed Army and Royal Air Force) aircraft deployed in the South Atlantic, reference should be made to the very comprehensive *'Falklands – The Air War'* published in 1986 by the British Aviation Research Group.

III – *Royal Marines units in the South Atlantic during the period 14 June – 1 September, 1982*

Royal Marines units of 3 Commando Brigade, commanded by Brigadier J. H. A. Thompson O B E, all left the South Atlantic for Britain soon after the Argentine Surrender. Departure details for the principal units are given below: those for the Army's units serving in the Brigade are given in the Army Annex.

1 *3 Commando Brigade Headquarters and Signal Squadron* (Major R. L. C. Dixon R M)
   Sailed from Stanley aboard S S *Canberra* on 25 June.
2 *40 Commando* (Lieutenant-Colonel M. P. J. Hunt R M)
   Sailed from San Carlos aboard S S *Canberra* on 24 June.
3 *42 Commando* (Lieutenant-Colonel N. F. Vaux R M)
   The Commando, less M Company, sailed from Stanley aboard S S *Canberra* on 25 June. M Company (Major J. M. G. Sheridan R M) sailed from South Georgia aboard the M V *Nordic Ferry*.
4 *45 Commando* (Lieutenant-Colonel A. F. Whitehead R M)
   Commando Headquarters, together with X and Y Companies, sailed from Stanley aboard the R F A *Stromness* on 26 June. The remainder of the Commando sailed from Stanley aboard the S S *Canberra* on 25 June.
5 *Commando Logistic Regiment* (Lieutenant-Colonel I. J. Helberg R C T)
   The main part of the Regiment sailed from Stanley aboard the R F A *Sir Percival* on 28 June. The Medical Squadron sailed aboard S S *Canberra* on 25 June, and other elements of the Regiment returned aboard various other ships.
6 *3 Commando Brigade Air Squadron* (Major C. P. Cameron R M)
   The Squadron sailed from Stanley aboard the S S *Canberra* on 25 June.

ANNEX F

Army units serving in the South Atlantic in the period 14 June–1 September, 1982

Unit	Dates	Commanding Officer
★ Medium Recce Troop, B Squadron The Blues and Royals (RHG/D)	dep late June	Captain R. A. K. Field
29 and 37 Field Batteries, 4 Field Regiment Royal Artillery plus elements of 41 Battery	dep July	Lieutenant-Colonel G. A. Holt
Elements of 55, 127 and 143 Batteries, 49 Field Regiment RA	dep July	Mainly additional 'OP' parties
★ 7, 8, 79 Batteries and 148 Forward Observation Battery, 29 Commando Regiment RA	dep end June	Lieutenant-Colonel M. J. Holroyd-Smith
Elements of 43 Air Defence Battery 32 Guided Weapons Regiment, RA	dep end June	Captain R. C. Dickey
9 Air Defence Battery	dep September	Major D. Issac
★ T Air Defence Battery	dep end July	Major G. F. W. Smith
Elements 58 Air Defence Battery – all from Air Defence Regiment RA	throughout	
21 Air Defence Battery 27 Field Regiment RA	dep early August but some elements throughout	Major R. G. Cowlishaw
137 Field Battery, 40 Field Regiment RA	arr July	Major J. S. M. Tulloch
58 Air Defence Battery, 12 Air Defence Regiment RA	arr September	Major P. A. Shahinian

Unit	Dates	Commanding Officer
HQ 36 Engineer Regiment and 3 Troop, 20 Field Squadron Royal Engineers	dep end August	Lieutenant-Colonel G. W. Field
37 Engineer Regiment	arr mid-August	Lieutenant-Colonel P. R. Ievers
3 Field Squadron, Royal Engineers	arr late June	Major M. H. H. Brooke
9 Parachute Squadron, Royal Engineers	dep end June/July	Major C. M. Davies
11 Field Squadron, Royal Engineers	dep August	Major R. B. Hawken
30 Field Squadron, Royal Engineers	arr early August	Major R. J. Little
50 Field Squadron, Royal Engineers	arr late June	Major J. R. Harrison
★ 59 Independent Commando Squadron, Royal Engineers	dep late June	Major R. Macdonald
60 Field Support Squadron, Royal Engineers	arr early August	Major S. W. Hesketh
61 Field Support Squadron, Royal Engineers	dep late August	Major R. C. Morgan to mid-June/Major W. T. R. Thackwell
69 Gurkha Independent Field Squadron, Royal Engineers	arr early August	Major J. G. Baker
★ 49 EOD Squadron, Royal Engineers	throughout	Captain B. Lloyd, Major G. S. Lucas, then Major J. Quinn
Detachment, Military Works Force, Royal Engineers	throughout	Lieutenant-Colonel L. J. Kennedy
Element 2 Postal & Communications Regiment, Royal Engineers	throughout	Major I. Winfield
Elements 30 Signals Regiment	dep mid-July	Major W. K. Butler
266 (Falkland Islands) Signal Squadron	arr mid-July	Major N. Fairley
2nd Battalion The Scots Guards	dep end July	Lieutenant-Colonel M. I. E. Scott
1st Battalion The Welsh Guards	dep mid-July	Lieutenant-Colonel J. F. Rickett

Unit	Dates	Commanding Officer
★ 2nd Battalion The Parachute Regiment	dep late June	Lieutenant-Colonel D. R. Chaundler
★ 3rd Battalion The Parachute Regiment	dep late June	Lieutenant-Colonel H. W. R. Pike
1st/7th Gurkha Rifles	dep mid-July	Lieutenant-Colonel D. P. de C. Morgan
1st Battalion The Queen's Own Highlanders, with a Company of the Queen's Lancashire Regiment under command	arr mid-July	Lieutenant-Colonel N. J. Ridley
D Squadron and elements Special Air Service	–	–
656 Squadron Army Air Corps	dep late July	Major C. S. Sibun
657 Squadron Army Air Corps	arr late July	Major A. H. Stansfield
Elements 17 Port Regiment, Royal Corps of Transport	dep late August	Lieutenant J. G. D. Lowe
Composite Port Squadron, 17 Port Regiment RCT	arr late June	Major J. M. Bowles
407 Troop, Royal Corps of Transport	dep late August	Lieutenant J. P. Ash
426 Troop, Royal Corps of Transport	arr mid-August	Lieutenant J. E. Brownbridge
16 Field Ambulance, Royal Army Medical Corps	dep end July	Lieutenant-Colonel J. D. A. Roberts
2 Field Hospital, RAMC/Falkland Islands Base Hospital	arr late June	Colonel T. A. M. Cook
81 Ordnance Company, Royal Army Ordnance Corps	dep mid-August	Major G. M. A. Thomas
91 Ordnance Company, Royal Army Ordnance Corps	dep mid-August	Major R. Smith
Falkland Islands Logistic Battalion	arr end June	Lieutenant-Colonel R. W. Hurles
10 Field Workshops, Royal Electrical and Mechanical Engineers	dep early August	Major A. D. Ball
2 Field Workshops REME	arr early August	Major N. S. Ford

Unit	Dates	Commanding Officer
Elements 160 Provost Company, Royal Military Police	dep early August	Major A. K. Barley
Falkland Islands Provost Unit	arr end July	Major A. J. Figg
Detachment, Royal Pioneer Corps	arr early August	Lieutenant F. Curtis

The '★' denotes the unit formed part of, or was attached to, 3 Commando Brigade for the Campaign. The dates given in the above schedule are approximate only, because those for the arrival or departure of different parts of a unit sometimes varied and full details are not available.

Annex G

Royal Air Force Squadrons and Units based on, or operating into, the Falkland Islands in the period 14 June–1 September, 1982

Squadron/ Unit	Aircraft/ Armament	Commanding Officer	Notes
RAF Stanley		Group Captain W. J. Wratten	Established 1 July
1 (F) Squadron Detachment	Harrier GR3	Wing Commander P. T. Squire/Wing Commander G. W. Honey (from 6 August)	Disembarked from HMS *Hermes* on 4 July and mounted Quick Reaction Alert (QRA) from 5 July
3 Squadron Detachment	Harrier GR3	Squadron Leader K. G. Grumbley	Deployed to RAF Stanley on 5 July as back up to 1 (F) Squadron
63 Squadron, RAF Regiment	Rapier/Blindfire	Squadron Leader I. P. G. Loughborough	Travelled with the Task Force and initially deployed to San Carlos. Redeployed to Stanley on 4 July complementing 9 (AD) Battery, Royal Artillery, until taking over the whole SHORAD task on 21 August
18 Squadron Detachment	Chinook	Wing Commander A. J. Stables/Squadron Leader R. Cuthill from 13–21 August	
24 Squadron 30 Squadron 47 Squadron 70 Squadron	Hercules C Mark 1	Wing Commander M. A. E. Sellers/Wing Commander B. E. Nunn (from 21 August)	The Squadrons provided elements making up the Air Transport Detachment based at Ascension.
55 Squadron 57 Squadron 232 Operational Conversion Unit	Victor Mark 2	Wing Commander A. M. Bowman/Wing Commander C. C. B. Seymour (from 15 July)	The Squadrons/Unit provided the Tanker Detachment based at Ascension
Tactical Communications Wing Detachment		Squadron Leader G. Jones	Reinforced the Task Force TCW Contingent from 13 July
Tactical Air Traffic Control Team		Squadron Leader G. R. Bush	A No 38 Group Mobile Air Operations Team (MALM A. Smith) ran RAF Stanley Air Traffic until 13 July

Squadron/ Unit	Aircraft/ Armament	Commanding Officer	Notes
Mobile Meteorology Team		Squadron Leader W. R. McQueen	The team deployed to RAF Stanley on 13 July but an individual Met Officer had arrived on 5 July
Mobile Air Movements Flight		Flight Lieutenant A. M. R. Holliday	The advance party of the MAM team arrived on 23 June
Tactical Supply Wing		Wing Commander W. S. Girdwood	TSW personnel from the Task Force provided refuelling facilities at RAF Stanley until the arrival of the advance party on 13 July

INDEX

A

Accommodation, British Forces 35–40, 145, 155

Ajax Bay: 52; ammunition 76, 78, 153; campaign 9, 125; visit 23; war cemetery 24, 160

Albatross, MV, BAS 96, 99–100

Albemarle Harbour 59

Albion Star Ltd 103

Allied Mobile Force (Land) 44

AM2 airfield surfacing: 37, 53–7, 123, 141, 146

Andrews, RQMS Andy, RE 52

Andromeda, HMS: 8; 108–13; Ascension 142; Force Eleven 108–10; life aboard 110–13; South Georgia 96, 101, 104, 106

Animals: disease 95; for food 52, 95; guanacos 95; importance of pets 95; llamas 113; mines 28; mine dogs 28, 136–7; 'Noah's Ark' 151; rats 95, 103, 124; sheep, mine clearing 29; shooting the mine injured 92–94; South Georgia 97, 100–1, 106, 164

Antelope, HMS 59

Argentine Exclusive Economic Zone 150

Argentine fishing activity 150

Argentine forces: 80–84; action at Grytviken 102; ammunition 32–3, 76, 81; attitudes 83; booby traps 32; Chinook 81; defences at Stanley airfield 22; equipment 69–70, 78, 80–2, 170–1; Fokker aircraft 52; Fox Bay 71, surrender 60, 86th Infantry Regiment 60; Fox Bay East ammunition 77; helicopters 81; Hercules 53; invasion 9; Las Malvinas 42, 83; mines and mining 26–7, 167, 169, mine map 134–5; Mirage 59; national airline 42; officers 43, 83; Post Office signs 42; POW mine clearing party 26–30; POW stories 83–4; pre-invasion 42; Pucara aircraft 10, 33, 81–2, 152–3; raising flag 41–2; rations 44, 83; repairs Stanley airfield 53; Roy Cove 67–8; SAS POW 72; scrap merchants 105, 106; Skyhawk 31, 60; Special Forces 43; Super Entendard 59; superstition 61; surrender in South Georgia 105–7; unwelcome 42; Virgin Mary on butts 81; YPF tank farm 47

Armstrong, WEA Graham, RN 112

Armstrong, Simon, FIDC 148

Army Air Corps: 12, 78, 143; 657 Squadron 120, shooting the animals 92–3; FIPZ 119; Teeny Weeny Airways 120–1; white-out flying 72

Army equipments: Bulldozer, D6, mined 22; Clansman radio 132; Combat Engineer Tractor mined 22, as tower 55; 'Cubic' detector 136; Emergency Fuel Handling Equipment 20-1, 47, 120, 124; Flail 28, 136; Forster Locator 134; Hjelper sledge 165; Irrado Detector 136; mine detecting 28, 136; REDFIRE 153; Rough Terrain Truck 123; SATCOM 132; Smalley excavator 164; stone crusher 22, 54–5

Army units – indexed under Regiment, Corps or other title

Artico, MV 175

Artuso, CPO, Argentine POW 103

Ascension: 13–16, 35, 56, 65, 142, 166; administration 15; BBC, Cable & Wireless 15; closure of Stanley airfield 56, 141; communications link 132; English Bay 15; Georgetown 15, 142; Green Mountain 13, 15, 142; locust threat 166; Long Beach 166; mail drop 125–6; route north 142–3; route south 13; Royal Marines 13, 15; sea lanes 62, 65; size 13; Traveller's Hill 166; USAF/NASA 15; Wideawake airfield 15, 142, 166

Association of Parents of Unmarried Sons killed in the Falklands 160

Astiz, Captain Alfredo, Argentine Navy 105, 107, 163

Atlantic Conveyor, SS 54, 156

HRH Prince Andrew: on *Invincible* 6; opens new airfield 146, 172, 176; pilot 59

Hunt, Sir Rex, Civil Commissioner and Governor: 19; FIDC 148; hands over 149; Knight 148; pilgrimage 160; returns 49; the man and Legco speech 85–9; weapon amnesty 137

Hunter, Corporal, RE 125

Hurles, Lieutenant-Colonel Roger, RAOC, CO F.I. Logistic Battalion 122

Husvik, South Georgia 104, 106–7, 163

Hutchinson, Bob, Press Association 144

I

Illustrious, HMS 77, 110

Infantry Brigades:
  No 1 98
  No 5 10, 25, 69, 98, 125, 132, 144
  No 19 36

Intelligence material 82

Intrepid, HMS 59

Invincible, HMS: 59, 61–2, 110–1; Chile TV 5–6; visit 63

Iris, CS 107

Isle of Wight 13, 50

ITM (Offshore) Ltd 156

J

Jaffray, Corporal Ron, RPC 124

James, Captain Jimmy, RN SNOFI, HQ BFFI 19

Jarwood, Sergeant Mick, RAOC 44

Jason's Island, South Georgia 105

Jenkins, Bombadier Jimmy, RA 36

Jenkinson, Captain Bob, RE 47

Jensen, Midshipman Lee, RN 111

Jewkes, Gordon, Governor F.I. 150

Joint Air Transport Establishment, Brize Norton 126

Joint Service Reconnaissance Team, South Georgia 163

Joint Services Movements Staff, HQ BFFI 123, 141

Joint Venture Consortium 172–8; film 176

Jolly, Surgeon Commander Rick, RN 23

Jones, Lieutenant-Colonel 'H', VC CO 2 PARA 24, 160

Jones, Private Mark, ACC 96

Jones, Mrs Sara, Falklands Families Association 160

Jukes-Hughes, Colonel Robin, RE 19, 172

K

Keeling, PO Di, WRNS 157

Kelly's Garden, San Carlos 159

Kelper Khronicle, The 130–1

Kemball, Air Vice-Marshal Kip, CBFFI 146–7, 149

Kendrick, Lance-Corporal Ian, RCT 123

Kennedy, Lieutenant-Colonel Leslie, RE, CRE Works 46–8

Kenrick, Wynn, Joint Venture 176–8

Keoghan, Des, Falklands Families Association 160

Keren, MV 155

Kidney Cove 92

Kidney Island 120

Kindersley, David, sculptor 161

King Edward Cove, South Georgia: 96; mythical cat 97, 100–2

King Edward Point, South Georgia: 96–7, 104

King George Bay 67

King Haakon Bay, South Georgia 164-5

Kitson, Linda, war artist 144

Knott, John, Defence Secretary, UK 142

L

Lafonia 114–6

Lane, Kathy, fiancée 116

Larsen, C. A., Co. 103

Latchford, Major Roger, RCT 123

Layman, Rear-Admiral Kit, CBFFI 147

Leather, Corporal Mick, RE 145

Lee, Robin, F.I. 71, 140

Leith, South Georgia: 163; Argentine surrender 105–7; mines and EOD 25, 152

Leslie, Lance-Sergeant Jim, 2SG 23

Limbu, Lance-Corporal Budhaparsad, 1/7 GR 32

Lindbad Explorer, MV 41

Lively Sound 185

Livingstone, Lieutenant Clive, RE 25

Lloyd, Captain Brian, RE 34

Locust threat, Ascension 166

Logistic skills, Army, preservation of 12

Louis, Lance-Corporal Kevin, RE 99

Lucas, Major Guy, RE 31–4

Luton, Captain Greg, QO HLDRS, South Georgia 96–7

Lyneham 141

M

MacDonald, Lance-Corporal Archibald, QO HLDRS 99
MacDonald, Lieutenant Murdo, QO HLDRS 70
Macdonald, Major Roddy, RE 25
Mackay, Private John, QO HLDRS 70
MacKenzie, Lance-Corporal Donald, QO HLDRS 70
Macnally, Second-Lieutenant Hugh, QO HLDRS 99–101
Maiviken, South Georgia 101
Malvinas Guest House 41
Manday, WEM Jim, RN 112
Marconi Communications Ltd 160
Mare Harbour 158, 174–5
Markham, George, Dean 90
Marr, Piper Graham, QO HLDRS 117
Mary Hill Quarry 146
Mathewson, Lieutenant Mark, 2SG 23
Maurice, Paul, IRN 144–5
May, Brian, F.I. 52
McCartney, Lance Corporal, RE 28
McGee, Tom and Moira, F.I. 67
McGregor, Captain Lorna, WRAC 158
Media tie 144–5
Meeson, Lieutenant Vernon, QLR 71–2
Menendez, General Mario, Argentine Commander 30, 60
Menzies, Sapper Ken, RE 36
Mercer, Crystal, F.I. 159
Merchant Navy vessels, indexed by name
Merchant Providence, MV Joint Venture 175, 177
Mexeflote 37, 54–5, 122–3
Mieville, Major Christopher, RGJ 164
Miles, Captain Ken 78
Millinson, Lance-Corporal 'Molly', RE 26
Mills, Lieutenant-Colonel John, PR, HQ BFFI 5–6, 19
Mills, Lieutenant Keith, RM 97,•102
Mines: 25–30, 152–4, 167–9; floaters 153–4; policy 26, 154
Ministry of Defence Report 'The Future Defence of the Falkland Islands' 152
Molkenbuhr, Claude and Judy, F.I. 92–3
Monmouth, HMS 90
Monsunen, MV 185
Montevideo, Uruguay 160, 185
Moody Brook: ammunition 76, 152; water plant 46–7, 49
Moore, Major-General Jeremy, CLFFI 19, 26, 87–8, 132

Morgan, Corporal 'Bas', RE 26
Morgan, Lieutenant-Commander Dai, RN 65
Morgan, Jack, Command Secretary, HQ BFFI 86, 91, 142
Morgan-Grenville, Captain Roger, RGJ 164–5
Moules, Captain Ken, RAOC 78
Mount Challenger 10–11
Mount Harriet 11, 19
Mount Kent: campaign 10–11, 19; flight 72; UXB 31
Mount Longdon: campaign 7, 11, 26–7, 83; mines and EOD 31–2
Mount Low 92
Mount Paget, South Georgia 105
Mount Pleasant airfield: building 172–8; NAAFI 158; opening 58, 146, 166; recce 19; site 57; worry 147
Mount Simon 43
Mount Tumbledown: campaign 7, 9, 11, 19, 80; Guardsman Williams 40; mines and EOD 31, 152; Ode to, 23–4
Mount Vernet, campaign 10
Mount William: campaign 11; ordnance disposal 77, 152
Mullin, Lieutenant John, RE 25, 27–30, 134
Mulliner, Leading WEM Philip, RN 111
Munro, CSM Donald, QO HLDRS 115
Murray, Snowfield, South Georgia 165
Murrell: bridge 132; mines 28, 120, 152; shooting the animals 92–4

N

NAAFI: bill 65; facilities 155, 158–9; staff 158
napalm 31, 34
Navy Point: NAAFI 159; visit 64; *Sir Tristram* 39
Neale, Barry, MOD (Lands) 91
Nesbitt, Major Margaret, QARANC 156
Nicholas, Major Richard, RE 47
Norland, MV 23
North Arm 114–5, 116
North Venture Shipping Agencies Ltd, Coastels 155

O

Ode to Tumbledown 23–4
Ogilvy, Second Lieutenant Alasdair, QO HLDRS 70

— 200 —

W

Walker, Staff Sergeant Keith, RE 47
War Cemetery 24, 160
War souvenirs 130, 137
Ward, Major Geoff, RE 154
Ward, Flight Lieutenant Jane, WRAF 166
Watson, Major David, QO HLDRS 116
Watson, Lieutenant-Commander David, RN 111
Watts, Patrick, F.I. 129
Weatherall, Captain Jim, RN HMS *Andromeda* 108, 110, 142
Weddell Island 71
Weddell Sea 164
Welsh Guards, 1st Battalion: campaign 10, 11; Memorial Badge 36
Wheeler, Colonel Roger, COS, HQ BFFI 19
White, Captain Hugh, RN HMS *Avenger* 59–60, 110
White, Sub-Lieutenant Mark, RN 109
White, Corporal Stephen, RCT 123
Wickham Heights 72
Wideawake airfield 5, 142, 166

Wild Life, preservation of: 94, 140, 174; Ascension 166; film 159
Williams, Guardsman Philip, 2SG 48
Willis, Captain Malcolm, RAMC (South Georgia) 97–8, 102–3, 105–6
Willoughby, Sergeant, RE 125
Wilson, Sergeant Derek, RM 164–5
Winfield, Major Ian, RE 125
Wireless Ridge: campaign 11; 19; mines 25, 27, 152–3
Women's Royal Air Force, Ascension 166; Falkland Islands 158
Women's Royal Army Corps 158, 166
Women's Royal Naval Service 157, 166
Woodward, Rear-Admiral Sandy, RN, Commander Naval Task Force 61, 88
Wratten, Group Captain Bill, RAF, Senior RAF Officer, HQ BFFI 19, 51–2
Wrega, Sergeant, RE 30
Wrigley, Able Seaman Graham, RN 65

Y

Yarmouth, HMS 185
Yorke Point, minefield 22

grand tamentella